Behind the Jester's Mask

To Corinne

Behind the Jester's Mask

*Canadian Editorial Cartoons
about Dominant and Minority Groups
1960–1979*

RAYMOND N. MORRIS

UNIVERSITY OF TORONTO PRESS

TORONTO BUFFALO LONDON

© University of Toronto Press 1989
Toronto Buffalo London
Printed in Canada

ISBN 0–8020–5806–X

Printed on acid-free paper

Canadian Cataloguing in Publication Data

Morris, R.N. (Raymond N.), 1936–
Behind the jester's mask

Includes index.
ISBN 0–8020–5806–X

1. Editorial cartoons – Political aspects – Canada.
2. Canadian wit and humor, Pictorial – Political
aspects – Canada.   3. Canada – Politics and government – 1957–1963 – Caricatures and cartoons.*
4. Canada – Politics and government – 1963–1968 –
Caricatures and cartoons.* 5. Canada – Politics and
government – 1968–1979 – Caricatures and cartoons.*
I. Title.

NC1446.M67 1989   971.064'02'07   C88–095205–9

This book has been published with the help of a grant from the Social Science
Federation of Canada, using funds provided by the Social Sciences and
Humanities Research Council of Canada.

Contents

Preface

This book has grown out of a long-standing love of cartoons. My interest in their potential as sociological material was first aroused by Perry Curtis's *Apes and Angels*, a splendid analysis of Victorian English cartoons about the Irish. Roland Barthes's *Mythologies* added enormously to my understanding of the messages carried through everyday channels of communication. The insights of Ariel Dorfman and Armand Mattelart, in *How to Read Donald Duck*, have also been an inspiration. In the spirit of their work, this book is a serious study of humorous material.

This will no doubt disappoint those who enjoyed Charles Press's witty writing about American cartoons, and those who would like to see the author's hundred favourite cartoons enlivening a text which is bound to seem dull by comparison. They will remark that here is another solemn professor intent on taking the fun out of humour. Dull and puritanical of soul must he be who can carefully and systematically squeeze the enjoyment and laughter out of cartoons, in order to show that a serious pulp remains. They will say that such a spoil-sport belongs in a dungeon with his patron saint, Malvolio.

These critics are right, to a certain extent. This is an analysis of cartoon messages, and not the humour in which they are wrapped. It is not a study of what is funny about them, or why. The best editorial cartoonists are not gag-writers who draw to amuse us; they are political commentators who use humour to show us what infuriates them about politics and politicians. While a few offer us gentle satire of ordinary people, most load their pens with acid to ridicule premiers, presidents, and prime ministers.

This volume looks at the nature of cartoons in a capitalist democracy. Press's work offers some valuable generalizations relating the cartoonist's work to the political conditions of the day. This book seeks to go further by relating those political conditions to their economic and social base.

This research centres on a question which may seem obvious yet does not appear to have been seriously asked. Why pick on politicians? Certainly the contrast between their promises and their performance is sometimes so wide that it is difficult to take them seriously. Certainly they have the power and legislative authority to upset us, harm us, and misuse our money. Certainly we enjoy laughing at the mistakes of our leaders and their efforts to inflate their own importance and effectiveness. Yet this is also true of many other occupations; schoolteachers, clergy, business executives, professors, doctors, plumbers, and mechanics all exercise power and are apt to promise miracles. None of them receives continuous lampooning, by highly paid professionals, on the editorial page of almost every daily newspaper. Business, in particular, occupies just as much news space as politics, but is presented in a very different light.

There is a major double standard here, between what is expected of public and what is expected of private figures. The book explores this double standard in the context of the press.

Caricatures of politicians have been around for several centuries. In earlier generations newspapers were strongly committed to a particular party and their artists concentrated on laughing at that party's opponents. Today most editorial cartoonists are non-partisan; they criticize whichever party is in power. They thus make fun of politics itself and implicitly contrast the disorderly foolishness of politicians of all persuasions with the orderly good sense of business leaders. I have therefore described them as the jesters of the bourgeoisie.

There is a risk that cartoonists will be offended by this description. They are rightly proud of their freedom from partisan political ties and of the progress they have made in establishing themselves as independent-minded contributors to the editorial page. Their critique of politics has been a powerful and incisive one which has served the public interest well. They have become specialists in political satire, and have set good priorities within the limits which their employers will tolerate. At a more personal level, they welcomed me warmly as a guest when I attended their convention and spoke with them about their work. Duncan Macpherson and Roy Peterson were particularly helpful. It would be discourteous to return their kindness by portraying them only as willing or unconscious tools of business interests. Some of them, indeed, would justly point out that they struggle valiantly to express a viewpoint which is well to the left of their paper's editorial position. My critique does not refer to their intentions, but to the limitations which are perhaps inherent in their situation.

I take the positive features of their work for granted, and have tried in this book to look at their work in the spirit in which they operate. I have studied their art with great care, while not becoming so close to them as individuals that my independence has been compromised. Just as they are outsiders looking underneath the red carpets of politics, I have tried to offer here an outsider's look under the rugs of their work. I have examined what is lost from view because these penetrating critics' sights are set exclusively on politicians. To point out this nether side is not to disparage what they accomplish. Their work speaks for itself daily across the nation's breakfast tables and in its buses and trains. They have won the admiration of those they caricature.

I salute them for their many achievements, and for the countless moments of delight which they have brought to me and so many others. They do not need my praises as a lay person, and I am no expert on the artistic quality of their work. In so far as I can give them anything of value in return, it is a portrait of themselves in the Spirit of Caricature, for it is at Caricature's shrine that we are fellow-worshippers.

In preparing this book I have benefited from the help of many people. Alan O'Connor was instrumental in introducing me to the work of Perry Curtis and Ariel Dorfman, and I am deeply grateful to him. Many other graduate students at York have shared their ideas, their insights, or articles they have come across. They are too numerous to mention individually, but together they have contributed a great deal. Charles Press's work has been extremely valuable, and he has been most helpful in sharing personal experiences. A wide range of colleagues have kindly shared their ideas and read sections of the manuscript: David Bell, Paul Bouissac, Northrop Frye, Lesley Harman, Richard Hoffman, Gilles Houle, Linda Hutcheon, Michael Lanphier, Jos Lennards, Thelma McCormack, Greg Nielsen, John O'Neill, Judith Posner, A.H. Richmond, Richard Schneider, Tony Wilden, and Anton Zijderveld. The careful and perceptive comments of the four anonymous reviewers are no less appreciated because I cannot thank them in person. John Fox and Sal Minkin played a major role in helping me to understand and apply log-linear models.

I have a special debt to Terry Mosher and Guy Badeaux, who compiled the remarkable collection of cartoons on which this book is based. For a number of years they inspired and cajoled their fellow cartoonists to contribute to a permanent collection of Canada's finest political art. Thanks to their untiring work there is now the basis for a Canadian Museum of Caricature. The help of Denis Castonguay and Raymond Vezina, in locating and reproducing material in the Public Archives, was crucial; without their dedication my task would have been much more difficult. The cartoonists who have allowed me to reproduce their work also deserve special thanks for their generosity. I also wish to thank the Star Syndicate for its co-operation.

Peter and Corinne Morris made major contributions to the work. Peter was both a conscientious and efficient coder and a very interested and insightful commentator on the cartoons. Corinne wrote some complex programs which allowed the data analysis to proceed smoothly, for both individual cartoon characters and for whole cartoons, on the family PC. Ruth, Sylvia, Douglas, and Joy Morris each provided important moral support and encouragement.

The editorial staff of the University of Toronto Press have been excellent midwives to a manuscript whose birth has been slow and difficult; special thanks are due to R.I.K. Davidson, Virgil Duff, and Diane Mew.

While the help of all these people has enriched and improved the book substantially, they are not of course responsible for the limitations which remain; those belong to the author alone.

R.N.M.

Behind the Jester's Mask

Introduction

When did you last take a careful look at an editorial cartoon in your favourite newspaper? Did you wrestle to uncover its layers of meaning, as you might struggle with the daily crossword puzzle?

These seem silly questions. We have always taken for granted that a good cartoon can be understood at a glance, and we dismiss it as a failure if we need to make an intellectual effort to see its point. A good cartoon is expected to conceal its artfulness by allowing us to identify the characters, incident, setting and commentary within a few seconds. We expect to skim or glance at it, grasp its message, laugh or groan, and move on. This book goes beyond what we take for granted about editorial cartoons, by examining their sources and messages in detail.

An editorial cartoon is a professional drawing, usually humorous and political, which appears on the editorial page of a newspaper. This working definition does not include the 'comics' section of the paper, though some of the conclusions might apply to certain comic strips. Nor does it cover 'social cartoons' about the many daily applications of Murphy's Law to family life, leisure, and work relationships.

It should also be stressed that this is not a study of humour. While many cartoons have a humorous side, a substantial minority do not. Those which deal with menaces to civilization in general, or to the cartoonist's country in particular, are extremely serious works. Similarly, many strips which appear in the comics section are earnest stories of heroes and villains. Consequently, this book will not apply the many theories of humour to the understanding of cartoons; its purpose is not to show why some drawings make us laugh while others do not. A focus on humour, indeed, distracts one from even raising the question which underlies the present research: why pick on politicians?

The question is disarmingly simple, and disconcertingly difficult to answer adequately. To begin the task, we need a theory which highlights the important questions and then disciplines our efforts to find answers. We also require a sample of editorial cartoons from which good generalizations can be made. The theory can then be partially tested.

Two broad approaches to a theory of cartooning show promise. The approach of communications theory is to generate questions about three key elements: the sender, the message, and the receiver. Study of the sender involves an inquiry into the operation of the capitalist press and the place of cartooning within it. The work of Charles Press appeared shortly before this research began, and that of Ericson, Baranek, and Chan in 1987, after it was concluded. Press made a thorough study of the technical and economic aspects of cartooning, and compared its products in different settings: under democratic, authoritarian, and totalitarian political regimes, and in times of war and peace. Ericson et al. analysed the contemporary news-gathering work of journalists, the social construction of news stories, and their organization into a daily paper or broadcast. The present research seeks to extend their work, by asking how cartooning relates to journalism, and how newspapers change in response to changes in material conditions and social expectations. One can then see the circumstances in which cartoonists are paid to make fools of certain public figures and policies. The structure and content of reporting can then be compared with the structure and content of cartooning.

Questions about the message concern the cartoons themselves: who is satirized and who is spared, from what perspectives are the cartoons drawn, what symbolism is used, and what messages are conveyed about public figures?

Questions about the receiver of the cartoons are given relatively little attention here. There have been occasional studies (Perkins and Hagen; Shaffer; Twer) of what viewers see in cartoons, but they are few in number and modest in coverage. In this respect we do not really know under what conditions the message which is received corresponds closely to that which was sent. Most researchers agree that the receiver participates actively in communication and does not merely absorb passively whatever is presented (Eagleton, 1976a; Hutcheon, 1984; Smythe, 1981). At the same time, the effort required is much more intense and sustained in some contexts than in others. The defence offered here for not studying receivers directly is a simple one: since cartoons are designed for very quick reception, their senders cannot afford to engage in subtleties. While there may be hidden messages which most receivers will not consciously notice, the principal message in a successful cartoon needs to be immediately apparent. Much of the artist's skill is devoted to ensuring that the receiver will rapidly recognize the characters, setting, and humorous incongruity. While some may miss the point, the cartoons are designed for quick comprehension by most adults, are more readily grasped than most art forms, and can therefore be studied without serious concern that receivers will regularly and substantially distort their meaning. The theory presented here, then, will focus primarily on understanding the sender and the message.

The problem of an appropriate term for the receiver of the cartoon continues to be troublesome, since none seems adequate to describe the particular expectations which accompany the reception of a cartoon. 'Viewer' captures the visual element but ignores the caption and the peculiar rapidity with which one seeks to get the point of the cartoon. 'Reader' applies poorly to a text which is mainly visual, and again ignores the important element of speed. Although they are not altogether satisfactory choices, the terms 'glance' and 'skim' are used interchangeably to describe this type of reception, and the receiver is therefore called the 'glancer' or the 'skimmer.' In their noun form these terms are unusual, but not unique. The implication of this choice is that one receives a cartoon in much the same manner as one receives the photograph and the major headline on page 1 of the newspaper.

The other promising approach to a theory of cartooning begins with a model or metaphor (M. Black; Brown: 77; Ricoeur: 84–90, 240–4), which applies knowledge and insights gained in one area to help us understand what is happening in another. Sociological theory has been developed by exploring such metaphors. Marxists treat contemporary society as if it were, first and foremost, a struggle between two conflicting social classes. Symbolic interactionists explore it through the analogy of a stage on which actors negotiate somewhat loosely prescribed parts as the play proceeds. On a more modest scale, this research relies on the metaphor of the jester and the fool show to shed light on the political satire of the editorial cartoonist. The principal insight from this metaphor, which will be explored in a variety of ways as the book proceeds, is that cartoonists are the jesters of the bourgeoisie. As the implications of this insight are understood, the significance of cartooning becomes much clearer. The drawing and the artist no longer appear as anomalies or eccentrics in an industry which derives its profits from the provision of information on current events. Cartoons and cartooning, and the recent changes in them, can be seen as consistent with other features of the newspaper business as it has moved into a more monopolistic phase.

Once the question and the approach have been outlined, and the object of study defined, the researcher needs a good sample of drawings. Newspapers nearly always include only one cartoon per issue. A researcher can see a series of related drawings only by buying an anthology, by browsing through old newspapers, or by inspecting the collections in archives and libraries. When cartoons are carefully compared, it becomes possible to answer questions about their common features and their variability. The present research used the national cartoon collection on which Peter Desbarats and Terry Mosher based *The Hecklers*. I have chosen all cartoons from this collection which appeared between 1960 and 1979 and which dealt with relations between a dominant and a minority group. Initially these fell into three categories: French-English relations, Canadian-American relations, and Canadian business-labour relations. The number of business-labour cartoons proved too small for analysis.

The fool-show metaphor is the theme underlying chapters 1 to 3. Several clear parallels between the fool show and the cartoons will be examined in the opening chapter. The second chapter examines some ideas from literary and cultural theory which place the jester and the fool show in their broader context of story-telling and social struggle. These ideas can shed further light on political caricature. Chapter 3 looks at research on newspapers, to generate a more complete picture of the immediate environment of editorial cartoons. It raises at greater length the central question: why pick on politicians as the special target for systematic fool-making? Political leaders are as likely as anyone else to act foolishly and to deserve lampooning. Editorial cartoons go further, however, connoting that politics is a special breeding-ground which produces a disproportionate number of fools, whereas other social institutions produce relatively few.

Chapter 4 derives and spells out the main hypotheses from the earlier discussion. The remaining chapters examine these hypotheses to see how far recent Canadian cartoons confirm them. Chapter 5 explores the extent of regional and language differences among the cartoons on French-English relations. Chapter 6 then analyses these cartoons, while chapter 7 studies those on Canadian-American relations. The final chapter summarizes the research and points out some of its wider implications.

1

The Fool Show and the Cartoon

This opening chapter focuses on the literature about jesters, and the value of the metaphor that cartoonists are their modern equivalent. A number of writers, beginning with Nock in 1928, have pointed to similarities between the two roles. Both have been widely represented as persons who have a licence to cut through conventions, surface appearances, and routine politeness. Both are believed to place a very high value on impartiality, distributing their darts equally to high and low, rich and poor, left and right. Both are regarded as wise, discerning souls whose freedom of speech is the other face of their duty to speak the truth even when it is painful. Their value as critics is widely believed to entitle them to protection against retribution by those whom they ridicule.

At least two experts on cartooning have echoed the same theme. Draper Hill described the early political caricaturist as the 'jester to the beau monde.' W.A. Coupe argued that 'the modern political cartoonist has largely been reduced to the level of a court jester, given perhaps the freedom to tell the "truth", but only on condition that he make us laugh in the process' (p. 90). These writers have generally argued from the similarities between the public images of these two occupations. Zijderveld and Welsford, on the other hand, have examined the historical evidence behind the popular beliefs about jesters. Their research shows that in reality jesters had quite limited freedom, and offers some useful insights for the present study.

MEDIEVAL SOCIETY AND FOLLY: THE ORIGIN OF JESTERS

Zijderveld in his 1982 study, *Reality in a Looking Glass*, made a bold attempt to understand medieval folly, the context in which jesters rose to pre-eminence, by placing it in the setting of modernization theory, and by using the metaphor of the looking-glass. Feudal society was traditional in nature, and defined the sinner or knave as the person who placed short-term earthly interests before long-term heavenly ones. Folly and deformity were respectively the mental and physical punishments which the Devil meted out to those who sinned. Medieval society was also figural, drawing a close parallel between events in the Kingdom of Earth and those in the Kingdom of Heaven. In Auerbach's words, 'an occurrence on earth signifies not only itself but at the same time another (in heaven), which it predicts or confirms, without prejudice to the power of its concrete reality here and now. The connection between occurrences is not regarded as primarily a chronological or causal development but as a oneness within the divine plan, of which all occurrences are parts and reflections' (p. 490). There was therefore great fascination throughout society about those whose folly and deformity were thought to signify divine punishment.

While everyone sometimes sinned, and therefore suffered from folly and pain, those who remained deformed or fools became part of a distinct social category. Zijderveld sees them as marginal persons, deprived of any legal status, and treated as a source of general pity and amusement. In return they were free from any responsibility for maintaining a social reputation or for earning a living within the feudal system. Many fools wandered around Europe, subsisting as best they could by displaying their deformity and folly to entertain those who could give them food and shelter in return. Some became skilled as classical or lewd poets, story-tellers, singers, or wits. Unusual and skilled specimens of folly lived at court and formed one of the displays and diversions which rulers enjoyed and offered their guests. In this respect they were a source of prestige.

The behaviour and appearance of the permanent fools defied the basic social distinctions of medieval Europe. They would step across social boundaries with nonchalance, ignore taboos, fail to distinguish between social opposites, and treat the profane and the outcast as equal in value to the sacred and the socially prized. In conversation, their unusual rejoinders might be thought very witty or might be received in dull silence. Sometimes their remarks seemed to be pure gibberish, unworthy of a normal person's attention and their actions irrational and irresponsible.[1] At other times they fearlessly pointed out unpalatable truths, showing deep wisdom about the shortcomings of conventional beliefs and the ineptitude of conforming behaviour.

Fools were thus attractive and repulsive at the same time. Through their words and deeds they offered society a mirror-image of itself. Where ordinary people were responsible, fools were irresponsible; what one revered, the other openly mocked. The religious corporatism of medieval society contrasted dramatically with the secular individualism of its fools. In trying to translate the idea of folly into contemporary terms, a number of writers have summarized it as the medieval representation of chaos, the opposite of social order (Arden: 144; Duncan: 125; Willeford: 15, 157–9). Zijderveld generalized this: he argued that fools were a vivid socially constructed portrait of the state of anomie or nature in diverse cultures. Traditional society saw itself as having emerged from nature, but as being in constant danger of reverting to its former state. Fools were both a warning and a living humorous demonstration to their contemporaries of the price of abandoning positive cultural values such as seriousness and social order (pp. 18–20, 149).

Although fools were treated as marginal, subhuman, and amusing, this was only one side of the picture. In other respects they were feared as superhuman and treated with awe. At times they gave evidence of superior insight or talents which defied normal social or physical restrictions. Some might, for example, see and speak the truth about social conventions and about those who held power, in a way that ordinary people would not dare to do. Others gained a reputation for predicting the future or for performing remarkable physical feats.

Their wisdom and power were thus quite different from those of the church and the aristocracy, the traditional defenders of the medieval social order. Through practising folly they seemed able to draw on alternative sources of power and to hold their own in the face of verbal and physical chaos (Willeford: 208–23). They seemed undismayed by any disorienting event, outlandish idea, physical or verbal impossibility which they could imagine or which others could use as a trick. They could invent riddles and situations which reduced the 'normal'[2] persons around them to helplessness if not despair (Charney: 168). Their actions and speech were thus a bewildering example of 'perspective by incongruity' (Burke, 1954: 69–70).

Their mental disorderliness and their openness to lateral thinking were interpreted as indications that they belonged to the adjoining kingdom of chaos. In popular medieval thought, the kingdoms of Earth and Heaven were exactly paralleled by the kingdoms of disorder which were their looking-glass images. While Mother Church and God ruled in one pair of kingdoms, Mother Folly and the Devil held sway in the other. The power of folly operated from the kingdom of fools, quite outside the comprehension or control of the conventional guardians of earthly order. If unchecked it could reach into every person and reduce the whole realm to chaos, by subverting the classification of medieval believers according to their estates (Arden: 74–7, 85–9).

The ruler who kept fools in court might hope to use them, not only for amusement, but also as ambassadors who would ensure good relations between his or her realm and this neighbouring world of disorder in which 'social rules and rational understanding are no longer effective but the fool's magic is' (Willeford: 35). Although they were considered useless materially, fools might play a sacred role in their society, as communicators with this significant neighbouring world.

Most writers on folly make a distinction between 'natural' and 'artificial' fools. Natural fools played the role because they had no choice. Their mental or physical deformity was regarded as permanent and merited. The only socially acceptable response was to acknowledge it, perhaps exaggerate it, and make it a resource in the search for food and shelter. Artificial fools were people who had the choice, and who elected to supplement their income or to support themselves entirely by folly. Zijderveld describes a number of social groups from which artificial fools were drawn in medieval Europe.

One of the most important was the church itself. Priests without independent means were often unable to live on their meagre benefices, and were obliged to augment their earnings. Students who wearied of theology or university life, or who exhausted their funds, chose a life on the road. Monks who became restless under the discipline of holy orders and priests who left parish work swelled the ranks of wandering friars and entertainers. They regularly poked fun at the higher clergy, satirizing their corruption, greed, simony, and materialism. Few of them offered schemes for reform or an alternative to the primary ideology of their age; they were equally ready to satirize the serious church reformers. Their goals were amusement and physical comfort, as exemplified in Orff's *Carmina Burana*.

The other principal source of artificial fools, especially in France, was the urban professional class. Fool societies formed among its members and put on *soties* and other humorous 'plays' during the Festival of Fools period which preceded Lent. At this season the lower clergy, law students, and similar groups engaged for a limited time in public sacrilege of church rituals, desecration of church property, and lampooning of the higher clergy. When the hierarchy tried to curb these activities, the performers justified them as a safety-valve for popular discontent. If the fools' criticisms were too pointed or their target too sensitive, the societies might temporarily be forced to keep a low profile, only to re-emerge with new ideas for evading censorship. During the carnival periods the *soties* were accompanied by widespread displays of unorganized folly among the general public (Bakhtine: ch. 3).

One of the critical differences between the natural and the artificial fools was the possibility of choice. The artificial fools were usually opportunists who elected folly as a way of life. Their folly was not so much a necessity as a strategy. Criminals might pose as wandering fools or friars. The fool societies were a means by which youthful professionals could safely laugh at the rigid feudal norms and values which were taught but not practised by the church.

Arden noted that the actors in the *sotie* covered their meaning with layers of folly and were continuously ironic, so that no censor could successfully ask them whether their words had a political meaning. To retain their freedom of speech they had to express their satire in the seemingly senseless chatter of the natural fool. Those whose criticism went too far might still suffer punishment, but they were usually able to disclaim successfully (Hewitt and Stokes) by a witty retort or by claiming a fool's licence. Since they were fools, only another fool would take their remarks and allegations seriously.

Similarly, court jesters might perform a skit in which they praised their patron, while using their baubles to make allegations that he or she was immoral, stupid, or feeble: 'the fool could ... address the bauble as though it were a [certain well-known] person and treat it with respect, although the reduction of that person to a bauble had already made a fool of him' (Willeford: 34). They also cultivated a vocabulary of great vulgarity, special mannerisms, and a unique costume of cap, bells, and bauble. These served to make it absolutely clear that they were portraying fools and should not be held responsible for the words which crossed their lips or the sentiments expressed. Within the clear ritual limits of this carefully constructed social world, taboo remarks could be made and taboo actions performed. The language of folly served as a specialized tongue in which otherwise unacceptable ideas could be expressed with relative impunity.

As a strategy, the fools' irony was double-edged. It permitted them to reveal unpalatable truths or to insult a social superior without incurring the violent consequences which would follow if 'normal' persons uttered the same words. At the same time, the folly claimed by the speakers generally discounted their credibility as commentators. In making fools of others, they accepted the very high risk of being seen as fools themselves.

Although it was often used only to ridicule the rigidity of the old ways, folly could also serve as the cover for more coherent and radical social criticism (Bakhtine: 233–9, 268–73). There were very powerful segments of medieval society, such as the emerging merchant class and the monarchs, who had a vested interest in undermining the ideology and the power of the church and substituting their own. These groups could covertly encourage the Festival of Fools and the natural fools' ridicule of official religion, at a time when they hesitated to attack it directly. Folly showed traditional society a mirror-image or negation of itself in one key respect: religious corporatism was transformed into its opposite, the secular corporatism of the absolute monarchy.[3] Later it became politically less dangerous to proclaim the self-interest and secular rationality of the monarch and the merchant class, and the fool show declined.[4]

Folly itself could not evolve into secular individualism, for it was essentially irrational and incoherent. In the hands of court jesters and monarchs, however, artificial folly could become an important tool in discrediting those institutions which opposed social transformation. With the jesters' participation, medieval thought was changed. First it turned from the religious corporatism of the church into the secular corporatism of absolute monarchy; then it was further transformed into the secular individualism of early capitalism. The next section examines the court jester and the fool show from this perspective.

THE COURT JESTER AND THE FOOL SHOW

The oldest records showing that fools received money or amenities date from the twelfth century; prior to that, they received payment in kind, but never formed part of the household economy. By the fourteenth century they were common in influential households, and their position reached its apex in the fifteenth and sixteenth centuries. Some jesters became highly skilled professionals, well paid and increasingly distinct from the natural fools who could still be found in marginal positions. The most famous ones were experts in parody, burlesque, improvisation, and repartee. While a few were natural fools, the later jesters were essentially witty courtiers whose folly had become increasingly routine and artificial. Some were employed principally to organize pageants. Meanwhile the Lord of Misrule at the Festival of Fools had been evolving into 'a middleman who conveyed the cap and bells from the shaven heads of the half witted into the creative imagination of the philosopher, the satirist and the comic poet' (Welsford: 219). The expression of folly, an integral counterpoint to orderliness in traditional medieval society, was thus transformed during the late Middle Ages into the professional imitation of folly, the specialized skill of an occupational group.

Changes in the meaning of folly also took place, as it lost its original spiritual significance and magical properties. By 1500 it was acquiring its current meaning of foolishness, the mirror opposite of political and economic rationality.

This section discusses the fool shows at their apex in western Europe. It deals briefly with their conditions of production, and with the pattern of relationships between monarch, jesters, courtiers, and church.

Successful court jesters were very popular with their rulers, and might be called on to perform every night. They underwent an elaborate and careful training from their keepers, who also supervised and protected them. The most eminent ones might have tenure for life, and were cared for in their old age. They had a place of honour in the court, often sitting next to the ruler or standing behind the royal chair at dinner. At the same time they were regarded as subhuman like the natural fools, and frequently slept with the monarch's favourite dogs. In many respects, Zijderveld concludes, they were treated exactly like beloved and expensive pets.

Jesters provided entertainment by exercising their licence in fool shows or by mocking members of the court during and after the evening meal. They made clever riddles and puns, which reduced their hearers to speechless incompetence. They took pride in being able to counter any insult, and to catch their victims off guard, even though the tenor of their remarks might be quite predictable. They provoked and played with verbal ambiguities, manipulating words and situations in ways which would eventually show the jester to be wise and the others to be foolish. Double meanings and inconsistencies in word usage gave rise to apparently logical demonstrations that people and things were the opposite of what they appeared to be. Jesters revelled in the arbitrariness of cultural attitudes and social categories. They relished the ambiguities and contradictions of polar oppositions between life and death, allegiance and rebellion, good and evil, nature and culture, order and disorder.

The fool show would set up an imaginary world into which members of the court were transported. There they encountered familiar persons in unfamiliar guises and relationships. Two operations were performed simultaneously by the jester. First, the leaders and setting were abstracted from their social context and simplified into stereotypes, to enable the jester to make a point more clearly. Second, their statuses were transformed through metaphor, so that the ruler or noble might be cast as a low-status person while the jester or bauble was cast as the ruler. These two operations were designed to reveal that the ruler's or noble's recent actions fitted much better with the transformed status of a fool than with the actual status of this person at court. As 'playwrights' the jesters could insert themselves into the drama, stand outside it, or enter and leave it at will. They could interact with the ruler and courtiers within the show or outside it (Goffman, 1974: ch. 5).

The court jesters depended for their licence and position on the favour of the monarch. It was critical to know this person's ideas, moods, and sense of humour, the court gossip, the current favourites and black sheep, and the points on which each person could be ridiculed. Jesters avoided political alliances and alignments, and remained apart from intrigues and factions. They were then free of any suspicion that their wit was being used to attain personal power or to plot against the ruler; and they could bestow their satire wherever it might gain royal favour.

There is much evidence that a favoured jester acted as the alter ego of the ruler. As dependants with no possibility of personal power, jesters did not represent a threat to the monarch, as did the courtiers and higher clergy. Their companionship provided relief from the cares of an extremely stressful and isolated position. An absolute monarch took considerable risks in sharing knowledge and power with nobles and clergy who might later use them against him or her, but one could confide in a jester. A fool could release the ruler's tensions by ridiculing enemies and those who were irritating. These persons' qualities and behaviour could be caricatured in a way which brought relief through laughter. The jester could utter words and thoughts or take actions which a wise ruler would have to suppress. Each grew increasingly dependent on the other as power became more firmly concentrated in one pair of hands. They were complementary parasites on the society of their day.

In relation to the courtiers and especially to the higher clergy, the jester acted as a fool-maker. With the ruler's tacit approval and protection, if not instigation, the jester would constantly set up 'fool-making encounters' (Klapp, 1964: 91) to humiliate them by his (or occasionally her) verbal superiority. They might receive ritual public beatings from the jester's noisy bladder full of dried peas, in recognition of their alleged folly.

In the plays of the subsequent period, jesters often made fun of a ruler who showed signs of becoming foolish. In reality, however, this was done only with great circumspection. Welsford is emphatic that they were tools of the ruler in relation to the church and court. The legendary licence of the jester was strongly oriented to the ruler's wishes.

The fool shows of the jesters served the interests of the ruler in several ways. First, they drew attention to the ruler's dominance. Jesters were traditionally fearful of power and those who possessed it. At the same time, as part of their licence they rejected social distinctions based on prestige, authority, or status in a hierarchy which might have mitigated power. Their ridicule thus tended to undermine the pretensions and social bases on which courtiers and clergy strengthened their positions, while exposing and respecting the power of the ruler. The courtiers were publicly reminded that their position was inferior even to that of the fool. The monarch's power was sometimes so strong that even the closest person – the jester who was the ruler's symbolic opposite – was strongly dependent on personal favour and protection. The fool shows thus reinforced social control at court, in the interests of the ruler.

Secondly, in so far as the jester's skill satirized the monarch, this served as a symbolic reminder that the myth of absolute royal power was only half true. When the ruler accepted criticism with grace, and admitted the validity of an accusation, the fool show served as an expiation ritual. The ruler who had treated social conventions irreverently was being treated with irreverence until the fault was properly acknowledged. The existence of the ritual recognized that the ruler was both important enough and foolish enough to justify a semi-public drama of repentance. In this manner the jester might protect the monarch from the effects of her or his own folly, while issuing a reminder that at some future point the all-powerful one would be reduced to the status of an old fool and replaced by a new and younger ruler (Willeford: 164).

The work of Duncan and Burke suggests two other services which the fool show rendered to the monarch. They see two basic human responses to a powerful national or mythical force such as chaos: pious awe and impious rebellion. The fool show is rebellious: it reacts against the terror of chaos by giving it a name and a human form. When thus reduced to manageable proportions, it loses much of its power as something unknown. The fool show is also impious. It personifies chaos not as a monster but as a fool, a character from the world of low comic entertainment whose worst actions are not the destruction of social order but such laughable familiar weaknesses as hypocrisy, smugness, or bad manners. By metaphorically associating chaos with low comedy, each takes on some of the characteristics of the other. While this may do little tangibly to resolve the practical problem of keeping disorder at bay in the realm, it often relieves anxiety, representing it in such a way that its terror is veiled.⁵

The fool can also warn through the use of drama. The ruler can be told a 'representative anecdote' about a particular situation. Its protagonist is a caricature, or 'a certain ruler who lived once upon a time.' The ruler is less personally implicated and better able to view the situation objectively. Since the mood is humorous, the monarch may be able to laugh at the folly in the drama and in the real situation.

During the period of the jester's greatest significance, the church slowly lost its political and economic power to an alliance of the monarchs and the merchant class. This alliance was relatively short-lived, however, and its success brought into prominence the differences of interest between them. The jester was of little value as the chief advisor to the ruler of an emerging capitalist empire. The allegiance of the feudal lords and the army was not a sufficient mechanism of social control in a realm based on trade. The jesters directly, and the ascendant bourgeoisie indirectly, held up a mirror before regal absolutism which exposed its foolishness. This mirror proclaimed as its opposite the ideal type of early capitalism, now associated irrevocably with the name of Max Weber. A system of bourgeois democracy gradually became dominant within the framework of states which the monarchs and nobles had erected.

The result, then, was the emergence of a new ruling class and a new capitalist ideology of modernity. It involved the negation of secular corporatism as a value in favour of individual rationality. The cumulative impact of the two mirror transformations was that seriousness and its close ally orderliness were restored to their central positions. In the course of this second transformation, folly itself was converted into foolishness or economic irrationality, which became the key form of deviant behaviour in the emergent capitalist society.

Zijderveld drew several conclusions from his thorough review of this evidence. First, court jesters played a unique role, inextricably tied to the peculiar institution of absolute monarchy, which they mirrored perfectly. Secondly, the main forces of modernization which swept traditional folly away – specialization and the generalization of values and meanings – are still at work. After producing and then rendering obsolete the court jester, they have produced still more specialized roles. Some of these, such as the clown and the mental patient, embody the disregard of social conventions. Others embody social commentary and criticism: the journalist, the intellectual, and the sociologist. Thirdly, this fragmentation represents a sufficient change to justify the conclusion that the court fool has not survived; the role is dead, never to return.

THE FOOL SHOW AND THE POLITICAL CARTOON

My research does not challenge Zijderveld's finding that traditional folly has no modern equivalent. Nevertheless, I would make the point that the fool show can serve as a model for understanding the contemporary concept of economic foolishness. While there have obviously been important changes and some discontinuity, a strong case can be made that the editorial cartoon is the modern equivalent of the fool show.

Several features of Zijderveld's analysis have perhaps led him to overlook this. First, the experiences he describes with Peppi, as a contemporary personification of natural folly, have clearly furnished deep and personal insights which have greatly enriched his book. At the same time, the possibility that Peppi was an extraordinary throwback to a natural fool has perhaps led him to underestimate the differences between artificial and natural fools, and the substantial evolution which took place during the several centuries covered by his research. Correspondingly, he may have overestimated the differences between the court jester and his modern equivalents.

Secondly, Zijderveld focused primarily on the monarchy, rather than on some other features of fifteenth- and sixteenth-century Europe, which may also have been crucial in understanding the rise and fall of jesting. There are good reasons for emphasizing the link with the monarch, but it may have led him to underrate the importance of other factors in Renaissance society. These include the imperialism, moral decay, and imperviousness to reform of aristocratic and papal power at the time. Such a constellation has been a major focus of satire in other epochs.

Zijderveld explains the uniqueness of the late medieval jester in terms of the needs of absolute monarchy. This explanation leads to two serious problems. First, as Welsford makes clear, jesters were also employed by wealthy merchants, town corporations, monasteries, and brothels. Possibly they served different interests in these settings, but it is not self-evident that absolute monarchy can best explain their presence. Secondly, the claim that king and jester were complementary opposites, the jester being a structural necessity in an absolute monarchy, implies that jesters and absolute monarchs are always found together. Zijderveld does not present evidence to support this claim, however. Folly in other societies is discussed, but not in relation to kingship.

A third limitation of Zijderveld's analysis concerns the adequacy of his search for functional equivalents. He might have examined jesters and kings in a broader context of power-holding and licensed criticism. The church ceased to be satirized as it lost its power, and the same is true of monarchy; yet satire as a literary and artistic genre has not been extinguished as these institutions have faded from centre stage. Other groups have come to exercise power, and the targets and social organization of satire have evolved correspondingly.

Fourthly, Zijderveld pays relatively little attention to the links between the emergence of the merchant class and the ideology of modernization. While the subtle shift from folly to foolishness was noticed, its implications were not fully appreciated. By treating modernization as the polar opposite of traditionalism, Zijderveld is obliged to treat social change as either progressive, if modernity were increased, or regressive, if it were reduced. To be progressive meant to favour more extreme specialization and more diffuseness of generalized values and meanings. Given this manner of conceptualizing progress, it is indeed difficult to imagine how medieval folly and further progress could fruitfully be combined, and hence to conclude that folly in the strict sense might return.

Modernization can also be seen, however, as an ideology whose evolution is closely linked to the dominance of the bourgeoisie. It would still have the same major accompaniments – specialization and generalized values – but its opposite then becomes foolishness or economic irrationality.

This opens up two scenarios which remain inconceivable within Zijderveld's frame of reference. First, modernization may reach the point where further specialization or generalization itself becomes economically irrational; indeed, some might argue that this point has already been reached in many organizations. Modernization itself would then become a fertile source of satire. Secondly, if modernization is tied to capitalist society or to a particular stage of industrialization, one can imagine a form of foolishness which is progressive. It would anticipate certain features of a society which has evolved beyond the early forms of capitalism or industrialization, possibly beyond capitalism itself. There is then ample scope for anticipating reincarnations of foolishness, if not of folly.

The fifth limitation of Zijderveld's analysis is that, by emphasizing political power and celebrity rather than economic power, he is led to look at politicians and star entertainers as the contemporary figures who might have had their own jesters if the institution had survived. These are both occupations with a strong symbolic component, which have been relatively resistant to the rational concept of a career (Klapp, 1964: 21–7). Had he looked at the bourgeoisie and their image-makers, the newspapers, he would have found a flourishing survivor of the fool show in the editorial cartoon.

THE EMERGENCE OF EDITORIAL CARTOONING

Political caricature first became popular in England during the middle and late eighteenth century, roughly one hundred years after the decline of absolute monarchy. It blended caricatural portraiture, which had hitherto been mainly heroic, with written political satire, which had been flourishing since the disappearance of the court jesters and which had reached its apex with *Gulliver's Travels* in 1725.[6] Most political caricatures of this period appeared as prints, and were produced in modest quantities for individual sale. They quickly evolved from romantic to mock heroic works, whose planned incongruity satirized either the ruler or certain leaders in the struggle for political power. While some were drawn as commercial ventures for the print shops, others were commissioned by influential people to mock their political opponents.

As royalty withdrew from involvement in major decisions, caricaturists increasingly focused on party leaders. The king and queen dropped out of the satirist's sights, to become national symbols alongside Britannia.[7] The same shift occurred later in continental European cartooning, as elected politicians established their pre-eminence over hereditary rulers as policy makers.

Cartooning spread to North America in the mid nineteenth century, the drawings appearing mainly in magazines at first. They generally carried a strong partisan political message. Thomas Nast's attacks on Tammany Hall politicians in *Harper's Magazine* are the best-known example.

By the 1890s they had also found a home in many of the daily and weekly newspapers, which were often run by or closely tied to political parties. Indeed, as late as the 1930s Robert Chambers, now the senior Canadian cartoonist, was hired by a newspaper at election time, specifically to ridicule the opposition. He was sufficiently successful that, after the election, the rival party's paper offered him a permanent position! During this period cartooning was a key form of communication with the newer and less literate segments of the electorate (Desbarats and Mosher: 13–15). For this reason, much of the cartooning was polemical rather than humorous, especially when presenting the viewpoint of the party in power.

CONTEMPORARY NEWSPAPER CARTOONING

Since the First World War the basis of newspaper ownership has moved rapidly from political advantage to corporate profit. Parties lacked the funds to invest in expensive printing equipment or the skill to sell papers to un-committed sectors of the public. They were gradually replaced, first by entrepreneurs for whom the paper was both a livelihood and a personal organ; and more recently by conglomerates with interests in many other industries.

These changes were followed by major alterations in the role of the cartoonist. Most successful cartoonists now work for newspapers. They must abide by frequent and tight deadlines, producing five or six finished works and sometimes as many as fifteen to twenty preliminary sketches a week. Their works occupy a place of honour to the right of the main editorial, or occasionally in a corner of the front page. The most successful have their work reproduced in other newspapers, and their better cartoons published annually in book form. National and international awards are given for the most outstanding creations.[8] They are relatively free to set their own work styles and environments as long as they meet deadlines, and are rarely confined to office or factory conditions.

Since the arrival of Duncan Macpherson in the late 1950s, Canadian cartoonists have greatly improved their status in the newspaper hierarchy and made important strides toward becoming a profession. In particular, they have won recognition for the principle of political impartiality: the freedom to lampoon the leaders of the day, regardless of their party affiliation. They are proud of their neutrality, and take steps to maintain it against intrusions.

Another aspect of their working conditions is the extent to which cartoonists may choose their own subjects. The best-known artists may sit on the committees which decide the content of the editorial page, or work in relative independence from editorial policy. The fortunate ones can take the initiative by submitting several ideas each day, from which the editor selects one which falls within the bounds of newspaper policy. The less fortunate are assigned their topics and possibly the points which should be made (Hewison: 63). The drawing is expected to be current and quickly recognizable, if necessary by the use of captions and labels. Most interviews with cartoonists in the Mosher collection[9] suggest that they have accepted the limitations imposed by their editor, or that they have found an editor whose restrictions they consider reasonable.

As a result, Press's work suggests that most American cartoonists are like columnists: they are not party propagandists but their work expresses the values of a certain social group with which they identify. Their drawings portray the political world as that group sees and experiences it; and in so doing they often cut across conventional ideologies of the left and the right. They tend to satirize those who are in charge politically, and exercise their freedom mainly from the perspective of their chosen constituency. Since they are commentators and not reporters, they are under no obligation as individuals to look at both sides of an issue, to give equal time to each, or to present outlooks which are different from their own. In so far as a fair balance of criticism is achieved, it is due to the cumulative efforts of many cartoonists, columnists, and their employers.

In English-speaking countries, cartoonists have had very broad licence. Legal retribution by those who have been caricatured has not been a constraining factor. Politicians generally admire their work and welcome the publicity and criticism which they offer. Cartoonists have defended themselves successfully on the rare occasions when they have been taken to court or when laws to restrict them have been proposed.[10]

In practice, the position of cartoonists has depended mainly on their employer, the editor or publisher who is responsible for newspaper policy. The employer in turn is guided mainly by real and imaginary fears about the possibility and the effects of offending readers and advertisers. The working cartoonist, like a journalist, is obliged to balance personal integrity against whatever restrictions the employer imposes (Ericson, Baranek, and Chan: 286–7, 318–22). When the employer has been a political party or a rugged individualist, most have toed the editorial line or gravitated to a paper whose outlook was reasonably close to their own. Breed found that every U.S. newspaper he studied had an editorial policy, which covered in particular the fields of business, labour, and politics. Unlike the sports or fashion correspondents, the cartoonist's work falls squarely within the areas where the publisher is most likely to take a stand to 'protect property and class interests' (Breed, 1975: 179–80, 193).

As newspapers become increasingly monopolistic, some changes may be occurring in this respect. On the one hand, it may now be more difficult for radical cartoonists to find a compatible newspaper. On the other, a monopoly newspaper tries to attract readers of very diverse perspectives, since its competitors are other media and not rival papers. It is therefore more likely now to include a medley of columnists and several cartoonists who will attract different kinds of reader. A loss of advertising revenues, however, is easier to anticipate and also more important financially, than a loss of readership. It is therefore to be expected that cartoons will freely mock the leaders of all political parties, but that business executives will be portrayed positively, when they are depicted at all. Exceptions will be found only among those business leaders who have clearly deviated from the values of their group.

Just as fool shows were the mirror-image of the serious business of running an absolute monarchy, cartoons in a western capitalist democracy are the mirror-image of serious government, as it displays itself in party election materials and official documents. Where political candidates and ministers present themselves in terms of romantic struggle between heroes and villains, cartoonists usually re-present them with the traditional comic vices of arrogance, cantankerousness, hypocrisy, and greed. Although a few artists, such as Daumier, have created serious allegorical works, most have preferred satirical commentary on current events and personalities.

If cartoons are the modern counterpart of fool shows, it can be hypothesized that they will have the same characteristics. They will often pun, or draw a political leader's actions and statements in a setting which brings out their irony or foolishness. Double meanings will sometimes be used to show that these leaders are the opposite of what they appear or proclaim themselves to be. They will often be re-presented as low-status persons whom one would not normally expect to see in office, or as animals or objects which would be ineligible. The cartoon will thus display familiar political figures in an imaginary world. They will have been simplified by caricature and given the guise of fools, children, or other incompetents. The cartoonist, as artist and fool-maker, can insert himself[11] into the picture, remain invisible, or be seen in the cartoon but outside the frame in which the political figures appear.

The caricaturing of political leaders and the quiet approbation of business figures is thus not accidental. It corresponds closely to the behaviour of the royal jester, mocking the courtiers and clergy while respecting the monarch. The mirror is now being placed along the axis of effectiveness. Politicians will consistently be shown to be ineffective, exemplifying traditional bourgeois foolishness. Business leaders will be portrayed, in their rare appearances, as clean and effective, models of the traditional bourgeois virtues of hard work, honesty, and dynamism. This depiction is central to bourgeois ideology: government is dirty and unproductive and interferes with profit-making; business people are clean and productive. They know how to run the economy and therefore the country. Politicians' special skills are exercised through words and symbolic gestures; they serve best when they concentrate on creating an environment in which businesses can freely pursue their own interests.

Cartoons, it is suggested, while often relatively impartial between political parties, will serve the interests of capital by their attacks on politicians. They will stress that power and effectiveness lie with business and not with political chiefs. Their general message will be that common sense and orderliness are characteristic of business and its executives, while foolishness and disorder are almost intrinsic traits of politics and politicians. If this insight about cartooning is accurate, the licence of its practitioners as fool-makers will be exercised in the interests of their employers, and more generally of the bourgeoisie. They will hold up a mirror which contrasts the ineptitude of the public and those whom they elect with the efficacy of those who through talent or inheritance have reached the corporate summits. The ideological message is clear: the corporate world knows best how to choose leaders, and the wise electorate will choose the golden deed over the silver tongue.

THE FOOL SHOW AND THE CARTOON IN POPULAR BELIEF

This section explores the metaphor further, examining whether the popular beliefs and legends which have become attached to the jester can illuminate the work of the cartoonist. Though some of these have only a limited foundation in reality, their persistence may give important clues about the significance of cartoons. Legends arise as popular thought transforms particular incidents or qualities into social types: the prophet, the fearless speaker of truth, the champion of witticism, or the broken-hearted individual who nevertheless puts on the motley to make others laugh (Klapp, 1964: 52–64). They also develop when audiences meet striking characters in operas or plays, such as Rigoletto, or the Fool in *King Lear*. These portraits are exceptional, but an audience which is unfamiliar with the role may conclude that they are typical.

The major beliefs about jesters concern their licence, impartiality, wisdom, and criticism. Jesters' freedom of speech is probably the strongest of these. It is underlined when politicians happily accept the artist's caricature, or when the courts acquit the cartoonist of libel. It is further reinforced by those exceptional cases where a cartoonist such as David Low could caricature much that was dear to his employer, Lord Beaverbrook. Literary works appear to have exaggerated the extent to which jesters were free to make fools of their masters.

Popular beliefs do the same in relation to cartoonists. Those who have specialized in drawings on minority topics and minority viewpoints, for example, have had very limited economic success. The biographies collected by Desbarats and Mosher include only a few artists who take radical positions on economic issues, and just one who focuses mainly on themes connected with native peoples. They have not found employment with mainstream newspapers, and are unlikely to see their work appear in book form. However high the quality of their art, it will not reach a mass audience. Similarly, there are at least two major cartoonists whose work clearly reflects their support for Quebec independence, but only one of them has regularly found a market for his art. In the years when there was no independentist newspaper their viewpoint was not freely represented.

The freedom of cartoonists, then, appears to be exercised in the same way as freedom of the press in general. Editors of major newspapers offer their readers several viewpoints, but within a restricted range. Freedom of the press is not taken to imply responsibility to give space to all perspectives, either equally or in proportion to their prevalence. Perspectives which lack wealthy backers or substantial readerships will probably be underrepresented or altogether absent, not only from individual newspapers but from the press as a whole. This topic will be considered more fully in chapter 3.

Finally, it should be mentioned that licence is a cultural phenomenon and is far from universal. Most authoritarian and dictatorial regimes censor cartoons; if, like absolute monarchs, they need the aid of professional critics with a sense of humour in running the country, they disguise the fact very well. The same is true of a regime at war. Popular beliefs about licence thus suggest, as a generalization, that the only socially acceptable political targets for the cartoonist are those office-holders whom it would be legitimate to defeat.

The second popular belief is that jesters distributed their barbs impartially among courtiers because they were free of alliances or alignments. Correspondingly, one would expect cartoonists to caricature foolishness in all parties. Some, indeed, were very insistent in the Mosher interviews that they carefully avoided personal contact with the politicians they caricatured, since a lessening of social distance might impair their freedom to be incisively honest.

In practice, however, the evidence collected by Press from the United States points to two generalizations about impartiality which are not altogether compatible. First, cartoonists tend to seek targets among those in authority. In this respect most cartoonists are non-partisan in their humour, concentrating on whoever currently holds office and makes decisions. One would therefore expect the opposition to receive less concentrated attention and possibly gentler treatment than the party in power. Secondly, they tend to focus on certain individuals, regardless of party: 'Most cartoonists have had to settle for victory on a smaller scale – victory that comes through sniping at some of the enemy, and occasionally winging one. This is not so psychologically satisfying as crusading. You may even have to face the ultimate pain, the discovery later that you were fighting for the wrong side, that you winged someone who deserved better' (Press: 183).

It is likely, then, that a roughly equal balance will be attained only where the swings of the political pendulum give roughly equal time in power to each party. Precise equality is probably not important to the operation of this form of social control. Both Welsford and Zijderveld perceived that jesters kept all courtiers on edge because the timing and direction of their darts was so unpredictable.

The third popular belief concerns the wisdom of the jester. Fools reputedly had the ability to expose the traditional comic vices and to see the simple truth through the complexities, abstractions, and secrecy with which political actions were sometimes surrounded. Correspondingly, cartoonists seek through art and metaphor to reveal in familiar terms the meaning of complex and distant current events, and the nature of political personalities who are remote from the readership. Constitutional debates may be depicted as domestic squabbles between (English) Canada[12] the husband and Quebec the

"What do you mean, you don't understand the question?"

© Rodewalt, *The Albertan*. Reprinted with permission

wife; or free trade negotiations as an unfair swap between two neighbours. The Quebec referendum campaign was represented by Rodewalt as a solicitation.

It would be difficult to imagine tests of the wisdom of cartoonists. Both Coupe (90–2) and Gombrich (128–30, 138–41) have seriously questioned this version of the pastoral myth – that simple souls untouched by politics have wisdom and insight which more urbane citizens lack. They argue that there are three dangers in the simplification which caricature involves. One is distortion, which occurs when the message displayed is itself incomplete or misleading. Striking examples include Soviet caricatures of the Jews or the Toronto *Sun*'s tendency to portray former Prime Minister Trudeau as non-cerebral – all mouth and no brain. Another is underestimation: if an enemy nation is portrayed as puny or blundering, it may induce a false sense of security in a time of hostilities. The third is the association of political leaders with primitive emotions or stereotypes by depicting them as hate-filled brutes, repulsive reptiles, or subhuman monsters.

The kernel of insight in this popular belief is the recognition that cartoonists, like jesters, span the worlds of politics and foolishness, sometimes to the point of virtually equating them. They transpose into the kingdom of foolishness at least one event from each day's news. Their wisdom differs from the conventional wisdom of politicians. They contravene the boundaries between heroic and villainous, left-wing and right-wing, loyal and rebellious politicians. They demolish distinctions between rival parties which claim to differ substantially from one another, showing that their leaders are equally foolish and often interchangeable. They ignore the niceties of political rhetoric and pull down the façades behind which temporary allies or opponents hide the expediency of their actions. They do not debate or offer responsible alternatives. They heckle, cause discomfiture, and laugh as they point out the irrationality of present political attempts to benefit the public.

WHEN DOES CARTOONING FLOURISH?

Press's survey of cartooning distinguishes three types of regime which profoundly affect the scope of this art. In the case of a dictatorship, the only cartoonists who may continue to operate are servants of the state, whose duty is to echo the official propaganda against public enemies and to chide citizens gently for their shortcomings. Since the dictatorship identifies itself with past heroes and the symbols of the nation, criticism of the state would by definition be unpatriotic and illegitimate (Press: 107–10). Dictatorships can have capitalist, pre-capitalist, or anti-capitalist outlooks; their cartoons will follow the state's official line in illustrating the virtues or sins of private enterprise.

Authoritarian governments, for Press, are recognizable by the fact that they have powerful, autocratic rulers who face strong and growing opposition. The greatest ages of cartooning, historically, have occurred in the twilight of such regimes. Press's prime examples come from Europe in the era when absolute monarchies were crumbling before the attacks of capitalist interests on both their power and their rationality. It is therefore difficult to know whether authoritarian regimes and great satiric art would be discovered together in other social and historical contexts. Since Press's conception of an authoritarian regime may have been based on the particular transition from feudalism to capitalism, it is very likely that the cartoonist critics were serving largely bourgeois interests. Their attack was perhaps simplified by the greater rigidity of an authoritarian than of a democratic regime. Press makes reference to cartoonists who were defenders of the status quo during this major transition (80–105, 115–20), but in general they were found only in Victorian England, when the industrial revolution was nearing completion and Britain was the chief capitalist power of the day. The evidence on contemporary American cartooning does not justify the conclusion that the chief capitalist nation is always staunchly defended by its indigenous cartoonists, however. A mood of laughing satire has characterized the mainstream of U.S. cartooning since the Civil War, with the brief exception of the Vietnam years.

The final type of regime which Press considers is the capitalist democratic state. Here the cartoons appear in major newspapers, and their self-defined role is to assess critically the performance of the government: 'They are especially useful when things are not going well and we don't know why ... Somehow their combined efforts in informing us about what it all means will, hopefully, keep the politicians money-honest and their policies to some degree responsible' (p. 51).

There is of course a close parallel between the cartoonist's predilection for foolishness in government and the newspaper's eagerness to print bad news. The insistence by cartoonists that a favourable portrait would be mawkish is the same argument as that of the reporter or editor who insists that tranquillity is not newsworthy. Both stem from the ideological position that the failings of the government are newsworthy and should be reported to its citizens, while its successes are not and should not. The supporting argument is that politicians themselves can be counted on to publicize their successes widely and to cover up their failures.

This plausible argument emanates from a particular social formation, in which cartoonists are employed by the bourgeoisie to make fun of one of the groups which can affect its power and resources significantly. Other organizations such as trade unions also do this, of course, but their impact is more specialized and their leaders are elected by much narrower constituencies. While politicians are undoubtedly responsible for a great deal of foolishness, this may be equally true of power-holders and, indeed, powerless people in many other institutional settings. What is distinctive in democratic capitalist and authoritarian proto-capitalist cartooning is the pervasive theme that foolishness is endemic to politics yet largely absent from other institutions and in particular from business.[13]

In general, then, the empirical data relating to authoritarian and democratic regimes demonstrate that cartooning has been associated with the rise of capitalist interests and with the ridiculing of the political systems which to some extent resisted their domination. When all three types of regime were compared, editorial cartoons emerged as generally respectful of the interests of their employers, patriotic toward their national symbols, and often very incisive in their caricatures of those who were defined as inimical to their employers' interests. In the specific case of newspaper cartoonists in capitalist democracies, they could aptly be described as the jesters of the bourgeoisie.

This line of argument raises one further important question. Marx generally regarded the state as the executive committee of the bourgeoisie, a body which faithfully promoted the interests of capital in all areas of social life where it was active. While more recent writers (Miliband, 1973; Panitch, 1977) have modified this colourful but one-sided statement, they have still documented the general congruence between the interests of the bourgeoisie itself and those of the bourgeois state. Accordingly, the opposition which cartoons present between sensible business persons and foolish politicians is itself largely fictitious. Chapter 3 will discuss the place which this fiction occupies in the ideological constellation of capitalist newspapers.

Cartoons operate as a social control mechanism exercised by the newspapers over those they perceive as the opponents of the bourgeoisie. They highlight the gaps between politicians' promises and their performance, while drawing attention away from similar gaps in the performance of business chiefs.

One should note, however, that their attack, like that of satire in general, may be two-pronged. In laughing at political figures on our behalf, newspapers may disempower ordinary citizens, pre-empting their efforts to do this in their own way on the issues of their choice. Thus the cartoon may not only legitimate public criticism of political figures; it may also appropriate this social control mechanism on behalf of the bourgeoisie, as the newspapers generally seek to appropriate the social control mechanism of news dissemination.

The situation is not, however, fully determined and unchangeable. Social control itself is an ongoing process and struggle, and not a permanently established fact. Most cartoonists perceive themselves, with substantial accuracy, as allies of the ordinary citizen in the struggle against the misuse of political power. They are perhaps unaware how far their militancy has been appropriated for the purposes of their employers. Many recognize, however, that they work with a basic contradiction: 'The validity and ultimately the popularity of their cartoons depend on their sense of moral outrage, but unlike authentic revolutionaries, they are supported by the established order' (Desbarats and Mosher: 19). The weapon they wield can be used for other causes; and indeed there have always been some radical cartoonists, though their history has yet to be written.[14] For this reason it is important to analyse their work to see how far one can detect what Kunzle has called 'the scowl of capitalist ideology behind the laughing mask' (in Dorfman and Mattelart: 11).

2
Literary Theory: Cartoons as Symbolic Action and Satire

This chapter examines a second body of theorizing which offers insight into the nature of cartoons. It outlines the main ideas of symbolic action as they have been developed in literature and political science. Symbolic action considers the fool show, the novel and the painting as socially constructed symbolic worlds. When applied to cartoons this has several implications. First and most obviously, they are not attempts to portray politicians exactly, as a photographer would. The cartoon characters must be recognizable but their features are deliberately distorted. Secondly, the distortions are not careless and random, but deliberate: they aim to convey certain messages about the person depicted, by associating this leader with certain symbols. A politician may be given a huge stomach or the features of a pig to symbolize greed. Thirdly, the caricaturing is usually consistent, and can be related to the values of the social groups with whose interests the cartoonist sympathizes. The characterization of the prime minister as pompous, scheming, a champion of the poor, or a defender of the rich will reflect perceptions of this person which are currently held in the group.

The cartoonist this engages in a kind of story-telling: 'Once upon a time there was a man called Trudeau who ...' The stories are satirical, humorous, and short – as a rule only one scene is shown. They take us into an imaginary world, which may have much in common with our perception of the real world of politics but which also distorts it systematically in several ways through the use of well-known symbols and stereotypes. This chapter therefore looks at the nature of imaginary worlds, at literary genres and particularly at satire, at social types in literature, and the use of metaphor.

At first glance, this may seem a complex and lengthy diversion. It might be argued that the propositions which will be tested in the later chapters could be derived straightforwardly from Marx's theory of class relations and ideology, once the key metaphor of the cartoonist as the jester of the bourgeoisie has been established. While this is substantially accurate, such a leap from general theory to propositions in a particular context is open to criticism.

In a paper presented in Moncton in 1988, Gilles Houle made a strong and convincing case that an adequate content analysis must take account of both the form in which the material is produced and the context in which it appears. This chapter, accordingly, examines the form of the editorial cartoon while chapter 3 will study its context, the newspaper.

Houle cited a number of instances from his experience where students given coding projects in research methods classes made elementary mistakes on factual matters because the form of the material, individual life histories, was subject to wide cultural variations which they failed to understand. He found that young, urban francophone Montrealers consistently misheard and misjudged the work histories and the ages of elderly rural Québécoises when asked to summarize the early life experiences of these senior citizens who had been reared in a quite different world, and who told their stories within an oral tradition which is vanishing.

In the same manner, the form of the cartoon and the expectations which skimmers bring to it have probably been responsible for the failure of previous research to ask why politics and politicians have been singled out for lampooning. If this is seen as obfuscation, one can of course draw on Marx's ideas about false consciousness, which assert that this is no accident. At the same time, these ideas offer limited insight into the mechanisms by which the cartoon conveys its messages. Literary theory is valuable in filling this gap, as it points to the creation of a symbolic world which is interposed between the skimmer and the sensory world, like tinted spectacles or corrective lenses. It follows that such an interposition will be more effective when the skimmer finds the political world disorderly and frightening, and when there are few alternative sources of information about politics, than when the world is perceived as safe and there are ample alternative sources.

The hypotheses which will be outlined and tested later are the ideological elements; this chapter and the next indicate how they are inserted or woven into a text. The interview as a form of data collection has been extensively studied; it has also been criticized, particularly from the perspectives of symbolic interaction and feminism, precisely because there is evidence that its form influences the content which will emerge and the perceptions of that content by others. There is an obligation to examine other forms of communication and to ask how the authority of the humorous drawing and its caption compares with that of the printed word. For present purposes, the focus will be mainly on the satirical and distorting elements in cartooning. The cartoonist does not claim to be an eyewitness and expert interviewer of informed sources, but does claim to be a perceptive person who has the interests of the public at heart and who can warn it, or confirm its prejudices, that politics is basically public foolishness. Ericson et al. have shown how journalists engage constantly in the negotiation and social construction of news, profoundly affecting what is produced. A similar investigation of cartoons as a literary form is necessary to show the mechanisms by which they convey consistent messages behind their immediate humorous points. Only by an examination of form can one begin to understand how populist and sometimes left-leaning cartoonists may faithfully reflect the broad lines of capitalist ideology in their work.

The chapter studies literary form through the symbolic action perspective of Kenneth Burke. This approach includes some of the key assumptions of symbolic interaction; it is best known to sociologists through the later works of Erving Goffman.

Symbolic action is grounded in the humanist conception that people relate to their world through the meanings they attach to objects, creatures, and behaviour, and through the goals they pursue. It has developed in response to the problems of analysing the content of one-way communication. Burke applied the symbolic action perspective to the analysis of literature and politics; Goffman used it to study advertising and news. As Goffman's research moved away from face-to-face interaction and toward image-making in the media, he placed increasing emphasis on the frames within which images were presented. In his 1974 book, *Frame Analysis*, he concentrated on the content of images, on the assumption that they drew on widely understood meanings which would change only very slowly.

An image is a scene from an imaginary world which is presented impersonally to a mass public. The stylized symbolic action within an advertisement, for instance, is treated as an episode from a larger drama. In one of the more frequent images, the victim Helpless Housewife is rescued from the villain Disorder or Dirt by the hero Brand-Name Product. Later, in *Gender Advertisements*, Goffman (p. 25) examined the composition of advertisements, the settings and poses used to show 'advertisers' views on how women can be profitably pictured.' In the same manner, this study explores the ways in which cartoonists and editors believe that Canada and its dominant and subordinate groups can be profitably portrayed. Occasionally there will be heroes and villains in the piece; more often there will be only fools and victims.

SYMBOLIC ACTION

Burke's theory of symbolic action begins with the premise that humans are distinguishable from other animals primarily by their dependence on, and their skill in, symbolizing. Even the most primary activities such as eating or sleeping are surrounded by a 'symbolic fog' of meanings which establish and justify the scope and limitations of their positions in the social order. The pursuit of social order itself shows this interrelatedness of the symbolic and the material; it 'makes for a tangle of guilt, mystery, ambition ... and vindication that infuses even the most visible and tangible material "things" with the spirit of the order through which they are perceived' (Burke, 1954: 288).

In Burke's conception, social order consists of 'necessitous' and 'symbolic' labour, which are always intertwined. Necessitous labour relates to tangible accomplishments; symbolic labour to success in representing and exemplifying certain values, motives, and goals. Leaders are judged by both types of achievement. At first glance the leader is in an unenviable position, as a performer who will be judged by two strikingly different standards. On closer inspection this double-headed criterion gives the leader two alternative paths to success as long as neither is overlooked completely. In the same breath it sets up two models of failure: the villain who pursues the wrong goals, and the fool who pursues the right ones but without making any discernible progress toward them.

While both types of labour are socially expected of every leader, one may predominate in a particular area of social life. In Burke's observation, symbols and symbolic leadership predominate in three areas – art, power, and order. This judgment, as Burke recognizes, overlaps to a large extent with prevalent capitalist thinking about what constitutes unproductive labour. Klapp (1964: 42–52) and Burke both insist, however, that symbolic leadership is productive in a different way. While practical leaders actively do things, symbolic leaders initiate feelings, orient multitudes, and assist audiences in moving to a state of mind and sometimes to a course of action. The symbolic leader is not an organizer but one who gives members of the audience a vicarious experience. The people enjoy the hero's triumphs, the villain's defeats, and the fool's ineptness, and gain a sense of security and well-being from these demonstrations that the world is still orderly and the right values will win in the end.

Consequently the arts and politics have many common features, and the literary critic can complement the social scientist's work by developing the metaphor of politics as public drama. Politics is, in Burke's view, the area of society in which major public decisions are acted out in an epic manner. Goals are personified as they become identified with the characters who appear to pursue them most vigorously. Thus political leaders become public heroes, villains, and fools and play their parts in dramatic sequences of conflict, suffering, atonement, and reconciliation (Burke, 1966: 38–9, 351–2; 1967: 37–48, 159). It follows that the reporters who condense political life into a series of 'stories' and the cartoonists who re-present it as a set of comical 'scenes' use a similar cluster of conventions to the dramatist. Their activities can best be understood through the concepts which have proved most effective in studying narrative and drama.

Symbols operate by condensing, summarizing, and simplifying social groups and their perspectives. A whole outlook on life is concentrated into a slogan; a badge portrays a set of virtues which the group is trying to appropriate. The symbol affects its believers and their opponents like a medicine because it is 'a formula for our experiences, charming us by finding some more or less simple principle underlying our emotional complexities' (Burke, 1964a: 49).

Symbolic power is not a hollow alternative to material power, something imaginary as opposed to something real. It is a different and complementary kind of power, neither being effective in the absence of the other. Where only one is attainable, however, symbolic or 'moral' victories are rarely despised. Becker, indeed, has identified a whole category of moral entrepreneurs who specialize in establishing laws which prohibit certain forms of behaviour, but whose interest in the technical issues surrounding their enforcement is quite limited (Becker: 147–62). These symbolic actions are concerned with the distribution of values, not material rewards, with the public honouring of certain groups and the public degradation of others. They organize the perceptions, attitudes, and feelings of the public by indicating 'the kinds of people, the tastes, the morals, and the general life styles toward which government is sympathetic or censorious' (Gusfield: 172). Status interests are as rational as economic interests, although they may be less amenable to compromise because their advocates are likely to believe that they are morally right while their adversaries are morally wrong (Gusfield: 179–84).

Burke has paid special attention to two major social processes which are heavily symbolic: sacrifice and persuasion. Sacrifice has been a prominent theme in both literature and politics, and it affords great insight into the nature of social order. The triumph of social order over disorder requires, on the individual level, a corresponding mortification imposed by one part of oneself upon another. The medley of negative reactions stemming from this internal conflict may be treated by externalizing and personifying it: 'hence the urgent incentive to be "purified" by "projecting" his conflict upon a scapegoat, by "passing the buck," by seeking a sacrificial vessel upon which he can vent, as from without, a turmoil that actually is within' (Burke, 1964b: 183).

On the social level, Burke noted that a corresponding cycle of sacrifice was frequently enacted. In *Language as Symbolic Action* he began his analysis with the observation that the concept of the negative is frequently found in the symbol systems of human life but never in nature. The existence of the negative means that human qualities and deeds have opposites, between which there is tension. Polar opposites each exclude the other, because they are incompatible. At the same time they require one another because each exists and is defined only by its opposition to the other. Symbolic action studies the ways in which society deals with social tensions and cultural oppositions through a dramatic cycle of sacrifice involving conflict, victimage, tragedy, and reconciliation, which is sometimes played out fully and sometimes interrupted.

Social tensions are frequently routinized, as when the opposition party in a parliament goes through the steps of calling for the censure of the government, charging it with foolishness, and losing its vote of non-confidence. The opposition members merit the title of fool, since the outcome is known to everyone in advance; yet this play is regularly repeated, with more or less enthusiasm and with minor variations, in every democratic parliament.

The social tensions will sometimes break out of this routine, however, especially when someone appears who intensifies them and refuses to rest until they are resolved. Eventually the party in power will muff its lines and take over the fool role, while the opposition will inherit the hero role from the government party. In this respect the foolishness of the opposition finally appears rational. It keeps creating caps and bells in which to dress the government, and if it is sufficiently dedicated and skilled in its foolishness, the fool clothes will at last be transferred to those who have been in power.

A cycle of sacrifice then ensues. When the government can no longer escape the appearance of foolishness, it will generally try to pin the responsibility on one minister who is expected to take the blame and resign. Not every minister has the makings of a successful victim: it requires a person who exhibits pride, superiority, or some other form of excess, who can personify the values which are to be degraded, who puts up an appropriate fight within the controlled setting of parliamentary debate, and whose departure can credibly bring the promise of general peace. Although the career of the victim will be set back and possibly even ended, the values which were defeated will continue to exist and to assert themselves. Their adherents, though degraded, will not be exterminated; and the victors will find other matters to absorb their energies. The viewpoint which was defeated will rise again and find itself confirmed in second place. The consequence of the cycle, then, will be a reaffirmation of the moral priorities of the majority over those of the minority (V. Turner: 294–8). Once a moral victory is assured reconciliation is likely to begin as both sides proclaim their allegiance to the underlying rules. The cycle will recommence as soon as one side sees a new opportunity for fool-making.

The cycle of conflict and reconciliation between opposites is also observable in the process of persuasion. Whereas sacrifice leads to an unequal valuation of the two opposites which are in conflict, persuasion seeks to stress that they are equally important. A president, faced with contradictory and piecemeal decision-making by the cabinet, may seek a slogan which reconciles its work 'either as an honestly ancestral title from which the specific policies may descend, or as a rhetorical misnomer that gives at least the appearance of substance' (Burke, 1962a: 391). The successful slogan may openly combine opposites in a manner which denies that they are opposed: 'progressive conservative' or 'benign neglect' are well-known illustrations.

Candidates often take full advantage of this flexibility in language to offer polar opposite policies without raising any questions about their compatibility. They promise to increase spending for defence and social services while reducing the budget deficit; to bring about full employment while reducing inflation; to move forward boldly while holding on to all that is best from the past. They can do this because they are speaking of ideals, designing and promoting a symbolic world in which the limitations of our world do not apply. In this world of typifications and not facts, opposing goals can be held in perfect balance, policies generated which can satisfy all parties, or issues redefined in a manner which transcends the present polar oppositions.

If this were pure fantasy, its consistent failure would ensure the disappearance of such rhetoric from the political scene. It has, however, certain elements in common with the riddle: it proclaims that what is insoluble or senseless at one level, in one perspective, or in one setting may be resolved when transformed to another (Maranda and Maranda: ch. 4). When a straight line is perceived as existing in only two dimensions, its two ends are seen as altogether opposite. When the same line is viewed in three dimensions, its ends appear identical on the new one. Burke gives the example of federalism, as an attempt to resolve the paradox of unity and diversity. The federalist philosophy refuses to impose a unitary form of government which would deny differences among the constituent states. Differences are recognized as legitimate; they are valued and perceived as complementary as long as the states have common economic interests. Federation is 'a marriage, and not an economic, military and geometric alignment' (Burke, 1962a: 399). The principles of unity and diversity both have a legitimate place, and neither should dominate the other in a federal system. Burke's analysis is clearly very different from that of Wilden, who asks whether this formal equality is simply a mask for inequality and oppression.

There are many points at which Burke's analysis of symbolism in political behaviour and language offers insights into political cartooning. Political leaders are persons who act out special dramas of good and evil, engaging constantly in representations of heroism, foolishness, or villainy. Cartoons evaluate their success in attending to both symbolic ends and material means simultaneously, and in correlating necessitous with symbolic action. A leader who ignores symbolic action is apt to be caricatured as dull and colourless; one who ignores necessitous action is seen as playing to the gallery while doing nothing; one who does not correlate the two is seen as incoherent.

Cartoons assist the public to participate vicariously in politics, by displaying some of the private motives and character of political leaders in their pursuit of a desired social order. They outline the meaning of political events or actions in familiar terms, often through personification or through allusion to myths. They comment in symbolic drawings on the language and drama which a politician uses in seeking symbolic and necessitous lines of action which will satisfy most electors. They help to ensure that readers have a version of both the symbolic and the material issues which are at stake in a particular controversy, if necessary translating freely from one to the other. The next cartoon illustrates this.

It is not clear how far Burke's view of art, power, and order as the main fields of symbolic action applies only to capitalist democracies. Politics may be by its nature a symbolic activity in every society, though Marxists would deny that social institutions such as politics can have an essence. While Burke's ideas have stimulated extensive work in North America (Bell, 1976; Edelman, 1962, 1971, 1977), it would be prudent to conclude that their relevance to non-capitalist societies has yet to be demonstrated. Cartooning takes quite different forms in non-capitalist societies.

Duncan has translated Burke's theory into a series of functionalist axioms and propositions referring to social order. The two central ones, for our purposes, relate drama to the creation and maintenance of social order, which Duncan sees as the principal function of politics. Once again, there is no overt suggestion that this is peculiar to capitalist society.

The first axiom asserts that social dramas are found in all the major social institutions, and especially in politics: 'Basic functions in society must be

© Roy Peterson, *Vancouver Sun*.

dramatized before they can be communicated as actions' (Duncan: 199). The second elaborates that these actions become crystallized; their form and content is gradually invested with a sacred character: 'Social order is created and sustained in social dramas through intensive and frequent communal presentations of tragic and comic roles whose proper enactment is believed necessary to community survival' (Duncan: 60–1). Social dramas may take seven different forms: games, play, parties, festivals, ceremonies, drama, and rites. These activities are the principal examples of symbolic action.

The basic functions of society are not subjects of everyday conversation, nor can they be discussed within the vocabulary of everyday language. Burke analysed the use of sacrifice and persuasion to show how symbolic language is used to reconcile a pair of goals or values which were important and at the same time incompatible. Similarly, Lévi-Strauss and Bouissac have shown how myths and circus acts are symbolic languages which reconcile the incompatibility and the importance of both nature and culture for social life. This is achieved by inventing incidents and characters which actively incorporate these contradictions: animals which teach humans their cultural skills such as cooking or fire-making, or clowns whose ugly features and clumsiness are coupled with extraordinary agility and musical talent. This approach offers the insight that cartooning is an attempt through humour to talk about the problem of social order and the threats to it.

Goffman's later work seeks to relate symbolic action to the processes which lie behind the finished cultural product which the public sees as an image. He remarks (1974: 1–2, 10) that definitions of the situation are not usually created by those who are in it; participants generally limit themselves to assessing what the situation ought to be and acting accordingly. A process such as victimization or reconciliation has a well-known form and content which participants can manipulate.

Goffman groups these manipulations of everyday behaviour and social rituals into two types: keyings and fabrications. A keying occurs when an activity which is already meaningful in terms of a primary framework 'is transformed into something patterned on this activity but seen by the participants to be something else' (1974: 44).

Three ways of keying everyday activities are relevant to cartoons: make-believe, contests, and ceremonials. First, politicians are sometimes depicted as persons who only make believe or play at representing the interests of their constituents. Secondly, they sometimes spend their time engaged in a popularity contest which may ensure their re-election. Instead of governing the country they concentrate on public appearances to plant trees, kiss babies, and make welcoming speeches. Finally, they are sometimes portrayed making purely ceremonial gestures to lessen unemployment, improve international relations, or increase social well-being. These keyings are not intended to deceive the electors but to replace a difficult if not impossible task by an easier one in order to embellish their claims to success.

Fabrication takes place when an activity is undertaken to induce in others a mistaken belief about what is going on. Cartoons sometimes portray political leaders engaged in hoaxes, con games, and open lies. They do so with the intention of exposing the fabrications, and therefore include some obvious clues, akin to stage whispers, so that the skimmer is not deceived even when others within the cartoon may be.

These insights parallel recent developments in literary theory, which has gradually changed as the novel itself has evolved. In earlier generations the model of communication through the novel was entirely one way. It was written by an author who had God-like knowledge of the innermost thoughts of the characters. The reader was expected simply to absorb and passively admire this wisdom (Hutcheon, 1984: 71–6). Contemporary novelists are writing much more demanding works. The reader may now have to make a considerable effort to link each passage to its location in time and space, to understand which character is speaking and what that person is 'really' like; in short, to make sense of what has been written. The reader is thus called on to direct and perform the novel in order to bring it to life, exactly as the cast and director perform a play. Once the importance of the reader's contribution is recognized, communication becomes at least a two-stage, if not a two-way, process. First, the author interacts with the text in constructing it. Then the reader interacts with it in supplying the descriptive or analytic details which the author omitted, in making sense of the characters' behaviour, in seeking a moral, and in evaluating the quality of the work.

Interestingly, Goffman does not mention the complex of related manipulations which has occupied so much attention in literary theory – parody, irony, and satire. The relationships among these three are by no means simple, and will be postponed until there has been a more general consideration of texts as symbolic worlds. It was asserted earlier in this chapter that a text is neither a faithful copy of the real world nor a precise reflection of the interests and perceptions of a particular social class. It is, rather, a model of a social world which has been simplified to highlight certain themes or messages. Frequently, but not necessarily, these can be directly translated into the present world. Ben Wicks's Outcasts or Pogo's swamp are imaginary places, but readers can easily see the characters and incidents as metaphors for what is happening in Canadian and American politics. Indeed, Wicks often labels his characters with the names of contemporary politicians.

SYMBOLIC WORLDS AND THEIR IDEOLOGICAL CONTENT

The symbolic or imaginary worlds which artists create have much in common with the experimental situations set up by social scientists. Each is a simplified and closed model of a world which operates in accordance with certain principles. Some features are highlighted, while others are eliminated, held constant, or controlled. Its structure and content have been carefully selected to permit a clearer focus on the particular problem which the author has chosen, and on the solutions which the author is comparing. It brings participants or characters together in a controlled setting and confronts them with certain changes. The creator of this imaginary world records the effects of these changes, and the efforts of those involved to make sense of them. The resultant work can be seen as part of society's efforts to understand and represent itself.

In setting up symbolic worlds, artists and social scientists may rely on different mixtures of literal and metaphorical knowledge. Literal knowledge is deductive, and is the end result of a sequence which consists of deriving hypotheses, testing them, and calculating the results to yield valid generalizations about a population. This positivist model has, until the last twenty years, been advocated as the most appropriate one for the social sciences to pursue in order to establish literal truth.

The artist, however, has generally sought metaphorical knowledge, while the investigator has preferred literal knowledge. Cartoonists are not like reporters in this respect; they frequently invite one to imagine a world in which talking animals, birds, mythical beings, or outmoded knights hold political office. While current leaders may be both physically and psychologically recognizable in these guises, they are shown as a different breed from other citizens. They may be represented as fanatical, subhuman, or evil, and therefore incomprehensible in terms of normal motives.

Allport and Postman distinguish between the two types of truth in discussing the metaphorical significance of rumour. Rumour is not valuable as information, for it does not accurately recount what has happened. It does, however, appraise: it signifies precisely the state of mind of the teller. A rumour about a wolf rarely describes it, but uses it as a label or metaphor for something frightening. By investing the wolf with the qualities one hates and fears, one can make sense of the hatred and fear one already feels toward it. Max Black and Ricoeur describe metaphorical truth as belonging to the logic of discovery, rather than to that of proof. It yields insights into the meanings which events, objects, and people have for the skimmer by showing the parallel between, say, women's dissatisfaction with traditional marriages and Quebec's discontent with its position in Confederation. A metaphor, according to Bruner, 'joins dissimilar experiences by finding the image or the symbol that unites them at some deeper emotional level of meaning' (p. 63).

The process of testing propositions cannot either confirm or refute the literal truth of a metaphor.[1] Lakoff and Johnson suggest that one may be more fruitful than another in the range of insights which it generates. One may be more or less meaningful than another; this may lead people to believe that its entailments are true, and to act accordingly. Other metaphors are then treated as false, and the insights which they might have offered are obscured or totally masked. The choice of which metaphors are dominant in a society, however, is not accidental, for 'people in power get to impose their metaphors' (p. 47) and the interests which they cloak.

The distinction between literal and metaphorical truth is easily exaggerated, however. Both versions of truth are socially constructed, and therefore are vehicles for ideology. The research on the relationship between symbolic worlds and ideology treats both as important (Eagleton, 1976a: 180–1; Goldmann, 1975: 9–15). It identifies the features of an ideology, and shows how art promulgates them. This demonstration is central in documenting that cartoons do indeed promote the values of the bourgeoisie in relation to politics. It will be made by examining the general conclusions of research about the effects of symbolic worlds on public images and behaviour.

Most commentators, as Streicher (1967: 427) notes, tend simply to speculate on these effects. Some generalize their personal reactions to the work, assuming in effect that they are typical of the best part of the audience. Some, such as Dorfman and Mattelart, analyse the potential effects which would result if the messages from the symbolic world were applied uncritically to the present world by the whole audience or by specified segments of it. Others – for example, Ericson, Baranek, and Chan, and Tuchman – study at first hand the practices of those who construct symbolic worlds, and infer conclusions about the effects of these practices on the reader. Finally, a few such as Berelson, have asked respondents what they missed when the symbolic world of the newspaper was temporarily unavailable. The processes by which ideology is transmitted can be grouped under four headings: ordering, orientation, legitimation, and criticism.

Ordering refers to the arrangement of values in a hierarchy. A myth is frequently an ordering mechanism: it demonstrates in story form how a value such as obedience and its opposite, disobedience, are both important to the society. It may also show that one of them is more important than the other, when a choice needs to be made, while stressing that neither can be neglected. The conflict between obedience and its opposite is dramatized, and later reconciled by the demonstration of their interdependence. Obedience to one's parents is extolled but the heroic person is the one who consistently obeys the gods, even at the cost of disobeying a parent. The values of the society are illustrated through a concrete example which holds one's attention while exemplifying their absolute and relative importance for all generations. A cartoon or a news story, similarly, exemplifies and orders competing values as it describes an adventure or a scandal and perhaps points out a moral.

The second process, orientation, refers to the structuring of information, attitudes, and behaviour toward an event or person. Opinion leaders take steps to bring events to readers' attention and to impose their informed definitions of these events and individuals before rumours and gossip among the uninformed do so. The entry of Soviet troops into Afghanistan, for example, quickly led to official definitions of the situation from both the u.s. and Soviet governments. Each was presented with conviction; each set this distant event in an unknown country in a familiar conceptual framework; and the two definitions of the situation were totally different in predictable ways. Cartoonists and reporters gave publicity to the event and then offered an overt or implicit interpretation. Motives were ascribed to the participants, and the incident was put in a context which gave it meaning. An attempt was made to organize popular sentiments and to arouse emotions while offering information. If the strategy was successful it would rally supporters and discourage or confuse opponents. An orientation is offered within a set of widely agreed conventions about the perspective of the author and reader. In the case of cartoons, Press considers that these include the values, hopes, and fears of the particular segment of society with which the artist identifies.

The third process, legitimation, refers to the containment of deviant attitudes and behaviour. Certain individuals or groups are presented as causing trouble in a basically satisfactory society, as the next cartoon illustrates. Legitimation involves reassuring readers that basically all is well, and that the political or social turbulence being experienced is only minor and temporary. It may involve persuading those who are frustrated or anguished that their woes are not the fault of the present political and economic system.

Ostensibly the fourth process, criticism, is the opposite of legitimation. Cartoons may openly undercut the official version, mock or degrade those in authority, and debunk their claims to status, truth, and integrity. The ridiculing of individuals, however, may imply support for society as a whole. The cartoonist who criticizes a government for not living up to its own ideals is upholding both those values and the system which claims to embody them.

In so far as a symbolic world offers any commentary upon the material and social world, it becomes a vehicle for ideology. An ideology is a self-contained and circular system of reasoning. Since it does not question its own assumptions, it is unable to see its own boundaries, limitations, and internal inconsistencies. It is oriented toward persuasion and not truth, to manipulation and not precision (Eagleton, 1976a: 96; Moreux; 9–15). It operates therefore to encompass and explain contradictory evidence, and there is no test or critical incident by which it would allow itself to be

invalidated. It may, however, be opposed by another ideology, which begins from the opposite premises, may ask different questions, and is an equally closed system of thought. In this case each takes for granted that it has appropriated the truth. The two cannot intersect; when they attempt to enter the same space their adherents simply talk past one another. They will continue to do this until one becomes dominant.

Eagleton defines a dominant ideology as 'a relatively coherent set of "discourses" of values, representations and beliefs which, realized in certain material apparatuses and related to the structures of material production, so affect the experiential relations of individual subjects to their social conditions as to guarantee those misperceptions of the "real" which contribute to the reproduction of the dominant social relations' (1976a: 54).

The artist, then, constructs an imaginary world, which may but need not closely mirror the social conditions of the time. In so far as it makes statements about this world, the work of art has ideological content. Realism, for instance, is ideological because it sees the contemporary world through a particular set of perceptions and meanings, and claims that its findings constitute truth and reality. To the extent that art moves away from denoting the current situation, it tends to connote some universal quality of human experience. Universal art is ideological because it treats the product of a certain historical situation as if it were a basic feature of human nature. Since cartoons always refer to existing people and events, from Eagleton's perspective they are necessarily ideological.

Inasmuch as cartoons and other imaginary worlds are pervaded by the dominant capitalist ideology, they will have certain core features. Six of these will be outlined here and will form the basis for the hypotheses about the content of the cartoons.

First, they will focus on the theme of culture and nature, social order and disorder. The dominant ideology will equate the dominant class, the dominant ethnic group, and the dominant political unit with social order and culture, while minorities will be equated with social disorder and nature. The former will be shown as representing goodness and stability, while the latter represent badness and threats to stability. Official definitions of what constitutes deviance will be accepted (Ericson, Baranek, and Chan: 28–31, 140; Fishman: 135), and the dominant world-view will be depicted as common sense, as moderation, as the national interest (E. Black: 259; Hartley: 104). Thus the dominant group's ideology will be shown as factual, and so obviously reasonable and true as to be incontrovertible. It is represented as timeless truth and reason, and thus beyond challenge or change (Barnett and Silverman: 21; Millum: 52; Williamson: 136; Worth and Gross: 29).

Price's 1980 doctoral thesis documented the taken-for-granted conviction among Montreal anglophone youth that their forebears deserved almost all the credit for having built Canada as a modern industrial nation, while francophones had contributed little or nothing.

Secondly, within this social space minority groups may occupy only two positions: they can be ignored as unimportant in cases where they exercise little power; or they can be represented negatively in cases where they offer any threat of change. Relative to spokespersons from the dominant group, they will be underrepresented in cartoons; and when they are depicted, they will be more likely than members of the dominant group to be shown unfavourably. This will apply to socially defined minorities such as women, ethnic groups, and deviants. It will also apply to interests which are defined as 'regional' or 'sectional' rather than 'national.' In capitalist and nationalist ideology these are viewed as narrow and selfish, benefitting a particular segment of the population at the expense of the nation as a whole, whose interests are equated with the goals of the bourgeoisie and the federal government. A strong central government is seen, accordingly, as an asset to Canada, while strong regional governments are seen as a liability. The national and federal elites are given moral priority over the regional elites. Cartoonists will therefore denigrate those provincial politicians who seek more power for their province at the expense of the federal government. Although the persons portrayed in the drawings are real, the relationships depicted among them may be largely imaginary (Williamson: 73–4).

Two exceptions might be found, however. Local politicians from the newspaper's own province may be seen as Davids valiantly defending 'our' interests against a dominating federal government. Canadian politicians may similarly be seen as heroes in their dealings with domineering American representatives. Within this conceptual scheme those who advocate independence for Quebec will be a doubly stigmatized minority. Their proposals will be depicted as economically foolish and morally bad. They will be seen as damaging national markets and freedom of trade, both materially and ideologically.

Thirdly, cartoonists, like reporters, will focus on the persons who occupy positions of authority and on the individuals whose deviance leads to the exercise of that authority. Cartoons will thus have a small cast of regular leaders and spokespersons for official interests and policies. Social change will normally be attributed in a capitalist society to outstanding individual effort and talent, and not to an advantageous position in the class structure. Social failure, correspondingly, will be attributed to individual ineptitude or deviance and not to social conditions. Heads of the government will be much more regular targets of cartooning than leaders of opposition parties. Shortcomings will be sought mainly in the major power centres; more attention will be paid to provincial than to local politics, and federal leaders will be caricatured more than those at the provincial level.

Fourthly, the individuals who represent dominant and minority groups will be portrayed as formally equal. Relations of conflict will appear as contests between equally strong opposites: unions and business, left and right, women and men, French and English, René Lévesque and Pierre Trudeau. This 'conveniently' overlooks the major advantages in power and access to resources which the bourgeoisie and its supporters enjoy over the proletariat, the right over the left, men over women, the English over the French, or Trudeau over Lévesque. These advantages permit inequality and the exploitation of the less powerful group to flourish. Furthermore, the emphasis on distinctions according to ethnicity, political position, and gender divides the proletariat and distracts it from dealing with the basic class division (Barnett and Silverman: 12–13, 24; A. Berger: 157; Nimmo: 147). This representation of exploitation as if it were rivalry has been the subject of an extensive critique by Wilden, who gave a wide range of examples. It is difficult, however, to judge how far his citations are representative of news coverage or editorials; this study will examine how far Wilden's claims hold true for cartoons on a range of topics.

Fifthly, although there is in practice massive overlap between the interests of the capitalist state and those of the bourgeoisie, the dominant ideology contrasts the two in some very important respects. It distances them by equating business with social order, while politics is identified with social disorder. Capitalists are generally described as sensible, orderly figures while politicians are represented as disorderly and foolish. The former are committed to effectiveness and constructive activity, while the latter are usually ineffective, destructive, and quarrelsome. Business alone engages in materially productive work while politics specializes in the manipulation of symbols, which is materially unproductive. In these key respects, business and politics are shown as diametrically opposed.

Sixthly, there is a contradictory portrayal of the voter. On the one hand there is a deeply held tenet that the consumer and the voter are the ultimate decision makers in economics and politics. The business or political leader can succeed only as long as these people express their collective satisfaction through favourable purchases or votes. On the other hand, they can be held accountable for the exercise of their responsibility. The voter can therefore be blamed if those who were elected prove to be foolish in their exercise of power. The cartoonist who expresses this ideology is therefore likely to portray voters as fools like the politicians they have elected, or as the dupes of orators who promised one result but who are delivering another which is distinctly less desirable. The citizen is, then, simultaneously shown as the king or queen and the fool; and the public is portrayed as being poorly served as long as it does not learn that business has a better model for decision-making than democracy.

In this portrayal of the public, the vast differential in time is ignored; the power of the voter for a single day during an election is equated with that of the politician every other day. So is the massive difference in the number of decisions made; once the voters have chosen one team over the other(s), they have little influence again until the next election. Finally, the electors are offered a choice between only two or three well-established teams; there is no opportunity to dismiss them all or to set up a new team.

TYPES OF SYMBOLIC WORLD: COMEDY, TRAGEDY, AND SATIRE

This section examines the insights about cartoons which can be gleaned from research by literary theorists on types of symbolic worlds. In his *Anatomy of Criticism*, Frye organized literary genres into a circular system, analogous to the seasons. Spring shares the major features of comedy, summer corresponds to romance, autumn to tragedy, and winter to satire. Although Streicher (1967: 431) virtually equated cartooning with satire, others have pointed out that it is not confined to a single genre. Comedy is likely to have an important place in cartoons dealing with the replacement of one government by another. Press notes that some cartoons are romantic and glorify their subjects; a few are tragic.

Many writers have studied the nature of comedy and tragedy. The present work can do no more than sketch some of the main points of agreement, and examine their relevance to cartooning. The central unifying myth of comedy, according to Frye, is 'the recognition of a new-born society rising in triumph around a still somewhat mysterious hero and his bride' (p. 192). Comedy deals largely in conventional characters and stock situations. It focuses on certain types of behaviour which it deems foolish: character rigidity, hypocrisy, smugness, selfishness, strict adherence to outworn traditions, arrogance, stupidity, envy, sloth, and an excessive portion of a single virtue. These qualities are treated by the author as offences against reason, common sense, and social bonds. In another societal context these excesses could lead to tragedy. Faced with laughter and reason, however, in comedy they lead only to ridicule and ineffectiveness.

There is a conventional happy ending, in which the young eventually marry and establish the supremacy of their own social standards over those of their elders. If the latter confess and reform, there need be no victim. The losers are expected to take defeat and offer congratulations in the heroic manner, pledging to be loyal and to harbour no ill-will against the victors or the system. This is also the model for the political loser.

Both comedy and tragedy, according to Burke, begin with a gap between the magnitude of the heroes and the challenge which their situation presents. Whereas tragedy resolves this by bringing out a greatness in one or more characters which enables them to match the challenge, comedy dwarfs the situation to match the characters. Comedy reduces virtue to politeness and appropriate dress, and marriage from a lifelong enterprise to a temporary conquest. Civility, youth, and cunning are emphasized and rewarded; the goals are to manage self, to manipulate objects and others, to outwit the opposition. Having the right style is more important than having the right values, in so far as a choice is required. Being young is also essential: age is viewed negatively, except when it is employed in the service of youth. The absurdities which isolate individuals from others are generally associated, in comedy, with the elderly.

Any moral judgment in comedy is offered with geniality; the final verdict is usually be happy and not be good. The social goal of comedy is integration, the triumph of the life force over the rigidities which attempt to block its flow. Revelry and the promise of happiness are the order of the day.

Tragedy occurs, according to Sorell, in a situation where responsibility and guilt are assigned to an individual, and not to the collectivity. It brings out human integrity, the triumph of those who are prepared to die for the values which they represent. When the protagonist fails, the failure itself brings forth nobility of character. The structure of tragedy is built on conceptions of a fatal flaw and an inevitable fate, which in turn presuppose an orderly functioning world. Tragedy recognizes the Establishment; it affirms the gods and stable social values. It evokes a predictable audience reaction and identification. These presuppositions are not easily credible in a society marked by contradictions and rapid changes, and some authors have argued that tragedy has largely disappeared from the literary scene as a result (for example, A. Berger: 172–3; Charney: 107, 175).

The tragic victim is one who is not satisfied with the more superficial solution represented by comedy. Such a person seeks more profound social change, whether forward or backward looking, and is ready to sacrifice the comic rewards of social integration and personal happiness in the hope of attaining it. The stance of the tragic victim is perceived by the majority as a preference for social change, even at the price of social cohesion itself.

Faced with the more fundamental threat of a conflict which has gone beyond the point of comic resolution, the majority tries through victimage to re-affirm the symbolic pre-eminence of social cohesion. In Burke's view it purges the social order by calling forth a sustained moral and physical effort to destroy the victim, who is too intransigent or deviant to accept the will of the majority.

Satire is the genre which has been most frequently invoked to categorize cartoons (Coupe: 82, 89–93; Frye: 206; Hutcheon, 1981b: 293; Streicher, 1967: 429) because they share three common features. Both use devices such as irony for purposes of ridicule; both have a clearly identifiable target whose nakedness is exposed; and both aim to alter the conduct of their targets. The satirist may range from a child-judge, who innocently and laughingly notes contradictions, to an inquisitor who metes out symbolic killings. Often satire exposes littleness, ugliness, and evil with high moral motivation. At other times it may take no clear moral position but still treat the misfortune as an indication of human foolishness.

Frye has perhaps given the most comprehensive account of satire, depicting it as the opposite of romance. Romance features heroic figures who undertake perilous journeys and crucial struggles in search of a golden age which will be initiated by a victory, discovery, and/or marriage. A better world is created as innocence and goodness combine with spiritual wisdom to defeat evil. Romance generally reflects in a childlike nostalgic way the ideals of the ruling social or intellectual class.

Satire inverts the Renaissance view that humanity is essentially great and can look forward to steady progress in scientific knowledge and earthly happiness. Its central myth is 'the sense that heroism and effective action are absent, disorganized and doomed to defeat, and that confusion and anarchy reign over the world' (Frye: 192). The protagonist is depicted as unheroic and perhaps inferior to the reader. Far from actively establishing a better world, the chief character is failing and mired in the present one. The characters are all grey, having lost their innocence, ideals, and leadership. They are associated with the qualities of darkness, confusion, sterility, and a moribund life. The symbols of satire and winter are grotesque, absurd creatures. They include the old king, impotence, and death. The enemy is not a villain but a spirit in society which defeats heroism and tragedy. The author is treating society itself as a sterile monster which cannot generate heroes. For Kingsley Amis, contemporary satirists have much in common with the portrait of the fool presented in the opening chapter: 'Their attempt has been to combine the violent and the absurd, the grotesque and the

"Would you mind giving this to Joe?"

May 23/79

The morning after the election that saw Joe Clark's Tories elected to power with a very small majority: looking around at the situation, Pierre Trudeau must have felt that there were some consolations in losing.

romantic, the farcical and the horrific within a single novel' (quoted in Dooley: 27).

Satire may take a high, low, or medium aim. Low satire attacks individuals, according to the principle that the larger they are, the more easily they fall. The author exposes their alienation from common sense and conventional standards. Medium-range satire ridicules the conventions themselves, when they have become rigid and inappropriate. It aims at 'breaking up the lumber of stereotypes, fossilized beliefs, superstitious terrors, crank theories, pedantic dogmatisms, oppressive fashions, and all other things that impede the free movement ... of society' (Frye: 233). High satire involves alienation from heroism itself as a way of life. It distrusts even common sense, and in the tradition of the medieval carnival it may use tabooed expressions and obscenity to attack more basic social dogmas. Its enemy is not human weakness but the non-human foes which have destroyed humanity.

As a genre, satire exaggerates; in Sorell's phrase, it strives to hit the bull's eye by aiming beyond it. It chooses 'to blow up reality to the point of excess and distortion in order to show the hollowness of reality' (p. 19). In doing so, it puts effectiveness and brevity before fairness, giving the impression that the cartoonist is a misanthropist. The satirist may simultaneously praise and vituperate, in a harsh or gentle, compassionate or misogynistic manner. As a result, satire is a double-edged weapon, which may backfire and create sympathy for the target which it attempts to mock.

Irony is closely associated with satire. It was originally considered a figure of speech, a rhetorical device in which one dramatically understated, overstated, or said the exact opposite of what one meant. Gradually its meaning broadened, and today it is generally considered to signify a mood or perspective towards the topic. There are many ways of achieving an ironic effect, and three will be mentioned here. In antiphrasis, the reader learns from the context that the speaker means the opposite of what is being said. In dramatic irony, the audience and the author clearly know something that is concealed from certain of the characters, and which would cause them to change their conduct radically if it were known. Finally, situational irony is found where one or more characters find themselves in a position which confounds their predictions and causes them to retract their statements of principle, by furnishing a striking exception or by placing them where they will suddenly perceive matters quite differently.

Irony differs from satire in two important respects. First, because it is a mood, it has no clear target, and for this reason Hutcheon (1981a: 154) has argued that cartoons are not examples of irony. Secondly, it lacks the militancy of satire. The ironist does not attack from a clear moral position, but undermines by dropping large seeds of doubt. If a new certainty springs up from these seeds and the author leaves it to flourish, the irony is said to be 'stable.' If this and subsequent new certainties are in turn undermined, until the reader has no idea what the author believes, the irony is called 'unstable' (Booth: 5–6). Doubt can be sown by revealing new information, by introducing a new perspective, or by a choice of words which now degrades what had previously been described positively, and flatters that which had earlier been held in contempt. Irony is the perfect vehicle for the paradoxical aspects of reality. It can therefore be expressed through such contradictions as animals which talk, or judicial language in a poem about birds (Tiefenbrun: 91–110, 150, 156).

Stable irony involves a close collusion between the author and those readers who share the same values and can therefore appreciate the incongruity. The author may realize that some will grasp the irony while others miss it, and may play off one section of the audience against another. One segment may hear in a speech only those elements which buttress cherished beliefs, while another hears only those which are critical of them. Irony breaks down the relationship of trust between author and reader, however, in two cases. When it is unstable, the author's apparent changes of perspective leave the reader unsure and suspicious. In melodrama, the reader or audience may begin to view its exaggerated climaxes ironically, as hilarious.

Klapp sees the anti-hero of satire as 'the ideal symbol for the alienated person, expressing the kind of work and the kind of heroes he sees' (1962: 169). At the same time he notes with regret the decline of heroism in favour of pseudo-heroism (success by any means) and mock-heroism (the dominance of steady, efficient little people). He connects these changes to alienation, though he does not pursue the analysis by linking alienation to capitalism (1964: 10–12, 53–86).

OPPOSITE SYMBOLIC WORLDS:
THE POLITICAL BROCHURE AND THE CARTOON

Further insight into the nature of the political cartoon can be gained by examining its documentary opposite, the political brochure. The prototype brochure is a leaflet which appears at election time. It includes the name, portrait, affiliation, and relevant experience of the candidate, and urges the reader to vote for this person. The brochure also includes some slogans from the party's platform; they constitute a naive allegory. In Victorian times an assortment of statues representing such troubles as Sedition and Discord would have been pictured as the property of the opposition party. Another set representing the virtues of Sound Government and Encouragement of Trade would then have been claimed as the property of 'our' party. While the approach today is subtler, the structure of the argument is unaltered (Frye: 90–91).

A political platform presents a symbolic and not a practical solution; it therefore imagines a reconciliation of opposites. The party claims to be the best equipped to govern on behalf of the people. It claims that it can articulate and implement a national interest to which loyal subjects will gladly subordinate their sectional interests. It tries to dispel any suspicion that it favours any particular region, ethnic group, or social class. In addition to these ideals, it offers benefits for everyone.

These generally reflect the prevailing bourgeois ideology that the issues and problems facing a government are both separable and soluble (P. Hall: 65–6), typically by private enterprise with some help from government contracts and subsidies.

A political brochure identifies the party's platform with the local candidate, by inserting him or her into this ideal way of life. Those features of the candidate which best exemplify the ideals will therefore be presented and stressed. A political image will be developed and publicized, if necessary at the expense of a private character which is quite different. The candidate is thus invested with the skills, experiences, and qualities necessary to the party image. There may be allusions to the candidate's private life which are corroborative.

Barthes (pp. 91–2) argues that today the platform is frequently insignificant by comparison with the portrait. A political portrait, he claims, shows a morphology, a posture, a way of dressing: 'It tends to replace politics – a set of problems and policies – with manner-of-being, a social and moral status.' Instead of the candidate's plans, it transmits her or his deep motives, family, mental and erotic circumstances, 'all this style of life of which he is at once the product, the example and the bait.' The candidate gives the impression of being the owner of the dominant value-system, ready to offer the voter 'his own likeness, clarified, exalted, superbly elevated into a type.' The voter is thus heroized and invited to elect himself or herself: sanguine, well-fed, genteel, insipid, sanctimonious, good-looking, virile, and healthy.

Finally, the brochure seeks to appropriate the electorate for the party, through bridgeheads which stress the similarities between what the party has to offer and what the voters want. The two are presented in idealized form, as if they were identical; the candidate epitomizes the stable government, imaginative change, or personal integrity for which the public yearns. Capitalist parties interpret the task of selling a party to voters as only marginally different from that of selling a product to consumers. They appeal to electors to choose a member of their own group, someone who satisfies their taste in politicians. At the same time they are promising that this group member will have access through the party to magic powers for controlling budgets and directing bureaucracies toward that group's goals. As Williamson observes, they take the electorate's ideals, personify and package them, and then sell them back to the voters as attainable through an extremely simplified ritual act which is surprisingly akin to a purchase.

Bennett has taken this line of analysis further. He argues that elections are melodramatic rituals which downplay issues and exalt competition for the support of voters. Parties are judged more by their previous success in vote-getting than by their translation of policies into practice. Policy, he argues, is not the result of electoral decisions, because elections are symbolic acts whose products are other symbolic acts, such as shared public images and promises. These problems serve mainly as inputs which reinforce social images; for those which fail can still be used to legitimate the conclusion that the party's analysis was correct and the goals must be pursued with renewed vigour.

The political portrait, then, carefully selects the most favourable poses and characteristics of the candidate, with the object of identifying him or her in the viewers' minds with the ideals which they accept as basic. It places this political figure centrally in what Gamson and Lasch call an 'interpretive package' and what Hewitt and Hall call a 'quasi-theory': a set of ideas and symbols which are brought together in a more or less harmonious cluster to give a particular interpretation to events and to justify a particular stance in response to them.

The political cartoon can fruitfully be viewed as the mirror-image of the political portrait. Both rely on a combination of artfully contrived pictures and pithy statements to make a political point. Each takes the rituals and bodily features of the politician and artfully distorts them, selecting only those which underline the message. Each portrays a carefully chosen scene from the person's public or private political life, such as a happy meeting with a group of constituents or a friendly conversation with the party leader. The candidate is both the Friend of the People and the Close Confidant of the Politically Powerful. The cartoon and the brochure are both produced for mass consumption, to be 'taken in' rapidly by a population whose attention span is presumed to be very short and whose major life interests lie elsewhere.

Each shows a posture, a way of dressing, a social and moral status. Each depicts a version of the candidate's deep motives and moral norms, so that he or she becomes elevated into a social type. To the degree that they present problems or policies, these are reduced to slogans or one-liners, presented in isolation from one another. Each associates the politician symbolically with a particular interpretive package. The candidate in the brochure does not seek office alone, but claims to be the standard-bearer of many organizations and social groups.

In one key respect, however, the cartoon is the obverse of the political portrait: it is generally unflattering. It reveals the seamy side of the candidate, the contrast between aspiration and practice, and in this regard it counters the messages emitted by the political portrait. The cartoon invites the voters to look at the sorry consequences of electing themselves. The emblems with which the candidate aspires to be surrounded are replaced by a degrading set which likens the office-seeker to a pig, a puppet, or a clown. Where the political portrait showed a sanguine, well-fed, and energetic person, the cartoon shows one who is often discouraged or emotional, obese or scrawny, elderly or jaded. The good looks of the candidate are subjected to multiple disfigurement; and where the successful portrait evoked admiration in the viewer, the successful cartoon evokes laughter. Just as there are few limits to the self-inflation in which political portraiture may indulge, so there are few to the deflation which a caricaturist may inflict.

SOCIAL TYPES IN THE CARTOON: HEROES, VILLAINS, AND FOOLS

Klapp's study of contemporary American social types, *Heroes, Villains and Fools*, elaborates the relevance of symbolic action to the analysis of cartoons. He illustrates how social types and legendary figures are created from social dramas which capture the public imagination: Martin Luther King and George Wallace, Margaret Thatcher and Arthur Scargill, Pierre Trudeau and the FLQ terrorists. As the title of his 1962 book suggests, Klapp focuses on three main social types: the hero, the villain, and the fool. He sees them representing three important exceptions to the usual degree of social control: those who are better than, those who are dangerous to, and those who fall short of the norm. While this typification is widely observable and useful, Klapp's explanation is not very clear or convincing. [2]

The hero symbolizes the principle of social order and the qualities which the culture is striving to preserve. The villain, conversely, symbolizes the threat of social disorder emanating from the opposite qualities, which the culture is striving to restrain within acceptable limits. The two are depicted as polar opposites, but this is quite misleading. Too much selfishness certainly threatens the social order, and a minimum of unselfishness is necessary to its survival. At the same time, too much unselfishness is also threatening, and a minimum of selfishness is necessary. The status quo requires a rough balance, in which unselfishness is prevalent but selfishness is moderately widespread. Correspondingly, symbols of both heroism and villainy are needed; both should be strong, but the heroic should be noticeably stronger.

In the context of contemporary capitalism, the hero is obviously the business leader whose energy, dynamism, constructiveness, and talent for creating employment are highly valued. The meaning of villainy is no longer as clear as it was in earlier generations, when societal values were less diversified and segmented (Ungar; Vatter: 188–92). The current villains are clearly Socialism (in Canada) and Communism (in the United States). They exhibit a similar energy, dynamism, and talent for creating employment, but they see the destruction of contemporary capitalism as a means to achieving social justice. Foolishness, meanwhile, represents a different type of threat to social order. Whereas evil means seriously pursuing the 'wrong' goals, foolishness is a reluctance to take the 'right' goals seriously. In contemporary society, it means economic irrationality.

Public figures are fitted into these social types through media publicity, as their performances in public dramas are reported and judged. They are cast as heroes, villains, or fools when disorder threatens to break loose (Klapp, 1964: 66–100, 169–71, 208–9; Ericson, Baranek, and Chan: 38, 51).

There are certain underlying dramatic scripts which the protagonists may try to follow. They may hope to typecast themselves and draw their opponents into a performance of 'The Hero Conquers the Evil One,' 'The Villain Who Turns into a Martyr,' or 'The Over-Confident Candidate Is Upset by the Underdog.' Cartoons are a significant part of this process, since they present real or imaginary social dramas in a vivid medium where the message is grasped almost instantly. Artists may wage a laughing or punitive campaign to impress on their skimmers the particular qualities and shortcomings they see in a certain public figure.

THE USE OF METAPHOR

Cartoonists and other creators of symbolic worlds work with metaphors in conveying meaning quickly to their glancers. Although the large and rapidly growing literature on metaphor cannot be reviewed here, a few remarks are essential.

A metaphor is a unit of relationship. In its classic Aristotelian form, it is a comparison involving four terms: A is to B as C is to D. A and B in the comparison stand in a relationship of metonymy; they are placed or already belong in contiguity to one another. A and C are in a relationship of metaphor; they are brought together tritely or imaginatively to make two points. First, A stands in the same relation to B as C does to D. Secondly, A is like C, and one's understanding of A can be enhanced by cross-fertilization from one's understanding of C. A metaphor about politician A thus aims to give the skimmer either new insight or confirmation of existing ideas. It places A in a new sign system with C and D, fusing the two realms of experience A/B and C/D for the receiver (Lakoff and Johnson; 36–9, 151–4; Maranda and Maranda: 116–18; Turner: 25, 29).

Metaphors are powerful rhetorical tools. They enable emotional and value-laden themes to be invoked in support of distant, abstract, or puzzling actions. Politicians may persuade their hearers to buy inferior or expensive local goods, in the name of patriotism. Advertisers try to establish a link between their product and a social value or subconscious desire, to convince the viewer that purchasing the object or service will fulfil the dream. Metaphors may serve the process of domination more often than that of enlightenment.

The elements brought together in a metaphor may differ in important ways which are concealed by their juxtaposition. When a politician is portrayed as a fox, this tends to emphasize certain qualities such as cunning and ruthlessness, while distracting attention from others such as intelligence, patience, or devotion which the person may possess (Goodin: 105). The emphasis on similarities also leads to the fallacy of argument by analogy: that since two things are similar in some respects they are also similar in certain others. Carney and Scheer point out that in some ways metaphorical and logical reasoning are opposites: 'The rule is that the stronger the conclusion of an analogical argument, the less likely [that] the argument is [logically] correct, whereas the weaker the conclusion, the less likely [that] the argument is not correct' (p. 155).

Metaphors are shorthand means by which the subject of the cartoon can be located in a wider symbolic structure. When a political leader is drawn as an outmoded warrior or a technological wizard, a whole set of associations and oppositions is offered to the skimmer. Skimmers will of course vary widely in the amount of knowledge they possess about knights and magicians, and hence in what they can draw from this analogy. They may fail to grasp the details of the costume, or may reject the implications angrily. The comparison which the cartoonist intends may be superficial or profound. The successful allusion, however, carries in its wake an entire string of ideological propositions about the groups which this person represents. It brings to mind whole narratives and their attendant morals about what is good, evil, or foolish.

Sometimes the metaphors and their connotations are less obvious than knights and magicians. René Lévesque is frequently shown in (English) Canadian cartoons with several lighted cigarettes in various parts of his anatomy. They clearly denote that he carries smoking to excess, but what do they connote? The only real or imaginary creature which is well known for breathing fire and smoke is the dragon. One plausible hypothesis, then, is that Lévesque is being presented as a dragon. These cartoons would then be variants on the combat myth (Fontenrose: 57–78), of which the English story of Saint George is one well-known example.

Underlying the surface metaphors which are found in individual cartoons, one frequently finds a root metaphor which illuminates or distorts a whole series of drawings or speeches, or a whole area of social life (MacRae: 59–61). Relations between Quebec and (English) Canada have often been conceptualized in terms of those between a wife and a husband. It is the contention of this book that the root metaphor of politicians as fools is central to an understanding of editorial cartoons. This choice is part of a much broader pattern, as the book seeks to show, which presents politics and business as clearly different spheres of activity to which different social expectations apply.

Metaphors are used so widely because they bring together different realms of experience. By showing their common features, metaphors permit one to organize a bewildering and shifting mass of observations into a limited and manageable set of categories or models. Their power and versatility give them the potential to be strong ideological weapons. Citizens today need a great deal of information to make careful decisions about matters affecting their daily lives. Much of it comes through the media, from sources sufficiently remote that readers and viewers cannot readily verify it for themselves or grasp its implications and significance. Both the content of the news and the form in which it is presented therefore offer many opportunities for ideological blinkers to influence what is selected as information relevant to a particular segment of the public, and how it is perceived and organized. The next chapter explores this topic more fully by examining the available literature on newspapers, the setting in which nearly all editorial cartoons appear.

3

Newspapers: The Context for Cartoons

SOME MAJOR FEATURES OF NEWSPAPERS

The previous two chapters have set out ways of conceptualizing cartoons in general. This chapter looks at research on the daily newspaper, the setting in which editorial cartoons appear.

Berelson's early work identified three main services which newspapers perform: information, entertainment, and advertisement. Readers are offered information and entertainment, and in return give their attention at least minimally to the proclamations of advertisers. The Kent Commission in 1981 estimated that 78 per cent of Canadian newspapers' revenue came from advertising. The advertisers and not the readers are thus the major clients of the paper, and their contribution is crucial in keeping prices low and circulation high. Consequently, Smythe argued that newspapers serve to attract audiences and to deliver them to those who have something to sell. In addition to featuring advertisements on every page, they create a 'buying mood' by including whole sections on such topics as real estate, travel, and home improvements in which readers are given sales pitches and detailed counselling by advertisers (Smythe, 1981: 15).

Early in the twentieth century, newspapers passed from the hands of political parties to those of 'vigorous committed personalities' for whom they were both a livelihood and a personal forum (Rutherford: 12). The expense of technological changes and the dependence on mass circulation have since driven most of these 'characters' out of business, leaving the market in the control of a few conglomerates. The Kent Commission found that three chains owned 90 percent of the French-language market in Canada in terms of circulation, while another three owned two-thirds of the English-language market. Although most daily newspapers now enjoy a local monopoly, they face stern competition from radio and television; as a result their influence is declining and total readership is falling, especially among people in their early twenties. Some have tried to safeguard their position by buying the broadcasting outlets which were their main competitors. Others have diversified to the point where information is no longer their main product, and where their media outlets may be used to promote the interests of their other enterprises. These changes have put newspaper management increasingly in the hands of legal and financial specialists, who are likely to view papers as objects to be bought and sold according to their profitability.

Profitability for a local monopoly implies the successful appropriation of different local markets, and an approach to newsworthiness which stresses homogenization of coverage along with diversification of markets. The most extreme example of homogenization occurs when local news is 'bought up' by chains or wire services, transformed into a version which may have very different ideological content (Warner: 343), and then sold back to the local paper at a profit. Indeed, Bissonnette notes that the state may offer grants for such appropriations. Greater reliance on the wire services reduces a paper's need for a large contingent of journalists. Diversification of markets occurs when newsworthy items are found and features written in such non-traditional fields as the peace movement or ecology because they have become keys in attracting and holding important sections of the readership. The most successful newspaper, then, is the one which can attract and deliver both a mass audience for general consumer products and a selective audience for the advertiser who seeks a more specialized clientele.

In the English-language press these changes have been paralleled by changes on the editorial page. In the era of vigorous personalities and press competition, fulmination was the usual style. The cartoonist's task was to reproduce the editorial position with pictorial humour. By the 1920s, as monopoly became more common, there was more concern lest readers be offended, and a more tolerant, bland, reasoned, and inoffensive style of editorial began to come into favour. Eccentric and strong opinions became the prerogative of the columnist, whose articles were signed and did not usually represent the views of the publisher or editors. If a sizeable market arose for a particular viewpoint, a columnist could be hired to express it. Readers would include fans who read the columnist with enthusiasm, and devoted enemies who wrote furious rejoinders. It mattered little which side they took as long as interest was retained and papers were sold.

Press (33–49, 178–207) has given a fairly full account of the changing technical conditions of cartooning during this period, as mass production and monopoly ownership took over. He has also examined in some detail the three traditional constraints on a cartoonist's freedom: deadlines, editorial policy, and the fear of upsetting advertisers and readers.

Until recently, Canadian and American cartoonists were minor members of the editorial team, and were expected to accept editorially proposed topics, and in some cases to submit their drafts for approval. As a result, some critics have argued that until recently editors have restricted them to bland drawings which would not offend anyone (Breger; Klapp, 1962: 90–1; for other views, see Freund et al.).

Only at the beginning of the 1960s, following the lead and insistence of Duncan Macpherson, did Canadian cartoonists begin to acquire the privileges and responsibilities of columnists: choosing their own subjects without editorial supervision, occupying a significant part of the editorial page, and taking full charge of their own work. This practice is now generally accepted, and some Canadian newspapers have several cartoonists with very different styles and preoccupations.

Artists today generally take pride in their political neutrality. While a few may consistently attack one party, most insist on their freedom to expose foolishness in government, whichever party is in power. They still face the three traditional constraints, but for most practitioners these are not severe. Consequently, the search for their principal bias should be at the system and not at the party level. Their commission is to ridicule the foolishness of political life. Individual capitalists or the tycoons in a particular industry may become fair game when they exhibit the same foolishness as politicians, but as a class they are not caricatured in the daily press.

THE PRESS, THE STATE, AND BUSINESS

In general, the capitalist press shares the outlook of its advertisers on the capitalist state. Rutherford found this to be true even of the Canadian radical press during the inter-war years: its abuse was reserved for civic utilities and an occasional atypical capitalist. The mass press, meanwhile, 'popularized an entrepreneurial ideal that glorified the businessman as a national hero, acquisition as a public good, and competition as a progressive force. Time and again, this press urged the virtues of industrial harmony, ever ready to call upon the state to impose peace upon a warring Capital and Labour, an action usually against the best interests of the workingman' (p. 74).

Marxist political scientists, such as Fournier, Miliband, and Panitch, have shown that the state usually operates in the interests of the bourgeoisie, when they clash with those of the general public. It assists in supplying companies with services which are necessary but not profitable: transport routes, a trained and healthy labour force, and the suppression of social protests which might threaten profits, for example. It propagates nationalism, an ideology which creates a loyalty to the state and identifies the national interest with that of the ruling class. It then portrays regional and working-class interests as local and selfish ones which should bow before those of the nation as a whole, as defined by its ruling class. The state generally restrains only those capitalists whose activities threaten the interests of capital as a whole.

Nevertheless, the state is frequently seen and feared by capitalists as a rival whose power may be used against them. The capitalist state develops interests of its own, which it pursues in the same manner as private business. It seeks a monopoly on the loyalty and obedience of those whom it defines as 'its' subjects, on the use of violence in 'its' territory, on the right to make and enforce laws. It seeks to centralize power and suppress opposition where this is necessary to its goals. It appropriates other territories and citizens to increase its resources. It lives off the loyalty of those it defines as 'its' citizens in the same sense that a business lives off the productivity of 'its' employees. This is seen most dramatically when the state calls on young citizens to die in order to defend their state and the territory and resources it has appropriated, although these may be at the other side of the globe. It can increase its economic and political power over business by such policies as taxation or the manipulation of the money supply and interest rates, and by regulating business practices. Within the country, then, there is considerable potential for conflict, although in practice collaboration and consultation are much more common.

The state relies on its national bourgeoisie to appropriate national markets for their joint benefit, assisting it with subsidies, tariffs, and varied services. In Canada's case, Panitch (pp. 12–19) documents that the state soon realized the inadequacy of its indigenous bourgeoisie in most types of enterprise and invited foreign capitalists to develop its resources and to qualify as part of the Canadian bourgeoisie. It tried in this way to appropriate additional enterprises through an exchange of economic advantages for certain requirements of 'good corporate citizenship.' The result is a continuing and frequently unequal struggle between state and business in the national market.

In international affairs, the interests of business and political leaders are perceived as more closely aligned. Businesses try to co-opt government into aiding and underwriting their efforts to increase their share of international markets and their profits abroad. In return, governments try to co-opt businesses as means of appropriating territory and resources abroad, as sources of tax revenue for themselves and of employment for their citizens. Their rivals are other governments and those corporations which it defines

Northern Destiny . . . Southern Exposure

© Roy Peterson, *Vancouver Sun*. Reprinted with permission, The Toronto Star Syndicate

as foreign, who are seen as collaborating in the same manner. For this reason, national and commercial interests abroad are generally perceived as closely identified. A cartoonist who is expected to denigrate politicians in their internal dealings will be expected to display patriotism in external affairs, especially during a war (Press: 138–77). One might therefore expect elements of romance, comedy, and tragedy in cartoons relating to international affairs, as compared with a steady diet of satire on the domestic scene.

Nationalism as an economic ideology, then, favours the expansion of those enterprises which the state has appropriated for itself, and those which have appropriated the state for themselves. As a political ideology it depicts the relations among capitalist states. As Wilden points out, the nationalism of (English) Canada is defined in terms of an imaginary rivalry with Quebec in the political sphere, and a partnership with Quebec against the rival United States in economic and possibly in cultural life. Quebec independence poses two threats to this nationalism: on the political level, it is attempting to appropriate for itself a part of the territory which Canada has long claimed; and on the economic plane, it is trying to establish and support a Québécois bourgeoisie which will limit still further the power of Canadian capitalism.

Relations between the press and the state also focus on appropriation and property rights. The press certainly seeks to scoop information about the government's use of its monopoly power, under the guise of serving the public interest. The relationship is not simply one, however, in which the state tries to hide what the press is keen to reveal. Both claim the right to know what is happening in the state, and to decide whether and how this news should be released to the public. There are numerous instances where the state seeks publicity but the press refuses.

Disputes about the ownership of information should not, however, occlude the widespread collaboration which exists. Ericson, Baranek, and Chan have documented the extensive reliance which reporters place on official sources, and the extent to which officials initiate and structure the stories which are published. There are also cases where both agree to keep news out of the public domain (Breed, 1964: 189–98; Nielsen: 308–11).

On a different plane, the state's interest in control of information leads it to try to restrain the trend toward press monopoly by establishing royal commissions which deplore this possibility and propose legislation. It is claimed that news dissemination is a public service which differs from other forms of private enterprise because information is such a crucial commodity; and that this service is better performed when there are several newspapers in each city. The Kent Commission, indeed, reached the conclusion that monopoly and chain ownership rather than advertiser dominance were the main problems in the industry. This required considerable verbal gymnastics, including the observation that this 'monstrous' outcome was reached by a 'natural' process.

The press maintains a relatively firm distinction between public and private business. It tries to appropriate the lives of public figures, treating them as newspaper property whose on- and off-stage activities should be closely monitored for the public good. Those defined as significant power-holders in the public sector are fair game for reporters and cartoonists alike. The public-private distinction, which is central to capitalist ideology, serves to justify a double standard in this respect. Significant power-holders in the private sector are protected from such monitoring both by journalistic conventions of what is newsworthy and by libel laws which offer much fuller recourse against defamation to those in the private sector (Epstein: 102). Ericson, Baranek, and Chan (p. 38) stress that the double standard is applied even where public and private organizations are engaged in the same economic activities.

The best summary of relations between the press, business, and the state can be found in the phrase 'cleansing by publicity.'[1] Its double meaning neatly summarizes the stance which the press takes toward the two complexes. It concentrates on cleansing the state of unbusinesslike behaviour by giving adverse publicity to waste and incompetence by government leaders and officials, and to whatever it sees as unjustified intrusions by the state into private property. It concentrates simultaneously on cleansing business by giving its advertisers full scope to publicize claims for its products and services without refutation, and by not printing material which would harm its image and interests.

This policy would clearly favour political cartoons while precluding business cartoons, as Burke recognized: 'The strategy of our orthodox press, in thus ridiculing the cacophonous verbal output of Congress, is obvious: by thus centering attack upon the symptoms of business conflict, as they reveal themselves on the dial of political wrangling, and leaving the underlying cause, business conflicts themselves, out of the case, they can gratify the very public they would otherwise alienate: namely the businessmen who are the activating members of their reading public' (1967: 201).

HOW CARTOONS DOMESTICATE THROUGH METAPHORS

Having discussed cartoons as symbolic worlds, and the context in which cartoons are produced, the analysis now turns to the processes by which the dominant ideology of capitalism is transmitted. This will be done by applying Goffman's sensitizing concepts of domestication and hyper-ritual. Goffman's late work (Goffman, 1979; Gonos) draws heavily on Durkheim, treating such visual products of popular culture as photography, advertising, and political portraiture as collective representations.

He sees advertisements as hyper-rituals, or ritualized versions of ritual performances. They should be viewed, not as accurate depictions of reality, but as twice removed from reality into the normative. A ritual is a normative performance, a display of what people ought to do and be. A hyper-ritual is a display which shows how people ought to perform a ritual, as a director might show a performer how to display sadness. In an advertisement, sellers are re-presented as wise, helpful, powerful, and expert, while consumers are re-presented as foolish, helpless, weak, and ignorant. Political cartoons can equally be viewed as hyper-rituals: they re-present political actors in stylized form as personifications of elderliness, cantakerousness, and ineptitude. Voters are thus warned that by placing their trust in politicians of any party they are assured of trouble. Such idealized portrayals of the consumer, voter, business executive, or politician are sometimes simple and direct.

Frequently, however, metaphor is used as a clarifying or masking device which intervenes in the transmission of the message. Goffman refers to this, aptly, as domestication: 'a means of extending intimate comfortable practices outward from their source to the world' (1979: 9).

Press has discussed domestication at length, underlining the necessity of commentators, summarizers, and interpreters if democracy is to be maintained in a complex society. Most news concerns personalities and events which are distant and outside the everyday life of the reader. The newspaper domesticates this information by re-presenting it in terms of metaphors which show the equivalence of international news to local news, domestic situations, favourite stories, or stereotypes from popular culture. A surprising baseball team becomes a 'giant killer,' Quebec independence becomes the desire of a wife for domestic liberation, René Lévesque becomes an embarrassing brat, and Ronald Reagan becomes a cowboy applying Wild West morality to urban problems. While Press carefully explored the social assumptions made by individual cartoonists, he did not examine the possibility that a common ideology underlay almost all their work.

Similarly, Goffman firmly and incisively opposed the stereotyping of women as innocent, foolish consumers, while making only a very brief allusion to the possibility that this is done because it is profitable (1979: 25).

"IS THIS YOUR LITTLE BOY?"

Consequently he generates a sense of outrage among liberals, which he seeks to assuage by caricaturing the advertisers who have caricatured women. He invites the reader to take sides for women and against advertisers.

While the concepts of ritual and hyper-ritual are useful analytic tools, their explanatory value is limited because they stop short of indicating why hyper-ritualization is so widespread – whether in its economic form, where the ideal consumer meets the ideal product, or in one of its political versions, where the ideal foolish Canadian elects, and pays taxes to support, the ideal foolish government.

Advertisements can be adequately understood, as Williamson has demonstrated, only by showing how they fit with consumerism. Linkages can perhaps be made between the consumerism preached by the capitalist enterprise in furthering its own interests and the nationalism of the capitalist state as it appropriates symbolic public support for its policies (Breton). The twin slogans of the consumer and the voter as kings constitute one such link; the parallel selling of products and political candidates through slogans, artwork, and actors is another (Corcoran: 143). A third is the collaboration of business and political leaders in channelling local loyalties into support of such pseudo-local enterprises as major league sports teams. Bilingual advertising constitutes a fourth: where the state cannot unite French- and English-speaking Canadians into political harmony, private enterprise seeks to unite them into a common enthusiasm for the same consumer goods (Shell). Research is also needed into the mechanisms through which domestication acts as a conduit for ideology in the newspapers. The next three sections study three of these mechanisms: story-telling, rhetorical oppositions, and decontextualization.

STORY-TELLING AS A MECHANISM OF DOMESTICATION

The domestication work of cartoonists has been virtually unexplored, but an examination of the comparable work done by reporters sheds some light on it. The structure of news reporting has been studied at several levels: the newspaper as a whole, its organization by sections, and the single article. Some studies have expressed concern that a good structure for ensuring impartiality is threatened by the time and profitability constraints which capitalism imposes, or by a lack of professional self-discipline among journalists (Breed, 1964, 1975; Gieber). Some have gone further, suggesting that the structure of the media is itself inherently biased at each level (Golding and Murdoch). Others have viewed the news as socially constructed, the result of elaborate and often half-understood negotiations within news organizations as they convert an erratic foundation of events into a steady stream of stories (Ericson, Baranek, and Chan; Tuchman).

The Davey Commission asserted that 'If it is to be news, there must be a "story." And if there is to be a "story," there must be conflict, surprise, drama. There must be a "dramatic, disruptive, exceptional event" before traditional journalism can acknowledge that a situation exists. Thus the news consumer finds himself being constantly ambushed by events' (p. 9).

The transformation of events into stories and their successful mass reproduction in words and pictures for profit involve first shaking and then re-establishing social order, bringing a tale of chaos yet telling it reassuringly (Kevelson: 125; Thompson: 180–2). Klapp (1964: 14) and Warner (pp. 341–5) have illustrated the role of the media in setting up dramatic confrontations and generating legends about public figures. Although some events and personalities lend themselves more readily than others to this transformation, reporters and their editors exercise considerable control over what is noticed or ignored, what is emphasized, and what perspective is taken. The 'cultural power' exercised by the media as an institution includes the power to define which issues enter public communication, to define the terms in which these issues will be debated, to define who will speak to the issues and terms, and to manage the debate in the media (Connell: 139–40, 147–50; S. Hall, 1975: 143). Their task is made easier when readers have no personal knowledge against which the published accounts can be checked.

Reporters follow a framework of conventions relating to article, paragraph, and sentence length, order of presentation, balance between different viewpoints, and the exclusion of their personal opinions. Their articles generally distinguish between two types of material: facts and opinions. 'Facts' are pieces of information which are presented as indisputably true. They include much which is not controversial: the names of office-holders and their timetables during public ceremonies, and the scores in sporting events. Other material which is presented as factual has a more dubious status: personal estimates of crowd size or mood, adjectives describing events or personalities, and assessments of the origins of troubles or turning-points in a sequence of events. These add both colour and bias to what would otherwise be a much duller account. The functional distinction between facts as necessary information and facts as entertaining details, however, is frequently blurred by the conventions of story-telling, and by the challenge of presenting routine happenings dramatically enough to hold the attention of non-participants.

'Opinions' in a news story generally consist of statements by persons who have privileged access to knowledge of the subject. Reporters rely heavily on giving a balance of positive and negative partisan opinions. The views of the general public are rarely included, except for a specific purpose such as showing that leaders are out of touch with their constituents. Leading political and official actors are thus the centre of the narrative which highlights dramatic events and colourful remarks.

Unless the article is a feature, the conventions of neutrality and equal exposure are generally applied as part of the liberal ideology of fair play. This doctrine, which developed in an era of small organizations among persons whose resources were relatively equal, may have very different results in an era of monopoly capitalism. Most large and well-known organizations are viewed as trustworthy and may be able to state their case briefly because they are perceived as stable and orderly. A small radical group may attract publicity easily for unconventional acts, but may need much more space to convey the reasonableness of its position for several reasons. It is likely to be part of a whole outlook on life, and not an isolated stand. This outlook is likely to be unorthodox and difficult to grasp during a brief presentation. The group can attract media attention only for deviant activities, and consequently it cannot take any public knowledge of its views for granted. Finally, because it is unorthodox it is likely to be distrusted.

A story which was structured mechanically to show a dispute between two sides, each motivated by self-interest, would be poor drama, since it would not contain the seeds of its own resolution. The dispute is therefore mediated by the reporter and/or by experts whose position is taken to be non-partisan and to represent the public interest. The reporter and the expert thus insert themselves in the article as the advocates of realism, reasonableness, and compromise between two committed and often intransigent opponents. On close inspection this position of reasonableness proves to be the commonsense beliefs which hold the social order together (S. Hall, 1974: 22–5).

Story-telling is crucial to capitalist news reporting, as McLuhan recognized in his dictum that the news in the paper very quickly becomes stale. It should be noted, however, that lack of suspense does not inevitably mean a poor story: a familiar tale whose plot is known, and a romance whose outcome is largely predictable, are still popular. The capitalist emphasis on continuing mass sales to the same audience, however, does depend on firmly held popular values about staleness. News-vendors always stress that they are offering the very latest developments, implying that these are more valuable than news which is an hour or two old. Planned obsolescence was built into the news industry long before it became a key phrase in manufacturing: profits have always depended on the willingness of yesterday's readers to buy today's paper.

The most reliable strategy for achieving this has been to build incompleteness and suspense into as many stories as possible, while keeping them within a familiar set of narrative conventions. Sporting events generally fit well into this format. Nearly every day brings new baseball or hockey results to the enthusiast, each potentially crucial to the unfinished championship race. National and international political news items lack this organized regularity, and must be fitted into the conventions of the 'story.' The paper therefore truncates or stretches its reporting of events into a set of daily instalments of relatively fixed length about the doings of a limited set of 'regulars' whose motives and characters gradually congeal into social types. Old members of the cast die with due ceremony, and new ones are introduced with a suitable flourish.

In cartoons, similarly, the cast is relatively fixed, and the persons caricatured become old friends for the regular skimmer. There is some evidence (Beniger: 103–11) that television has assisted in making these regulars more immediately identifiable, thus reducing the need for cartoonists to attach labels to those they portray. They engage in an ongoing comedy compounded of goodness, evil, and especially foolishness. There is sometimes suspense in cartoons, because they depict vividly sources of fear and anxiety: the arms race, inflation, Quebec independence. There is more often reassurance, that fundamentally nothing has changed and that politics and foolish behaviour are still synonymous. Dexter argues this point tellingly in relation to a small-town mayor who achieved national prominence through the press: 'Muldoon's very appropriateness as a comic buffoon arose out of the fact that he was in no sense or manner a challenge at any basic level ... to national values – and therefore it was possible to blow him up many times larger than life by selective reporting' (pp. 339–40). Cartoons thus domesticate political action for the skimmer, elucidating its excitement and relevance while reducing its status from global drama to overgrown village or family feud.

As a witty columnist, the cartoonist seeks to highlight and interpret political events and personalities for the viewers. They are offered advice through picturesque metaphors on the appropriate attitudes to adopt toward circumstances which may be new, distant, abstract, and complex. The artist's focus on a modest number of well-known characters, however, makes the editorial cartoon less of an innovative commentary and more akin to a soap opera.

RHETORICAL OPPOSITIONS AS A MECHANISM OF DOMESTICATION

The importance of rhetorical oppositions in the social construction of meaning has been a major theme in semiotics and rhetoric, though it is also studied more peripherally in many other disciplines. The contrasting of facts and opinions has already been discussed; while most reporters and editors treat them as opposites, Park (p. 18) suggested that they can be more fruitfully perceived as parts of a continuum. The importance of balancing them has already been considered as central to the capitalist reporter's art. This section shows how the newspaper as a whole is structured around the rhetorical oppositions of good and bad, of serious and light news. This will be done through a review of the main issues in the debate on newsworthiness.

Critics of the press have long maintained that, with very few exceptions, it concentrates on conflicts and disasters. These are reported in detail, while happy events are generally, though not invariably, ignored. Failures and scandals are widely publicized, but success and virtue are not (Burke, 1967: 103; de Guise: 229; Kevelson: 70; Klapp, 1964: 147; McLuhan: 188).

Three main responses have been given to this charge. First, defenders of the press claim that virtue is not newsworthy, and that a paper which focused on the tranquil, happy events would be so dull that no one would buy it daily or even weekly. Readers seek excitement, which means suspense, conflict and disturbance in the social order. Ericson, Baranek, and Chan and Connell (139–41, 155–6) explain that news is socially constructed to mean the unexpected: whatever breaks from common sense and everyday middle-class experience. When the unexpected occurs, journalists and those whom they treat as credible witnesses and authoritative spokespersons come forward to explain and reassure the public. One might add that reporters also interview people whom they regard as less credible witnesses. Usually these are lower-status or deviant individuals, and the journalist indicates that they should not be taken too seriously.

Secondly, defenders claim that the purpose of the newspaper is to criticize. The government has extensive resources for publicizing its achievements, and the opposition is interested only in embarrassing it for partisan gain. The press is therefore needed as a watchdog, to offer criticisms which are independent of any political ambitions, and to point up weaknesses in the positions of each of the contenders for power.

Thirdly, researchers may counter that, on the basis of the evidence, the media serve mainly to reassure (Breed, 1964: 183–7; Gieber: 175–8; Epstein: 204; Gans: 52–61). The reassurance may take several forms. It may be conveyed through the matter-of-fact manner in which it is reported that two thousand people died and one hundred thousand were left homeless – especially if only one family is pictured, or if the dead were 'enemies' or non-Western people. The reader is often led to believe that the authorities can cope, and that adequate help is on the way. There may be reassurance in

the fact that the news comes from a distant place, and therefore by implication all is well in the reader's home area. Comfort may lie in the assurance
that the stories today are similar to those reported every other day, and that
the world has remained as terrifying as the reader expected.

This third point remains speculative and controversial. Others have argued
that the constant diet of bad news does not contain much reassurance. Many
news reports leave the reader depressed or in suspense, awaiting the next
instalment tomorrow. Cartoons remind one that politicians seem helpless
in the face of inflation, foreign domination, and most forces which are
socially defined as evil. Pursuing the analogy of the reporter as dramatist,
they conclude that the tensions created by bad news in the opening pages
are resolved only later in the paper, when the reader reaches the good news
of the advertisements. Here the 'happily-ever-after' story predominates.
Even if an advertisement begins with the bad news of suffering, it is altogether predictable that it will conclude with the good news that a solution
may readily be found by patronizing the company, service, or charity which
paid for the advertisement. In the poverty-free imaginary world of most
advertisements, the only source of discontent is the tension of decision-
making when several competitors make attractive appeals. Even for that,
the advertisement offers its own solution: patronize us.

McLuhan treats this balance as a dramatic necessity: 'In order to balance
off the effect and to sell good news (advertising) it is necessary to have a
lot of bad news' (p. 188). Burke makes the same point more picturesquely:
'Journalists and advertising men make a good team, since the one keeps us
abreast of the world's miseries, and the other keeps us agog with promises
of extreme comfort ... a crude, secular analogue of the distinction between
Christus Crucifixus and Christus Triumphans' (1954: 277). This theory of
dramatic necessity would of course offer an explanation for the relative
placement of good and bad news in newspapers. Kevelson and Duncan note
that there are several rhetorical oppositions here: advertisers make rental
payments to sell good news, while readers make subscription payments to
buy bad news.

The debate over good and bad news leaves out the opposition between
serious and light news. Not only do humorous items find their niche in the
newspaper, but a light-hearted approach to current events and personalities
is obviously fundamental to the cartoonist's work. The emphasis on socially
constructed heroes and villains should not blind us to the social construction
of fools in the media.

These oppositions at the level of the newspaper operate in the same manner
as the conflicts presented within the single story: they set up a triangular

framework on which to construct a version of social reality (see Chart 1). In the story the triangle has two dimensions: partisanship and favourability. The supporter and the opponent of any proposal are identical in being partisan, and opposite in their favourability to it. The reporter and/or expert are their opposites in that they lack partisanship, and are intermediate in terms of favourability.

A similar triangle can be shown to underlie the roles of hero, villain, and fool; the dimensions in this case are seriousness and goodness (see Chart 2). The hero and villain are identical on one and opposites on the other; the fool is their opposite on one and intermediate on the other.

The mechanism of rhetorical opposition is often used as a device to achieve two goals. First, the speaker's position is arbitrarily associated with what is good, while that of the opponent is linked to what is bad. Secondly, those

Chart 1. Rhetorical oppositions in the newspaper story

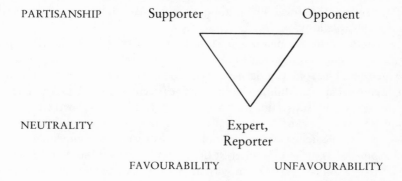

PARTISANSHIP   Supporter   Opponent

NEUTRALITY   Expert,
                               Reporter

          FAVOURABILITY   UNFAVOURABILITY

Chart 2. Rhetorical oppositions among Klapp's main social types

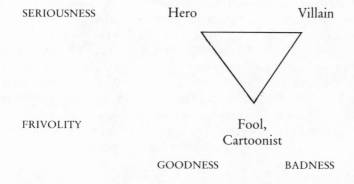

SERIOUSNESS   Hero   Villain

FRIVOLITY   Fool,
                              Cartoonist

               GOODNESS   BADNESS

who try to remain impartial are subjected to various kinds of pressure to take sides with the self-defined heroes against those whom they define as villains. Reporters generally seek to avoid these pressures by setting up the second rhetorical opposition, partisanship-neutrality, along which they are differentiated from both supporters and opponents and which legitimates to some degree their decision to reject both good and bad designations. They use the expert role as the intermediary through whose eyes they seek to view the conflict, or behind whose mask they hide their own views. Cartoonists likewise use the fool as their intermediary or mask in looking across at the turbulence caused by all the serious people.

DECONTEXTUALIZATION AS A MECHANISM OF DOMESTICATION

The third mechanism to be discussed is the practice of taking events and personalities out of their context in the process of converting them into stories. This practice is not peculiar to modern journalism; many traditional stories have been abstracted from time and space as if they were natural and true for all situations.

In examining the detailed organization of the parts of a magazine, Veron compared publications geared to middle-class and to working-class readers in Argentina. His conclusions are perhaps valid for other western countries and for newspapers. Middle-class magazines were found to be organized into sections and subsections in a relatively fixed manner which corresponded to their readers' everyday thinking about social institutions: business, sports, medicine, and education. This organization presupposed a readership which judged the interest of articles by their subject-matter, and tried to keep abreast of news in certain areas while treating others as less relevant and therefore lower priority.

For most magazines produced for a working-class audience by the same publishers, there was no such categorization. Articles tended to be clustered around a few events; they appeared as an accumulation of independent facts, connected only through 'human interest' and a personalized perspective which working-class readers were presumed to share. Each was taken out of context and treated as irreducible and singular. The world beyond the reader's everyday experience was thus portrayed as a constant stream of random but interesting incidents (Veron: 68–9; J. Berger: 55) with no underlying consistency. This emphasis on concrete and contingent events and a present time-orientation deflects the reader's attention from structural linkages between events which might present a meaningful critique of the current power structure if seen in conjunction with one another (Hannigan: 157–61; Tuchman: 179–80).

While this was most plainly true for working-class publications, fragmentation and a lack of historical and cross-cultural perspective are also observable in middle-class reading matter. Time and space constraints are a major contributing factor. A spokesperson may have spent twenty minutes giving the reporter a detailed picture from which the latter then extracts a few sentences. The reporter lacks both the time and the expertise to undertake detailed investigations, and is obliged to rely heavily on the information supplied by those in official positions. Since they will be serving as important contacts and sources of future stories, their continued collaboration is a very important asset.

A further element in decontextualization is the decline of local news. The Kent Commission concluded that one of the most observable effects of chain ownership was a greater reliance on news from the wire services. This implies a reduction in the attention given to local events in which the reader may have participated, or to local personalities who might be directly or indirectly known to the reader. Local news has generally had a poor reputation. It is often characterized as a means for gratifying local people by recording their presence at social events of purely parochial interest, and thus inherently dull. There is also a popular belief that local reporting is of poor quality when it ventures beyond lists of names and occasions to assess the quality of local activities or to report the substance of meetings. Whether these criticisms are valid or not, the local reporter does not face the same situation as one whose stories are prepared for people living at a distance. The local readership is more exacting because it already has independent sources of information about local events, and sometimes much more extensive background knowledge than the reporter. As a result, the writer has less scope for imaginative journalism, highlighting, or a personal angle (Edinborough: 19–20). Readers are unlikely to be influenced in their judgment of local affairs by the newspapers.

The significance of local news, then, lies in the fullness of the reader's context and its openness to verification from other sources. While a list of citizens at a gala is remarkably dull to outsiders, it may be very informative to those who know the participants and the setting, and who can compare it with other indices of social rank and activity. It acquires meaning from the reader's commonsense knowledge of this environment. This does not make it less ideological; but it does restrict the power of the newspaper to sell a different perspective than that which the local people already have.

There is much weaker competition from non-media sources when news items relate to distant areas, since local readers cannot quickly check their plausibility. Correspondingly, there is more scope for transmitting a picture of national and international developments which is removed from and irrelevant to daily experience – which increases the sense of local alienation.

SOME RESULTS OF DOMESTICATION

Two examples will be used to illustrate the results of domestication: the masking of inequality through the imaginary representation of opposite groups as equal, and the lampooning of politics and politicians from the vantage point of business and its executives.

In studying the ideology of the media, Wilden has illustrated two systematically opposed social constructions of Canada, which he calls the real and the Imaginary. He sees the real Canada as a capitalist country, characterized by class inequality and the oppression of ethnic, racial, gender, and other minorities. The domination of women by men, of non-whites by whites, of francophones by anglophone Canadians, and of the proletariat by the bourgeoisie are the most obvious but not the only examples. This portrayal is rarely seen in the media, however, for they generally present instead an Imaginary Canada in which these pairs of 'opposites' are equal and competitive rather than unequal and conflicting. When men and women, French and English speakers, or whites and non-whites are differentiated, they are socially constructed as rivals. There may be different levels of rivalry which form a structure: the francophones and anglophones who are portrayed as competing on relatively equal terms for power within Canada are expected to unite in order to compete on relatively equal terms with the United States for power in North America. Wilden stresses that the Imaginary Canada masks inequality and oppression when it redefines these oppositions as rivalrous, with the implications that the system is fair and that either can win. He rejects this implication, perceiving the system as strongly loaded in favour of the dominant group. These insights will be further examined in the context of the cartoons.

The second example of ideology in domestication focuses on the disproportionate attribution of foolishness to politicians. One can certainly point out that others are lampooned in different settings, such as the comics page or in humorous and professional magazines, but only on a much smaller scale.

The conceptual framework which underlies the present research is built around a paradox. On the one hand two major institutions, the polity and the economy, and their principal occupations are regularly selected by reporters as newsworthy. On the other hand only one of them is consistently presented by cartoonists as a major source of foolishness. There is consistency between the general absence of, say, clergy and teachers in the news pages and their general invisibility to the editorial cartoonist. There is similar consistency in the treatment of politicians. Yet the importance of business news contrasts strikingly with the absence of business leaders as a group from the cartoonist's world.

This central problem can be rephrased as the existence of a marked double standard which differentiates the public from the private domain. We have already commented that criticism which is libellous when applied to business is funny when applied to politics. From this it is easy to conclude that business is the spring for good and politics the fountain of bad news. Epstein has commented on the double standard in relation to self-enrichment, which is considered commendable for business people yet immoral for politicians. Executives' moral standards, private lives, and business dealings are not treated as matters of popular interest; politicians are open to scrutiny in all these respects, and the press resists and rails against their efforts to draw a veil of privacy around themselves and their subordinates.

Yet this vivid imaginary picture bears little correspondence to the contemporary scene, the real Canada, in which there is extensive overlap and many major similarities between big business and big government. There are substantial implications for one institution of any major decision made in the other; both are dominated by large, powerful bureaucracies run by technocrats; both argue that individual consumer decisions are their ultimate source of public input. Both seek to manipulate their consumers through extensive advertising and by controlling information; and there is a large-scale interchange of office-holders between the two. In these circumstances it would be easy to confuse political and business leaders, politics and business as institutions, if there were no mechanism for propagating and exaggerating their differences. Cartoons do this on the moral plane, by presenting politics and its practices as overtly foolish, trivial, and sordid, in implicit contrast with business and its practices.

This exaggeration of the differences between private and public enterprise artfully conceals the common capitalist nature of both. Political figures are shown as manipulating status through symbolic action, while those in business exercise power through practical activity. The distinction between symbolic action which is oriented to fame and public image, and practical action which is oriented to power and achievement, is not in itself imaginary. Ideology is introduced, however, when symbolic action is closely identified with politics and practical action with business.

Cartoons can express this imaginary opposition between business and politics in a more light-hearted, immediate, and holistic way than editorials, which rely on serious, gradual, and sequential reasoning. Cartoons enlist humour to slip across a serious message, appealing to and directing one's desire to laugh at authority figures and to express one's ambivalence about those who make decisions which affect one's life. By allying a picture with a text they activate more of the reader's senses. They thus invite greater involvement, offering a suggestive pattern to be grasped in its totality rather than an informative discourse which must be followed one step at a time (McLuhan: 20, 36, 86, 147–52). Their latent message may slip more successfully than an editorial through the filters with which readers protect themselves from ideas which may run contrary to their interests.

THE PRESS, THE STATE, AND ETHNICITY

This chapter ends with some ideas on the handling of ethnicity and ethnic inequality in the capitalist press. The treatment of ethnic relations and cultural variations in the media has often aroused accusations of prejudice. Singer's and Ginzberg's recent research on newspaper coverage of visible minorities continues this tradition. After noting that previous research found the depiction of native peoples to be very distorted, Singer examined native news during the early seventies in a major Canadian newspaper. Half the news referred to land claims. He concluded that according to the language chosen by the paper, 'The Indian is aggressive and involved in violent or illegal acts, while the Eskimo's behaviour is mild and dependent' (p. 234). Ginzberg has documented a steady pattern of racist remarks in some of the columns featured in the Toronto *Sun*.

In 1976 Siegel carefully documented the substantial differences in French- and English-language coverage of the October crisis in 1970. He found that 'the dissemination of the same basic information was socially divisive because it was organized in such a way as to emphasize particular interests coinciding with territorially-based language divisions' (pp. 154–5). The newspapers of the two language groups, even in the same city, often focused on different aspects of the crisis and stressed divergent values. As one moved further from the crisis centre, the English-language coverage became more hard-line and more divergent from that of the French-language papers within Quebec. Siegel showed, in general, that there were two versions of Canadian current events (just as Trudel and Jain have documented the existence of two Canadian histories). The English-language version was much more fragmented than the French.

It was argued earlier that in recent decades, as papers have become more monopolistic, their editors have become increasingly sensitive to the importance of retaining opposed segments of their readership. This has sometimes resulted in a more sensitive treatment of ethnic and racial minorities. Sometimes, however, as Ginzberg has shown, the persistence of racism can still be clearly documented. In yet other instances, newspapers may prefer to avoid ethnic and native news and their attendant controversies. As a result, cartoons about immigrants and native peoples were hardly ever found in newspapers during the period covered by the present research, 1960 to 1979. The sole exceptions occurred when a cartoonist from a particular minority made humorous allusions to the weaknesses of his own people, or when a cartoonist portrayed sympathetically the plight of native peoples.

While Canadian minorities were almost absent from the cartoonist's gaze, immigrants sometimes felt the stings of attacks on the government and citizens of their former homeland. Arab Canadians, for example, have not been the subject of caricatures, but Arabs have frequently been portrayed

"You'd think they'd have the decency to stay out of sight during 'Canada Week'!"

© Uluschak, *Edmonton Journal*

as fat and rapacious by Canadian artists, and the repercussions of this stereotyping have been felt by the immigrants (Mouammar). Similar indirect assaults are characteristic of French-English and Canadian-American relations, where ethnic and cultural differences are coupled with major claims to territory and nationhood. In these cases, ethnic and national hegemony has long been a central issue in politics and cartooning. The struggle to appropriate material and symbolic goods has intensified as government intervention has become more widespread (Breton).

The theory of ethnic relations under monopoly capitalism has until recently remained seriously underdeveloped. Traditional Marxism, like functionalism, has generally assumed that ethnicity would disappear after about one generation, as culturally diverse immigrants assimilated into the host society and ceased to be distinguishable. This belief has been demolished, however, by the resurgence of ethnicity in the third North American generation, the persistence of racism in American industrial centres, and the reemergence of regional nationalism in the communist countries and in many regions of western Europe. There have recently been a few studies linking racial and economic exploitation, offering sketches of the particular forms which race relations take in advanced capitalist societies (Green; Lawrence). They have pointed out the parallels between internal and international colonialism, and the use of immigrants and migration patterns in the class struggle. These have concentrated on their impact within the labour market, and have paid less attention to their effect on consumption patterns or on politics.

Cultural diversity complicates the task faced by monopoly capitalism in pursuing its interests, just as monopoly capitalism imposes its own contradictions on the internal structure of ethnic groups and nations. In the short run, efficiency and profits can be increased if, as a result of massive assimilation, production is geared to a single homogeneous market, operating in one language and within a single culture. However, in a highly diversified world, the focus on one language and culture limits the possibilities for appropriating the profits to be made from markets which operate in other languages and cultures. The search for short-run expansion therefore leads firms of one nation to take over those of another, appropriating their knowledge of the local culture and the profits from the local market. In this manner, the moral energy and material resources of ethnic consumers and businesses are harnessed and exploited by those of the dominant group.

In the longer run, the objective of a world-wide monopoly in a single homogeneous market generates heavy pressure toward cultural conformity among consumers, as a means of resolving this contradiction. If they could all be persuaded to buy the same goods, regardless of their varied backgrounds, profits would be greatly increased. The heaviest pressure, therefore, is exerted in trying to produce a homogeneous consumer culture. Much of the groundwork is already accomplished by the time immigrants enter Canada: surveys of their reasons for coming show that the desires for greater economic opportunity and a higher standard of living are paramount. While many are also seeking greater political freedom, the two overlap considerably: those who sought entry to Canada in the 1960s and 1970s in order to escape political restriction and oppression were more likely to be accepted if they were fleeing from a left-wing government than if they were escaping from one on the right (Marchand: 40–1). Even if their own desire for economic comfort still runs along the channels of their own culture, their children are rapidly induced into North American consumption patterns and motivations through the media and the schools.

Cultural diversity, meanwhile, has three major effects on the labour market. First, it facilitates a policy of divide and rule by employers. If labour is divided along ethnic and racial lines, and especially if it is possible to import substantial numbers of 'foreign' workers who willingly accept lower wages, union organization and working-class solidarity are much harder to maintain. The immediately visible threat of the rival employee who may take one's job attains greater prominence than the more hidden threat of an employer who manipulates the labour market to the worker's disadvantage. The social control of labour is tightened as a result.

Secondly, a diverse labour market brings greater problems of communication and work socialization. Maximal exploitation is possible when only unskilled labour is required, but the advantages to capitalism may diminish when communication and interpersonal skills are at a premium. To avoid this situation and to mitigate unrest in the traditional work-force, it may be profitable for employers to discriminate, segregating the minorities in low-status, low-paying positions and promoting only enough of their number to provide them with supervision in their own language. Since many lack Canadian experience, it may be regarded as appropriate that their social mobility should be low. Occupational and ethnic segregation are thus able to reinforce one another.

Thirdly, the homogeneity of the economic elite is protected, as mobility for minorities is restricted to those high-risk industries which the dominant group is reluctant to enter (Kelner; Clement: 260). Discrimination is legitimated with the claim that minority groups are economically incompetent, so their restriction to family and marginal enterprises is made to sound entirely rational. The ideal situation for profit is one in which the value of hard work generates a productive labour force, while cultural diversity pre-empts its drive toward solidarity.

The state practised a similar policy of divide and rule during this period. After the report of the Royal Commission on Bilingualism and Biculturalism it offered funds to promote the cultural, though not the economic, activities of minorities. Initially these were for organizing ethnic festivals, writing ethnic histories, and organizing cultural clubs. Ethnic groups competed for these funds, and became rivals in a zero-sum game. The greater the success of one, the less money was allocated to another. Subsequently policy shifted from cultural events to combating discrimination, and visible minorities were to be given preferential treatment if they proposed schemes to achieve this goal. This set up a new series of rivalries and conflicts of interest, in which minorities saw each other as adversaries in the quest for government funding and employment opportunities.[2] Minorities which are dependent on government for funds have in any case a strong incentive to support that government electorally, and to suppress any unrest among their own members.

The dominant ideology places its major stress on the benefits of hard work and the consumption of Canadian products: a happy alliance of docile productivity, consumerism, and nationalism under the joint auspices of capitalism and federalism. Newspapers are one of many mechanisms reinforcing this hegemony.

4

The Main Hypotheses and Methods of Analysis

The material reviewed in the previous three chapters has generated a substantial number of ideas. Chapter 1 elaborated the operating metaphor of the cartoonist as the jester of the bourgeoisie. Chapter 2 examined literary theory as a way of understanding the form through which editorial cartoons communicate their message. Chapter 3 considered the structure of newspapers, the context in which these cartoons are uniquely found. Concepts were introduced, such as the domestication of distant events and personalities, hyper-ritual presentations, and the interposing of an ideological filter between the event and the skimmer. These processes take place in a setting where the public has virtually no direct access to the events being described.

Many of these ideas are not currently testable against an alternative framework; this is especially true of those relating to the form of cartooning, which has not been previously studied. While they are good sources of insight, their status remains largely speculative. Those relating to the newspaper as the context of cartooning will not be tested, since they are based on a substantial body of existing research. The focus, then, will be on the dominant messages which can be found when a whole series of cartoons on the same topic is examined together. These messages can be reliably extracted only if one remembers that cartoons are the final products of a long series of operations and negotiations, using a particular form in a particular setting.

The messages of the cartoons will be discerned through an analysis of the ways in which dominant and minority groups, business and political leaders, are portrayed as different from, or opposite to, one another. It will then be possible to see how far the main features of the dominant capitalist ideology are transmitted through such drawings. Six principal features were outlined on pp. 45–8; they will now be rephrased in the form of hypotheses.

1: THE SOCIAL ORDER HYPOTHESIS. *Many cartoons will be commentaries on the themes of culture versus nature and social order versus social disorder. In them, (English) Canada will consistently be identified with culture and orderliness, Quebec and the independentists with nature and social disorder. In turn, Canada will be shown as nature and social disorder in comparison with the United States, which gravitates toward culture and social order. The minority will be consistently shown as a destabilizing element in its relations with the dominant group.*

However, in the case of conflicts between representatives of the cartoonist's province or country of residence and those of a larger political unit, there will be a substantial minority of romantic cartoons. The premier will then be shown as a hero in relations with the federal government, as will the prime minister in relations with the United States.

2: THE MINORITY GROUP HYPOTHESIS. *The richness of the politician's environment will be thinned by the exclusion of minority groups such as women, ethnic and racial minorities, representatives of local and regional interests, members of opposition parties, and Quebec independentists, except where they are shown posing threats to the social order.*

3: THE CAST OF REGULARS HYPOTHESIS. *The symbolic world in the cartoons on a given topic will be limited to about ten unlabelled 'regulars' and some labelled 'visitors.' In principle, these characters could be caricatures of well-known individuals, symbols of nations or human qualities (such as Uncle Sam or 'Greed'), or representations of social forces (such as War or Inflation). In practice, individuals will be much more numerous than symbols or representations, because capitalist ideology attributes success, failure, and foolishness disproportionately to individuals.*

4: THE IMAGINARY CANADA HYPOTHESIS. *The participants in partisan or national conflict will be depicted as formally equal rivals, similar in size and power, and not as adversaries with quite unequal resources. Cartoons will thus perpetuate the myth of the Imaginary Canada. If third parties are present, they will be depicted as bystanders or as moderating influences who take a position between the two sides. They will be shown to be hurt by the dispute.*

5: THE DOUBLE STANDARD HYPOTHESIS. *Business leaders will be portrayed much less regularly in cartoons than political leaders. The percentage of foolish and disorderly people will be much higher in portrayals of politicians than in depictions of business executives; the former will engage much more in keying, fabrication, and disputes.*

6: THE PASSIVE CITIZENS HYPOTHESIS. *Ordinary citizens and politicians will be depicted as foolish in about the same proportion of cases. However, the depiction of politicians as active will contrast with the portrayal of ordinary citizens as their passive audience. In general, politicians will be shown as having little contact with those who have elected them.*

Before these six hypotheses about cartoon messages are tested, a number of methodological issues need to be addressed. First, although this is not a study of the impact of cartoons, it is founded on certain assumptions about the work which one performs in skimming a drawing. These need to be clarified if research on their form, content, and context is later to be related to work on the reception of cartoons. Secondly, a discussion of cartoon conventions is necessary, to enable the reader to check the inferences about content which are being made. Artists frequently depict their characters as nervous, arrogant, angry, or unable to understand. Such qualities are an important part of their message; if they are to be effectively conveyed, there must be a commonsense stock of conventions and artistic knowledge which make them readily recognizable: shaking knees, looking down one's nose, furrowed brows and a snarl, or a blank expression.

Thirdly, the possibility of unravelling ideology objectively from a text has recently been a topic of debate; a few remarks on this subject are therefore necessary. Fourthly, the relationship of literal and metaphorical readings of the cartoons on various levels is considered; these include the psychological, the aesthetic, and the sociological level. The broad analytic categories to be used are then outlined. Finally, the nature of the sample is considered. Some details and comments on the coding scheme which was finally adopted will be found in Appendix A.

ASSUMPTIONS ABOUT THE GLANCER

This research does not focus on the impact which a cartoon has upon those who skim it, and has not attempted to add to the limited data on this topic. None the less, it is necessary to set out the assumptions which are being made about the perception of cartoons, since they underlie and determine the kinds of conclusion which can be drawn. There is a widely held belief that skimmers glance at a cartoon but expect to move on to other features within a few seconds. If its message is not grasped in the course of a very swift search, the cartoon is likely to be dismissed as incomprehensible. This belief is supported by the cliché that a picture is worth a thousand words. These comments refer to the rapidity of visual communication; it is less clear that they claim greater effectiveness for it. Taken together, these two statements comprise the conventional wisdom about the impact of cartoons.

Behind these beliefs lies a whole set of assumptions about the relations between the sender and the receiver of a message. Two broad theories of communication have been proposed. Although they are intended to apply equally to any form of mass communication, they will be expressed here as models of the relationship between a cartoonist and a glancer.

One popular theory treats the cartoonist as a skilful communicator, while most skimmers are like sponges, soaking up whatever claims the artist makes. Fears are then expressed that they can easily be manipulated and stampeded into believing whatever messages they receive from the cartoon. In this theory, only a minority of enlightened people, including of course the theorist, are too intelligent to take cartoons at their face value.

Three facets of this theory are notable. It is profoundly pessimistic about the credulity of the general public, and very optimistic about the acuity of such people as the theorist; the wise minority is perceived to be much smaller than the gullible majority; and it places on the minority a heavy responsibility to issue corrective material which will be equally persuasive. This theory of a sponge effect underlies many of the objections which have been raised to the concentration of the media. It also underlies the desire for a code of ethics for journalists and television reporters.

In addition to flattering the theorist, the sponge theory greatly simplifies the researcher's task, because whatever the cartoonist asserts will be accepted by most glancers. Analysis of the content of cartoons can ignore the characteristics of the mass audience, since any message will be accepted uncritically. Whatever is sent will be accurately and trustingly received by the majority, and its impact can be accurately assessed by looking objectively at its content.

The other popular theory rejects the idea that skimmers are sponges, and assumes instead that they have some competence and critical ability. They can recognize the characters shown and grasp the relationships depicted among them. Messages are not blindly accepted, however; they are compared with the glancer's existing stock of social knowledge. If a straightforward reading of the cartoon message clashes with this existing knowledge, the skimmer may jump to one of several conclusions about the drawing. The message may be dismissed altogether, treated as ironic, regarded as a rare exception to the general rule, or welcomed as an 'eye-opener' which extends the skimmer's conventional thinking or shows its limitations.

This theory points to the necessity of understanding the search procedures which skimmers might use in making sense of a cartoon. Three attempts to examine these search procedures will now be discussed: those of Goffman, Dondis, and Eagleton. Goffman (1974) uses the metaphor of searching for a key. Faced with a cartoon, the skimmer uses various common typifications as keys which might unlock the mystery which the new material presents. Twer (1972) has analysed some illustrative examples, taken from discussions between pairs of students who were asked to describe to one another a series of jokes and photographs which were placed before them. Goffman identifies five main types of key which may be used if the scene does not 'make sense' when 'read' literally: make-believe, contests, ceremonials, technical re-doings and re-groundings. Their common feature is that they transform a meaningful activity 'into something patterned on this activity but seen by the participants to be something else' (1974: 44). Children may play at fighting with such realism that passing adults are misled until they are given the key: 'we're just pretending.' Similarly, in a cake-making contest, cakes are produced; but this is not done for the joy of eating them with one's guests. A visitor who does not grasp this key may be puzzled that only a tiny sample of each cake is being eaten. The cartoon skimmer, similarly, tries various keys until one is found which makes sense of this depiction of the characters and their relationship.

Dondis's conception of a viewer's search procedures is very different, deriving from gestalt theory and psychological research into the perception of art (pp. 22–37). A sense of balance is the most important goal for the viewer. Imbalance and eccentricity create stress and inhibit the repose which the viewer is seeking. He or she begins to search for it by imposing vertical and horizontal axes on the picture, to determine the centre of gravity around which it is balanced. In a balanced picture, this is located in the centre, and the axes are parallel to the lines of its frame. If the picture is not balanced, the eye next inserts the main diagonals and the mind seeks to establish whether the centre of gravity lies along one of these. Once the presence or absence of balance is determined to the viewer's satisfaction, attention is turned to harmony.

A sense of harmony is conveyed by the use of symmetry and modest tones; asymmetry and striking colours create a sense of disharmony. The viewer receives a clear emotional message from either balance and harmony or from imbalance and disharmony, and ceases to search further. When no clear emotional message is received, the eye pursues the picture further, focusing first on the area which is lower and to the left of the centre of gravity. After the centre itself, this is the area of lowest stress. It gradually proceeds upwards and to the right toward the area of highest stress. Shapes located in this area will hold the viewer's attention longest; and if they are irregular in shape they will increase visual stress. The same procedures are presumed to apply to the parallel and possibly simultaneous search which the skimmer conducts to identify the people, events, relationships, and viewpoints which constitute the point of the cartoon. The greater the visual stress which the skimmer encounters, the greater will be the need for relief when the search is completed. An imbalanced and inharmonious cartoon thus evokes stronger reactions than one which is balanced and harmonious; heartier laughter will be one of these.

Eagleton's ideas about search procedures (1976a: 64–8) begin from a different analogy. For him, the reader is a theatrical producer who takes a text and transforms it into a unique and irreducible performance, in which the text and reader interpenetrate one another. This performance is more than a reflection, expression, or reproduction of the cartoon; and it is not a refraction, revitalization, or enactment of it. The reader both activates the work and interprets it within the framework of artistic conventions and social classificatory schemes.

In the context of advertisements, Williamson makes a similar argument. The reader *becomes* the (missing) person in the advertisement through an act of imagination, temporarily adopting this person's viewpoint and following the script which the advertisement lays out. Where it poses a question or asks a riddle, the reader works to supply the answer which is expected. The reader may be persuaded that this answer, which is correct in the imaginary world of the advertisement, is also true in the real world. Where a scene is presented, readers similarly work to relate themselves to that scene – imagining that they might own the ownerless vehicle shown, be the missing date of the model who looks so inviting, suffer from the ailment portrayed, or aspire to play the role illustrated. In these cases the advertiser may be able to tap the viewer's dreams and plant the idea that this product can satisfy them (Cossette: ch. 8). When this happens, the viewer takes over and performs without salary the work of selling the product (Williamson: 50–3, 70–5). The cartoonist similarly places the glancer in a setting and tries to evoke certain emotions and typifications, relying on humour rather than beauty. Seeds are planted which the receiver will be incited to water and nourish subconsciously. Gombrich (138–41) argues that in the cartoonist's case these seeds are messages about the moral worth of politicians, which are conveyed by showing them as smiling or snarling, tidy or untidy, commanding or defeated.

There are certain difficulties with these two theories when applied to the skimmer. They are much too general to yield testable propositions about the conventions which will attract certain types of readers, or which will induce them to perceive certain messages while missing others. And they do little to indicate what message is conveyed by the omission of certain groups from cartoons.

Some steps toward a third theory about skimming can be developed by combining the work of Duncan with that of Press and Goffman (1974). Duncan (pp. 78–81) proposed that there are five types of author-audience relations, which he called we, they, you, it, and me. In the first type, the author is addressing the Establishment, the guardians of community values; in the second, the general public. In the third, the message is aimed at significant others within the author's own group; while in the fourth it is beamed toward the author's ideal audience. The final type of audience is the self whom one addresses in a soliloquy. Press found the third of these to be the crucial audience whose welfare was of special interest to the cartoonist. The objective of mass communication is to establish a working consensus among this critical audience with regard to the situation or persons being portrayed (Goffman, 1978: 175).

The cartoonist relies on the shared conventions and stereotypes of this reference group to ensure that messages are faithfully transmitted. A broader consensus among the general public may be much more difficult to generate. The cartoonist may hope that others will receive the intended message accurately, while making little effort to check that they do. In this perspective, the intended audience can only be inferred, from the statements of the artist or the content of the works themselves. Most cartoonists take the view that they are drawing for the ordinary person in the street, or against foolishness in government. Any more elaborate analysis of their skimmers must come either by inference from the content of their work or by questioning potential skimmers. The former approach is used in this research, but it would be very desirable to supplement it by use of the latter.

CARTOON CONVENTIONS

While several books advise the young artist how to draw cartoons, there has been little systematic study of the conventions through which cartoon messages are conveyed. These conventions are nevertheless very important for an art-form which aims at almost instant transmission. To say that cartoons are highly conventionalized does not mean that the artists copy one another and fail to develop personal styles, or that their drawings are always simple. Where there are elaborations, however, they will generally repeat the central theme.

The major conventions of cartooning have been studied by Gombrich (pp. 138–40), who emphasizes three of them. First, spatial syntax serves to spell out social relationships: socially superior persons are drawn larger, more centrally, or higher in the picture than their subordinates. Secondly, portraits and symbols are fused, so that the figure one sees is both a particular animal and a certain person who shares its main traits. Lastly, and most important, physical appearance and facial expression are used to show character and moral worth. Long hair, an exaggerated nose, a glint, or a massive row of shiny teeth each send a powerful message about the person depicted. The more detailed set of sub-conventions by which character is deduced from appearance is therefore a crucial set. These sub-conventions are not rigid: there is no mechanical correspondence between, say, a jutting chin and the quality of determination; but features are exaggerated, expressions and poses selected, in order to convey certain messages about that person.

Duncan Macpherson was interviewed by Desbarats and Mosher about his use of costume to denote character. His caricatures of John Diefenbaker showed an astonishing range: Charles I, Nero, Captain Ahab, and Batman, among others. Their common theme was that the Conservative chief was the crazy ringleader of a national circus – a showman, an evangelist, and a third-rate actor all combined. Increasingly wild eyes, disorderly hair, and prominent front teeth were drawn to accompany his antics. Macpherson consistently perceived and dressed René Lévesque as a member of the 1837 Paris Commune. His supporters were given top hats, rosettes, and wooden clogs to express the artist's indignation, puzzlement, and feeling 'that separatism was a ridiculously antiquated and somewhat seedy expression of Gallic radicalism' (Desbarats and Mosher: 155).

Other insights about cartoon conventions can be gleaned from studies of the parallel literary practices, in particular those associated with satire and irony. The most distinctive convention in satire is the creation of distance between the author and the narrator/hero, or between the latter and the reader. Visually this means that the artist is included as a separate character in the cartoon, or is represented by a bauble. Barron, Girerd, Uluschak, and Yardley-Jones, among others, regularly include a dog or cat within or outside the frame of the picture; it gives the artist's comments on the characters. In other cases the obviously unflattering depiction of the principals tells the glancer that he or she and the artist have the maturity to laugh together at the foolishness of their political leaders. Exaggeration, stage whispers, captions, and parodies are among the devices which convey this to the skimmer. In some cases the separation is achieved by placing the politicians in a frame within the frame of the picture. They may be portraits on the wall, or actors or puppets performing on a stage while the artist is shown as a member of the audience.

A second relevant satirical convention lies in the use of opposition and identity: 'The structure brings together [certain elements] in such a way that their roles must be either opposed ... or equivalent' (Culler: 70). A political party may be shown with two evenly matched leaders or factions which, while firmly joined together, are vigorously pulling in opposite directions. When the NDP held the balance of power between the two larger parties, some cartoonists depicted its leader as almost indistinguishable from the prime minister. The paradox of being simultaneously joined together and incompatible is one means of showing that the main characters can be understood as both opposed and equivalent at the same time.

A third satirical convention which is observable in cartoons is a particular manner of using metaphor. In satire, metaphor focuses mainly on the grotesque and the taboo. Swift, Smollett, Hogarth, and their successors created monsters and systematically offended their contemporaries in order to draw attention to social evils. The politicians in editorial cartoons are similarly grotesque in appearance, and their activities are sometimes taboo. Consequently some readers find the art of caricature itself offensive.

Finally, irony may be adapted from literature for use in cartooning, and may take a number of forms. There may be antiphrasis, a glaring contradiction between the words and the deeds of the speaker, or between the message which is sent by one character and the translation of it which is forwarded to the other (Dolle: 344–7). More frequently, there may be dramatic or situational irony: a striking incongruity between the person and the setting, or between a policy and its fruits (Groupe Mu: 431–3).

IDEOLOGY IN CARTOONING

Each of these artistic conventions can be a vehicle for rhetoric and hence ideology. Oppositions, identities, and metaphors are superimposed on one another, building a structure of associations which contains a strong imaginary element. Goodness may be identified with Englishness and with culture, while badness may be equated with Frenchness and with nature.

When these particular associations are emphasized and exaggerated, others are ignored. Barnett and Silverman (pp. 12–13, 24) note, as illustrations, that capitalist rhetoric masks the fact that the nations which call for freer international trade are those which exercise imperialist domination over international markets. Conversely, the term 'property' is used in relation to both individuals and corporations in a way which conceals major differences between individual and corporate property and which allows corporations to benefit from the property rights accorded to individuals.

There is considerable debate over the potential of content analysis to be an objective method for revealing the ideology in texts of any kind. Most Marxists begin with a clear conception of bourgeois ideology and then study how far verbal and visual texts embody its key tenets. They focus on the ways in which meaning can be transferred or stolen (Barthes: 145). They identify the major tricks of bourgeois rhetoric, notably the practice of depriving an object of its history and context in order to treat it as natural and therefore eternal. They then seek examples of these tricks in the text, such as an elision between the denoted and the connoted meanings of the word or picture. In advertising, the consumer is tempted to believe that what is denoted (purchase of the product) will necessarily bring what is connoted (happiness or security) (Williamson: 87).

Critics of the Marxist approach, such as Molino and Nattiez, point out that it is by no means simple to infer ideology from associations and oppositions. There is no neat formula for extracting ideology, nor need a major ideology be consistent in its vocabulary and use of key words. Where speech aims to mislead or give false reassurance, the straightforward reading of its content will not suffice to uncover its intentions; and knowledge of the context will be necessary to show convincingly that the deception is intentional. Irony similarly seeks to convey a double message, and is open to misreading. Its covert message undercuts or flatly contradicts its overt statement. Metaphoric speech in general can be problematic, since it is open to both a literal and a figurative interpretation. Indeed, only straightforward ranting, which is very rarely found in western cartoons, is not subject to these difficulties.

However, literary devices can be used effectively in cartooning only if they are quite transparent, at least to members of the cartoonist's reference group. The metaphor must be immediately recognizable and the irony quite unmistakeable if it is to have an immediate impact. The satire and double meanings must be kept self-evident.

Ideology can also lurk within the visual conventions used. Spatial relationships can misrepresent the social relations among those who are portrayed, can leave certain key social groups out of the picture, and can exaggerate the extent to which individuals influence events. Symbols and portraits can be fused in a misleading manner, and appearances manipulated to deceive the skimmer about the moral qualities of the persons shown. Ideology is thus pervasive, and can be unambiguously disentangled only if one operates with a clear and generally static concept of the opposition between reality and its ideological representation.

LITERAL AND METAPHORICAL READINGS OF CARTOONS

Culler (pp. 60–2) and Levin (pp. 131–2) outlined two basic approaches to a text which contains strong metaphorical elements, as a cartoon does. It can be treated as poetry, which depicts a metaphorical world. In this case the analyst examines the nature of such a world by discovering what the consequences would be if every detail of the metaphor were literally true. What would happen if the country were literally ruled by puppets, or by pigs interested only in fattening themselves from the public trough? Objects and people from earth may be transported into this imaginary world; along the way the reader is asked to suspend any disbelief. 'Editorial cartoonists ... create their distinctive worlds. The universe of a Herblock is distinctly different from the vision of a Jeff MacNelly' (Harrison: 67).

When Joe Clark is portrayed as a person trying to sell second-hand vacuum cleaners to the occupants of a medieval castle, the skimmer may laugh at the incongruity of realizing that the appliance would literally be unworkable in that setting. The joke can be enjoyed, however, only by those who are willing to set aside the anxiety of questioning how and why he would have transported it there. This literal approach is valuable in bringing out the denotations of the principal objects and people. The literal purpose of buying a vacuum cleaner is to remove dirt; the attraction of a second-hand model is its economy. However, second-hand and door-to-door salespersons have seedy reputations; one who combines both attributes therefore appears particularly unsavoury. The seller relies on the vulnerability of the stereotypical purchaser, who is a female caught off guard and alone in a house which is less than spotless, by a male who arrives unexpectedly with a bargain machine and a talent for persuasion. The implications are clear: the Québécois are being seen as female, cheap, vulnerable, and less than spotless by the seller and those he works for.

The cartoon can also be seen as linguistic, a metaphorical representation of our present world. In this case each element in the drawing should not be taken as literally true. Each is part of a metaphor, a model through which

FREE TRIAL OFFER !
ABSOLUTELY
NO OBLIGATION, FOLKS.

March 31/79

© Macpherson, *Toronto Star*. Reprinted with permission, The Toronto Star Syndicate

the unfamiliar can become known. The cartoon just described might then be summarized:

If you want to understand Joe Clark's dilemma, try to put yourself in the shoes of a second-hand vacuum-cleaner salesman. If you want to know what is he up against, try to imagine yourself, defenceless and on a ladder, selling this equipment to the occupants of an enemy castle. Finally, if you want to understand how the Québécois nationalists view the Conservative party, imagine yourself as a medieval serf whose castle walls are being scaled by an alien with an altogether strange contraption.

The strength of this last approach lies in bringing out connotations. The intrinsic qualities of the vacuum cleaner and the castle are not then crucial. Any modern appliance and any dwelling from a totally foreign culture would convey the same meaning. The vacuum-cleaner metaphor is more piquant only because it brings additional connotations of pests who disturb one's privacy to sell unwanted objects. The castle evokes such adjectives as medieval, with its connotations that Quebec's thinking and technology are hopelessly out of date. It locates them half-way between modern glancers and those whom they consider 'barbarians.' Since it deals more in connotations, this approach is likely to yield less reliable findings than the first. There is more risk that personal values and meanings will be injected, but in return it promises additional insights. Each approach complements the other and will be used to help draw out more fully what a cartoon entails.

Analysis of a cartoon is the opposite of glancing at it. Skimming completes the process which the artist began: a complex and psychologically distant phenomenon has been domesticated, through reasoning by analogy, into a simple everyday scene. The purpose of analysis is to reverse this flow, separating out the conventions and layers of meaning which have been gathered and condensed into a single picture and punch line. One cannot expect to trace all the threads which have entered the picture, or to reconstruct its full history. One can nevertheless explore the main unifying themes and contradictions which come out in the finished work. It may also be possible to discover some of the elements which were omitted in the course of the simplification.

A rich and unified cartoon will emit parallel messages on each of three levels: the aesthetic, the social psychological, and the sociological. The aesthetic level refers to the style, materials, and technology which the cartoonist uses, and to the artistic effects which are produced. It is customary to exaggerate certain features in a caricature, making them keys to who is being portrayed and to the qualities which the cartoonist ascribes to this person. A drooping mouth, for example, represents a pessimistic outlook, a long nose is seen as a desire to be dominant, and an exaggerated plastic smile denotes insincerity. There is considerable dispute among experts on art perception over whether these and other aesthetic conventions are culturally bound or universal (Fisher; Aveni et al.)

On the psychological level, the cartoonist may include symbols which evoke a social role rather than a single quality. Generally the sign used is one which draws on a widely held stereotype, since the allusion must be caught almost immediately. A person may be drawn on a broomstick to elicit the stereotype of the witch, or with a cowboy's hat to imply that this person's behaviour and attitudes are like those of a cowboy. The messages at the psychological level are more holistic: this person is (like) a puppet, an alley-cat, a clown, an uncontrollable monster.

On the sociological level, there may be a parallel argument about the nature of the groups which have chosen these people as their representatives. An unfavourable portrait of a premier or the prime minister entails a negative judgment on those who elected him. At times, however, cartoonists are careful to dissociate the politician from the people by drawing them as separate figures, symbolically relieving the population as a whole of any blame for the actions of their present leaders.

The content analysis of these cartoons which follows will be organized under five headings: spatial syntax, harmony, associations, social relationships, and major myths and themes. Spatial syntax concerns the location of the persons in the cartoon – their positions toward the top or bottom of the picture, in the centre or toward the edge, and in the foreground or the background. It also includes their relative size. These elements are the main guides to the social status and relative importance of the characters who are portrayed. Harmony and contrast examine the extent to which the cartoon engenders stress or repose, applying the standards set out by Dondis. Although this is one of the more subjective aspects, it is sometimes possible to indicate whether the cartoons are drawn to influence the viewer toward one state rather than the other.

Under the heading of associations and oppositions, the focus will be on the social construction of ethnicity: what other qualities are associated with Frenchness and Englishness, and what qualities are seen as equally characteristic of both groups? There may be inconsistencies in this respect within a cartoon, or between one cartoon and another. Curtis found that Victorian English caricatures fostered at least two seriously incompatible symbols of Ireland: the passive, beautiful, peaceful, feminine Hibernia, and the active, ugly, terrorist male Paddy. These inconsistencies are as interesting as the areas of agreement. Willeford sees the jester and the fool show as personifications of the contradictions in the society, while Eagleton (1976a: 35) refers to the ideological silences which cover up contradictions. Since cartoonists are the modern equivalent, it is reasonable to see their work as an expression of these inconsistencies. Places can also be outlets for these contradictions: Hamelin (p. 147) showed that Anticosti was simultaneously regarded as both paradise and hell in the last century.

Social roles and relationships are more fully elaborated through the dress, poses, actions, and facial expressions of the principal characters. These features not only reinforce the equality or inequality which the cartoonist illustrates through spatial syntax; they also indicate attitudes, claims, and the specific social types in which these leaders are being cast (Meyer et al.: 22–3; Millum: 56). Goodness, initiative, and indifference are among the other qualities which may be portrayed. Roles and relationships in turn lead into the main myths and themes through which cartoons represent the nature of Canada and its major ethnic constituents: the parental myth, the marriage myth, and the combat myth, among others.

In concentrating on spatial syntax, harmony, associations, social relationships, and major myths, other aspects of cartoons are necessarily ignored. Most notably, little attention is paid to the measures of political integration or attitudes to the political systems which are central to the work of Press and Streicher. Cartoons are not discussed as part of a complex package of political rhetoric, as in the work of Edelman, Gamson and Lasch, and Hewitt and Hall. The focus here is on ethnicity and nationhood as two galleries in which capitalist representations of the state are displayed.

SAMPLING AND STATISTICAL CONSIDERATIONS

A suitable sample was needed to test the hypotheses outlined earlier. Most previous research has been disappointing in this respect. Groupe Mu, Floch, and Tardy, for example, give no indication that they did anything more than select a very small number of interesting illustrations of their points. Gombrich's selection was much wider, but not necessarily more representative. Posner (p. 472) claimed that sampling was unimportant, because all the Buck Brown 'granny' cartoons were essentially the same. Streicher (1965) does not indicate whether or how he sampled the Colonel Blimp cartoons of David Low. Press (pp. 31–2) alone discusses in some detail the difficulties of ensuring representativeness. It is likely that he sought this with care in his sampling of recent American cartoons but it is much less clear what can be claimed for his samples from other nations and earlier periods.

In each of these instances, then, the reader has no means of knowing whether a different selection of cartoons would have yielded similar conclusions. This procedure is acceptable where the author simply intends to explore a new medium with fresh techniques and has no wish to generalize. Yet each of these authors drew some conclusions about the nature of cartoons in general, while being unable to assure the reader that they were valid beyond the particular set of cartoons being analysed. This is not a trivial consideration: Press's work shows clearly that the whole nature of cartooning is strongly influenced by the kind of government which is in power, and by the prevailing conditions of peace or war. Conclusions which are sound for a democratic regime in peacetime may have little relevance to cartooning when the same regime is at war, or to its counterpart under an authoritarian or dictatorial government. Furthermore, it is likely that the topic itself has a major effect on the frequency and kind of cartoons which appear. Certain subjects are taboo, others need to be treated with care, while yet others are always 'fair game.'

Meyer et al. and Beniger resolved this problem by taking complete populations of cartoons from specified sources. Meyer used every Fourth of July cartoon in five major u.s. papers from 1870 to 1976. Beniger included every cartoon in February of a leap year in five major u.s. papers from 1948 to 1980.

Questions of sampling are important, though not simple, if the results are to be generalized. The present researcher was extremely fortunate in having access to the collection of cartoons made by Terry Mosher, Guy Badeaux, and their assistants for the documentary and book *The Hecklers*. This collection had two big advantages over other public and private sources, including any sample which the author might have drawn specially for this research.

First, it was assembled with the help of the artists who had drawn the pictures. It included the best of each cartoonist's work, as selected by the artist and Mr Mosher. A quality control was thus applied which ensured the elimination of works which were judged inferior by the artist or by another leading professional. This quality control was a major strength of the sample, but it could not be applied with perfect evenness for several reasons. In periods when the level of cartooning was not particularly high, standards were lowered to include the best examples of the time. Some cartoonists were very critical of their work, and considered only a small proportion to be worthy of inclusion, while others were more liberal. Some worked for newspapers which had the resources to publish an annual collection of their best drawings, others had little or no access to such outlets.

Secondly, the authors' position within the profession, and the widespread support for the project among their colleagues, enabled them to assemble an unusually complete population of cartoons from which to choose the best. All work which had appeared in book form was included in the collection, and nearly all these books formed part of the sample used here. Even where much of an artist's best work had already appeared in books, however, other extant work was carefully considered for inclusion. The only serious gap involved the earlier work of those whose personal collections were seriously incomplete. Some artists store everything, while others destroy or give away their works liberally. In one case, the cartoonist's newspaper had accepted responsibility for storing his work but had inadvertently destroyed most of it during a move.

With these provisos, however, there was good reason to believe that Mr Mosher's collection represents the best population of Canadian cartoons that could be obtained, in terms of both quality and representativeness, from the beginnings of Canadian cartooning up to early 1979. It is estimated to contain about seven thousand cartoons.

In preparing this material for publication, Desbarats and Mosher divided the collection into two parts. They chose 1,905 for use in either the film or the book, and these were carefully indexed.[1] The remainder were filed under the artist's name but have not been indexed. Selection for the film and the book was made partly on the basis of quality, but the main criterion was originality. Priority was given to works which had a unique topic or a creative angle. Those which could be considered duplicates were fairly ruthlessly eliminated, with preference being given to the artists who would otherwise be less well represented in the book and film. The total collection of seven thousand cartoons was judged more suitable for the present research. Since the aim was to obtain as representative a sample as possible, duplicates should be included; and the greater numbers permitted finer subdivisions and more elaborate analysis.

The field-work involved examining all seven thousand cartoons, and then photocopying for the initial sample each one which met three conditions: it was published during the period 1960–79; its topic could, broadly, be classed as inter-group relations in Canada, or Canada's relations with the United States, France, or Britain; and there were at least ten cartoons in the initial sample on this topic. It was thought likely that the topic of a cartoon would be an important influence on both its form and its message. It was therefore decided that drawings on different topics should be combined for analysis only in exceptional cases; while the number ten was, quite arbitrarily, taken as a reasonable minimum indicator that a topic was sufficiently popular to justify separate analysis.

With the complete and courteous co-operation of the Iconography Division of the Public Archives in Ottawa, these cartoons were photo-copied. They were then sorted according to their topic and the language of the newspaper in which the cartoon first appeared.

They proved to be distributed as shown in Table 1.

When the composition of the initial sample became clear, the decision was made to concentrate on comparing French- and English-language cartoons according to their subject, and where possible to examine regional variations in the content of the English-language cartoons. The unevenness of the numbers of cartoons placed some restrictions on the subsequent

TABLE 1
Cartoons in sample by topic and language, 1960–79

	English cartoons	French cartoons
1 Constitution, national unity	58	9
2 Ottawa vs. Quebec	120	36
3 Effects of Quebec separation	44	11
4 Relations with France	43	108
5 Relations with United Kingdom, royalty	42	21
6 Federal bilingualism	69	14
7 Quebec unilingualism	56	28
8 Referendum debate and result	20	32
9 Quebec provincial politics	24	17
10 Canada and the U.S. military	37	0
11 Canada and the U.S. economy	160	7
12 Ottawa vs. all provinces	34	0
13 Ottawa vs. an English province	25	1
14 Symbols of nationalism	56	1
15 Canadian flag debate	39	5
16 English provinces vs. Quebec	13	2
17 Native peoples	55	3
18 War Measures Act	18	5
19 1976 Quebec election	16	2
20 Quebec and the Progressive Conservative Party	27	6
21 Labour	23	5
22 Business	31	6
23 Minorities and immigrants	25	5
24 RCMP, armed forces	25	4
Total for these subjects	1,070	329

analysis. The original intention of comparing cartoons on French-English relations from English-language newspapers with those from French-language papers could be pursued only for certain topics.

The first seven topics in the first column were chosen for more detailed analysis in chapters 5 and 6 because they met two criteria of adequacy: they focused on topics within a common theme of French-English relations, and there were at least nine cartoons on this topic by artists from each language group. The choice of nine as a minimum was again arbitrary, but seemed reasonable and ensured a considerable range of topics. The eighth and ninth topics were excluded from these chapters because on closer inspection they depicted only francophones within Quebec, and therefore did not treat relations between the two language groups. The tenth and eleventh topics focused on Canadian-American relations and will be studied in chapter 7.

There were ample drawings for an analysis of English-language cartoons on these topics, which could be treated as constituting a single theme. The other topics could not be grouped as readily and were rarely depicted by francophone artists.

Two general types of comparison were possible. The simpler type compared French- and English-language cartoons on the same topic, to see if there was any pattern to the differences which were found. Their portrayals of the relations between Ottawa and Quebec, or of the projected effects of Quebec independence, were of this type. In both cases Mann-Whitney U tests were used as a simple test of statistical significance.

The second type was a four-way comparison of English and French artists' responses to their own and each others' cultural symbols or behaviour. It was possible, for example, to compare francophone and anglophone cartoonists' portrayals of francophones and anglophones, to see whether each concentrated on depicting their own people, while ignoring the other group. It was also possible to judge whether individuals of the cartoonist's own language group were shown more positively than those of the other group, and whether such indications of prejudice were stronger or weaker among francophone than among anglophone cartoonists. To assess the extent of differential prejudice, log-linear analysis was used (Fox; Reynolds). In this way it was possible to compare the amount of difference between language groups on a measure of prejudice with the amount of variation from one topic to another, and to judge whether there was interaction between these two. If the French-English differences and the interaction proved to be small, it would be advantageous to combine the French- and the English-language cartoons on the same topic for the remainder of the analysis. It was also possible, by the same technique, to study the extent of regional differences among English-language cartoonists' work, comparing variability by region with variability according to the topic of the cartoon.

5
Regional, Topical, and Ethnic Variations in the French-English Cartoons

The last chapter set out the guiding hypotheses which emerged about the ideological content of recent Canadian editorial cartoons. It also outlined the research methods which would be used in testing them. The next three chapters examine the findings from the analysis of these cartoons. A single volume cannot do justice to all the richness which they contain. This present one will focus on establishing or modifying the main underlying proposition – that cartoons in the capitalist press are the fool shows of the bourgeoisie. Once the validity of this main proposition has been determined, subsequent work will explore in much more detail the metaphors and sub-messages through which the overriding message is expressed.

The data analysis proceeded in several stages. It began by exploring the extent of regional and topical differences among English-language cartoons on French-English relations. It was recognized that regional or ethnic differences might be marked among cartoons on one topic, yet negligible on another. The analysis therefore used two independent variables: the topic of the cartoon, and the region from which the newspaper came. The dependent variables would be the features of the cartoon and its constituent characters.

The emphasis on region and language as independent variables arose from the possibility that cartoonists operated within separate regional and language markets. There is some syndication in Canada, and smaller city papers may rely on drawings reproduced from the major dailies. There is also a limited amount of cross-fertilization when the *Toronto Star*, for example, reproduces cartoons by Aislin or Roy Peterson. In general, however, most glancers see cartoons only from their own region and language group.

Differences were sought in the structure of the drawings, in the roles and qualities which were attributed to the cartoon characters, and in bias toward or against one's own ethnic group. Since the details of this analysis are highly technical, they have been relegated to Appendix B, and only a brief overview of the findings is given in the text. If large differences were found between the English-language drawings from eastern, western, and central Canada, the hypotheses of Chapter 4 would need to be tested for each region separately (Reynolds: 135–9). Similarly, if large differences were found from one topic within French-English relations to another, the hypotheses would be tested separately for each topic. Where, however, the regional and topical differences were negligible, the analysis would proceed to the second stage.

In the second stage, the English-language cartoons were combined whenever no topical or regional differences had been found. They were then compared, as a whole, with the French-language cartoons on the same set of topics. Differences were again sought in structure, roles and qualities, and bias; details of the findings are given in Appendix B. If large differences were found at this second stage, the hypotheses would be tested separately for the two language groups. Where no regional, topical, or language differences were apparent, all cartoons would be combined before the hypotheses were tested. The results of these two stages in the analysis occupy the present chapter. In reviewing them briefly, we shall highlight the ways in which regional and ethnic differences in Canada become expressed through cartooning.

At the third stage the hypotheses were tested. The organization of the data for these tests, as has been suggested, depended on experiences in the first and second stages. Regional, topical, and ethnic differences were respected: on certain measures it would be necessary to conduct the same test separately for each topic, for the several regions, or for each major language group. The results of this stage will be reported in Chapter 6.

REGIONAL DIFFERENCES IN THE STRUCTURE OF THE CARTOONS

At the first stage of the analysis, there were only two regional differences among artists in the structural features of their cartoons about French-English relations. The attributes which were studied are listed in Appendix A as items 1–26. They did not form a pattern but were relatively isolated differences.

There was a greater tendency to concentrate all their satire on politics among Ontario cartoonists than among those who worked in the East or the West. There were also joint effects from region and topic on the bilingualism theme. Maritime and English-Quebec cartoons took a similar stance toward both the federal and Quebec language issues, treating both as examples of general foolishness which merited medium satire. While Ontarian and western artists also treated federal bilingualism in this manner, they tended to respond to the Quebec language issue with low satire, as an illustration of the foolishness of certain individual leaders.

LANGUAGE DIFFERENCES IN THE STRUCTURE OF THE CARTOONS

Since the regional differences were minor, the next stage in the research on cartoon structure was to combine all the English-language cartoons on a topic and to compare them with those by francophone artists on that topic.

Following the metaphor of Canada as a three-generation family which had emerged from my earlier work in 1984, the seven topics relating to French-English relations were grouped according to three themes which derived from this metaphor. The 'in-law' theme treated relations between Canada and its two 'parent countries,' France and Britain (topics 4 and 5 in Table 1). The 'spousal' theme dealt with relations between the husband and wife, (English) Canada and Quebec (topics 1, 2, and 3). The 'children' theme concerned relations between the federal government and its French-language minority, or the Quebec government and its English-language minority (topics 6 and 7).

Language differences on the 'in-law' theme were striking: artists belonging to the two language groups gave very different portrayals of official visitors from Canada's two parent countries. There were also quite strong differences on the spousal theme, but none on the children theme.

It would be an exaggeration to say that these differences constituted distinct French- and English-Canadian models of cartooning. They nevertheless deserve some comment. The much simpler style of most French-language cartoons, and their gentler treatment of 'excesses' by Quebec nationalists, were noted by Desbarats and Mosher (pp. 188, 190). Since the present research used a subset of their cartoons, it was to be expected that these impressions would be confirmed by the present, more systematic, study. Three other differences were notable.

First, English cartoons were more likely to include an exposition of the foolishness of conflict or a plea for collaboration in policy-making. Cartoonists of the two language groups differed widely in their choice of issues to be presented as disputes between two sides. Each was much more likely to see the symbols associated with its own group as the foci of dissension. English-language cartoonists were more likely to perceive discord rather than harmony surrounding the queen's 1964 visit and the federal government's policy on bilingualism. Those working for French-language papers were more likely to see discord in President de Gaulle's visit and the Quebec government's language policy. Similarly, relations where francophones had recently been taking the initiative to bring about changes were more often represented as areas of dispute in the French- than in the English-language cartoons on the spousal themes.

A few cartoons made a plea for collaboration within their own ethnic group, for instance between those (English) Canadians who supported and those who opposed the federal bilingualism policy. Usually, however, the dispute pitted francophones against anglophones. The message was not that the other group's symbols and distinctiveness were a source of conflict or ridicule, as in traditional humour against an ethnic minority. Rather, the other group was portrayed as argumentative and disloyal when the symbols of the cartoonist's own group were featured, at a time when it was felt that they should have been collaborative and loyal.

Secondly, English-language cartoons on the in-law and the spousal themes were consistently and significantly less stressful in their composition than those in French. This was not the case, however, on the children theme. The less relaxed compositions in French on the in-law and spousal themes may point to the anxiety which affects francophones as a result of their position as a minority group. There is perhaps a parallel here with the simpler, starker drawings by American black children in comparison with the richer portrayals by whites of the same age and nationality. The French-language cartoonists' work was also more stark in terms of its target. Those working for English newspapers appeared more content to let the glancer decide who was being lampooned.

The third French-English difference concerned the identifiability of the characters. Cartoonists assumed consistently that skimmers' ability to recognize leaders from the other language group would be quite limited. Accordingly, francophones were more likely to label anglophones in their drawings; and correspondingly, anglophones were more likely to label francophones.[1]

These pointers showed a pattern of French-English differences in relation to the symbols of parenthood and domination, but otherwise did not suggest major dissimilarities between the frameworks used in French- and English-language cartooning. As was argued earlier, the relationship of newspapers to the capitalist system is similar for each language group. In practice this overrode their different relationships to the centres of political power.

REGIONAL DIFFERENCES IN THE CARTOON CHARACTERS

This section turns from the cartoons as complete works to the sets of characters in them. The analysis focuses on who was drawn, and on the qualities attributed to the major personae in each cartoon. A list of the qualities studied is given in Appendix A, parts III and IV.

In general the regional differences were far outweighed by the differences according to topic. Indeed, only one consistent regional difference emerged from the analysis: Ontario cartoonists were more likely than those from other regions to concentrate on drawing members of the dominant group on issues relating to language. On all other questions and themes, the regions could be combined for the comparisons in the next section.

LANGUAGE DIFFERENCES IN THE CARTOON CHARACTERS

With the one exception just noted, anglophone cartoons from all regions could be combined and compared with francophone cartoons.

When cartoons on different topics were compared, it was found that artists from both language groups portrayed members of a language group more often on those topics where that group was symbolically dominant than on those where it was not. The queen's visit, the constitution, and federal bilingualism were the topics on which anglophones were the principal subjects. Francophones were the main characters in relation to President de Gaulle's visit, the effects of separation, Ottawa-Quebec relations, and Quebec language policy, for artists of both language groups.

Three differences related to ethnicity emerged from the comparison between francophone and anglophone cartoonists' work. First, on any given topic francophones were more likely than anglophones to portray francophone characters, while anglophones were more likely to portray anglophone characters. Secondly, their satire was more likely to depict leaders of their own group as fools and the leaders of the other group as villains, though this tendency was weaker for the English- than for the French-language artists. Thirdly, the English-language cartoonists were more often veiled about the object of their satire. Among cartoons whose target was clear, however, those by anglophones were more likely to concentrate all their fire on one ethnic group or the other; French-language artists would more often blast both groups together.

REGIONAL BIASES IN THE CARTOON CHARACTERS

The last two sections of this chapter examine the question of bias in the cartoons. How far did cartoonists depict their own group's leaders more or less favourably than the other group's leaders? Was this more true for artists of one region than for those of another? The data had to be organized in a different manner to answer these questions. Once more, the details are given in Appendix B; the text outlines only the main conclusions.

This analysis revealed moderate regional differences, nearly all on the dimension of foolishness. The Ontario cartoonists consistently showed more francophones and showed them less favourably than did the cartoonists from other parts of Canada. Ontario artists were also likely to show the British as more foolish than the (English) Canadians; whereas (English) Canadians were given a less favourable image than the British among cartoonists from the other anglophone provinces. The differences were not striking, however, in comparison with the consistent and major differences between topics, and in nearly all cases they can be ignored.

ETHNIC BIASES IN THE CARTOON CHARACTERS

There was a general tendency for artists to depict their own ethnic group more regularly than the other one, and to concentrate most of their energies on exposing foolishness within their own ethnic circle. They dealt mainly with intra- rather than inter-ethnic humour. When badness rather than foolishness was the focus, the results were less clear, and there was some evidence of hostility, especially in anglophones' depictions of francophones. The presence of French visitors was an occasion for negative verdicts about francophones in English-language cartoons. The presence of British visitors generally led French-language cartoonists to offer slightly negative verdicts about their own leaders and slightly positive sentiments toward the anglophones. With the exception of certain portrayals of René Lévesque, there were very few cartoons which depicted ethnic or national leaders as evil, in the style of anti-Zionist cartoons in the Soviet Union (Nir). The portrayal of Lévesque as a scapegoat will be considered in more detail in the next chapter.

The general conclusion of this preliminary exploration of the data is that the topic of the cartoon has a major influence on both its structure and the portrayal of the characters shown. For purposes of generalization, the combining of topics, even within the same theme, is the procedure most likely to obscure important sources of variation. Language was the second most influential of the three variables; combining French- and English-language drawings involves some risks, but they are much less serious than those entailed by combining cartoons on different topics. Region was the least influential and the risk of combining cartoons from different regions of (English) Canada was the mildest. As far as practicable, these sources of variation will be respected in the next chapter when the hypotheses are tested.

Our analysis has shown that, in terms of very broad regions, the existence of separate local cartoon markets makes relatively little difference to the messages about French-English relations which skimmers receive. Similarly, the existence of two clearly defined language markets has a major effect only when the symbols and in-laws of the two ethnic groups are depicted. In most cases, then, one may talk of a national market in the sense that the drawings for regional and language markets generally differed little in the essentials of their structure and their depictions of the main characters. As far as numbers permit, the hypotheses will nevertheless be tested separately in those instances where important regional and language differences were found.

The problem of combining topics proved more complex, because it was related to the goals of the analysis and not to statistical considerations. The purist position was clear: there were usually major differences according to topic, even within the same theme. Valid research must take these into account by showing whether the hypotheses were sustained in certain pre-cisely defined contexts. It would not be legitimate to generalize across topics until one had demonstrated that the conclusion held for each one separately.

At the same time, it is doubtful whether the skimmer distinguishes clearly between topics in constructing an overall impression of cartoon messages. The theme of federal bilingualism, for instance, may dominate cartoons about French-English relations in a given year and may hammer home the message that Pierre Trudeau is being duped by René Lévesque. This message may scarcely be present in other French-English cartoons, yet its centrality on the topic which is shown regularly may override its absence elsewhere. A general and undifferentiated image of federal fool and provincial fool-maker may be conveyed as a result. It is important to notice such general images through an analysis which combines all topics, as well as specific images which occur only on certain topics. It is also important not to confuse the two, because they are based on different kinds of generalization and lead to different conclusions.

The appropriate statistical strategy, then, is to treat each topic as an independent test of the hypothesis, or the proposition within a hypothesis. Where all regions and language groups are combined, there will generally be seven such tests; where the language groups but not the regions are separate, there will be fourteen; where language groups and regions are all separate, there will be twenty-eight. While this sometimes means very small numbers, the replication added considerably to the reliability of the analysis.

6
French-English Cartoons as
Capitalist Slogans

Chapter 4 outlined a series of hypotheses about the cartoons. Chapter 5 found that there were widespread differences among them from one topic to another, but quite limited differences in the messages they offered to Canada's distinct linguistic and regional markets.

The analysis for each hypothesis will be based on the combined results of the various independent tests which can be made. It was indicated at the end of the previous chapter that these would usually range in number from seven to twenty-eight. These global results ignore the possibility that the hypothesis is confirmed only for relations with in-laws, spouse, or children. Where numbers permit, the existence of such variations from one theme to another will be examined.

It should be stressed that the unit of analysis will always be the cartoon and not the individual character. The portrayals in a single cartoon are not independent of one another; the presence of a hero implies a villain, the fool-maker implies a fool. They cannot therefore be considered in isolation from one another for statistical purposes. Where a cartoon shows several business chiefs as heroes or villains, it will be treated as a stronger statement than a drawing which shows only one in this light, but it will still be counted only once in any table. It follows that a cartoon may be classified as ranging from four positive and no negative portrayals of a certain social or ethnic role, to no positive and four negative depictions. The mid-point is a neutral situation in which the number of positive portrayals equals the number of negative.

I: THE SOCIAL ORDER HYPOTHESIS. *Many cartoons will be commentaries on the themes of culture versus nature and social order versus social disorder. In them, (English) Canada will consistently be identified with culture and orderliness, Quebec and the independentists with nature and social disorder. In turn, Canada will be shown as nature and social disorder in comparison with the United States, which gravitates toward culture and social order.*

The minority will consistently be shown as a destabilizing element in its relations with the dominant group.

However, in the case of conflicts between representatives of the cartoonist's province or country of residence and those of a larger political unit, there will be a substantial minority of romantic cartoons. The premier will then be shown as a hero in relations with the federal government, as will the prime minister in relations with the United States.

The data relevant to hypothesis 1 will be presented in several parts. First, the depictions of nature and culture, social order and disorder will be examined. Then the special case of the double threat of Quebec independence will be considered, as seen by cartoonists from anglophone provinces. Next, attention is focused on cartoons from other provinces about Alberta's oil policy. The results of these two sections will then be compared. The final section compares Alberta and Quebec cartoons on their own premier's assertions of independence from Ottawa.[1]

Four oppositions occurred with reasonable frequency: English-French, Canada-parent country, Canada-province (including Canada-Quebec), and federalist-independentist.[2]

Overall, representations of culture and nature were readily visible in 44 per cent of the cartoons where an oppositional pair was shown: 50 per cent of the French-English comparisons, 42 per cent of those comparing Canada with one of the parent countries, 35 per cent of the cartoons which contrasted Canada with one or more provinces, and 47 per cent of those which distinguished federalists from separatists. There were again wide variations according to topic, but the numbers were too small to justify an analysis by topic.

Contrary to the hypothesis, the English were significantly more likely than the French speakers to be identified with nature.[3] The pattern was the same on each of the three topics where more than nine cartoons could be assessed. During President de Gaulle's visit, francophone cartoons in particular associated English Canada with a decaying Confederation and with uncontrolled emotional responses to Québécois self-assertion. Confronted with bilingualism federally and with French language laws in Quebec, anglophone Canadians were generally shown as uncultured by comparison with francophones, unable to cope with a language other than their own. Anglophones were the ones who would die as a result of their incompetence if French became a working language of pilots. They would rely on brute force if necessary to maintain the dominance of English, an attitude which some cartoonists portrayed as reminiscent of cave-dwellers. Francophones, in contrast, were generally shown to be acting as civilized persons when

TABLE 2

Representations of opposing pairs as nature, culture: all topics

	Number	Per cent
English-French Comparisons		
English as nature, French as culture	46	38
French as nature, English as culture	15	12
Both shown, but neither as nature, culture	60	50
Number of comparisons	121	100
Parent Country–Canada Comparisons		
Parent country as nature, Canada as culture	8	10
Canada as nature, parent country as culture	26	32
Both shown, but neither as nature, culture	46	58
Number of comparisons	80	100
Canada-Province Comparisons		
Canada as nature, province as culture	10	11
Province as nature, Canada as culture	21	24
Both shown, neither as nature, culture	58	65
Number of comparisons	89	100
Federalist-Independentist Comparisons		
Federalist as nature, separatist as culture	4	5
Separatist as nature, federalist as culture	31	41
Both shown, neither as nature, culture	40	54
Number of comparisons	75	100

they made peaceful and parliamentary demands for equal rights within the federal system.

In relations with both parent countries, Canada the child was pre-eminently associated with nature,[4] although the numbers were much smaller. Culture was presented as coming from the two European heritages, while Canada by comparison was still a frontier, a place where nature was the dominant influence on social structure and personality. Royal and presidential visits were therefore occasions to overlay nature and disorder with a layer of culture and order. A red carpet for the royal pair is rolled over the protesting bodies of Quebec dissidents. The enormous torso of de Gaulle is untouched by the mud which English-speaking politicians hurl at him. The politicians stand with fingers crossed as the queen enters a fissure-ridden Olympic stadium.

The third pairing, of Canada as culture and the provinces as nature, was significant only at the 0.10 level.[5] Most of the relevant cartoons referred

QUEBEC MILITARY REVIEW

either to the provinces as a whole in relation to the constitution, or to Quebec in its relations with Ottawa on other issues. Where the constitution was the focus, cartoonists identified the provinces slightly more often with nature than with culture; when Quebec alone was the opposing party, it was depicted as natural in ten cases out of twelve.

Nature symbolized the absence of culture and socially approved behaviour in the artist's repertoire. One might conclude tentatively that Canada's interests received slightly more positive evaluations than those of the anglophone provinces, which in turn were portrayed more positively than those pursued by Quebec. This rank-order was clearer if one isolated the independentists from the federalists, rather than combining all Quebec representatives.[6] The independentists were nearly always identified with nature if this metaphor was used, and were sometimes shown in its extreme forms as fanatics, unkempt hippies, barbarians, or wild animals.

In summary, editorial cartoons followed political but not ethnic power lines. The symbols of culture were generally ascribed to the more powerful political unit: France or Britain in comparison with Canada, Canada as against one or more of the provinces, federalist Canada by contrast with independentist Quebec. The less powerful unit was generally compared to nature. In each comparison, culture was thus synonymous with power and the metropolis, nature with weakness and the hinterland. When the distinguishing categories were ethnic, however, the reverse was the case. Anglophones were depicted as symbols of innocence and confusion, while francophones were comparatively sophisticated and co-ordinated. In so far as these were depictions of power, Québécois were shown as well organized power-wielders while (English) Canadians were depicted as powerless and in disarray.

The nature-culture distinction has been briefly presented as a metaphor for goodness and then for power, on the basis of its everyday associations with these traits. A third possibility, in light of Burke's analysis, is to view culture as a metaphor for social order, with nature symbolizing social disorder. To test this carefully, a re-examination of all the cartoons was made. The same four pairs of oppositions were used, to see how far one pole was identified as a source of social disorder and the other as able or unable to restore order.

This analysis did not simply reproduce the results in Table 2. In some instances it resolved difficulties which had arisen in examining whether nature or culture was associated with a certain political or ethnic unit. It had been found that some drawings could not be included in Table 2 because they contained a dynamic contrast. The English, who were traditionally associated with culture, might be reduced to nature by the action of the French. The latter were thereby able to show that they were cultural and not natural, as had been thought. The simple, happy-go-lucky minority had shown itself to be sophisticated and ambitious, causing the once cultured dominant group to lose its emotional self-control and its social orderliness. The static culture-nature analysis missed the richness of this dynamic portrayal by insisting that culture be identified exclusively with one group and nature with the other.

The re-examination differed from the initial analysis in two important respects. First, the categories permitted a more dynamic study, in those instances where the outcome was clearly displayed.[7] Secondly, the question of threats to social order was addressed directly and not through the culture-nature metaphor. The coder was asked to judge who initiated the disorder which was observable in the drawing, and whether order was restored by the other party. No judgment was made on the justice or authenticity of the restoration itself. It might be the result of trickery, it might involve the suppression by force of the rebel minority, or it might occur because the dominant group was able to proceed as if nothing had happened. Each of these was judged to be a successful counter-initiative, even if the cartoonist was obviously depicting it as foolish or unfair.

Once more the numbers were too small to justify separate analyses for each topic.[8] Some cartoons were excluded, usually since the artist had not shown both members of any opposing pair. Among the 434 drawings where two such parties were included, 79 per cent featured a threat to social order,[9] whereas only 44 per cent had depicted one party as culture and the other as nature. The concept of a threat to social order thus proved to be a dominant element in the structure of these cartoons. Four out of five could be regarded as bearers of bad news underneath their humorous surface.

Relatively few overlaid this with reassurance of the restoration of social order. Where the threat to social order came from the minority, the dominant group was shown as able to re-establish it in only 23 per cent of cases. Where the dominant group posed the threat or initiated the change, the minority group was depicted as restoring it in only 13 per cent of the drawings.[10] It should be added that the artists did not necessarily represent the current social order as admirable, just, or beneficent. In some instances, they clearly showed that they would welcome the change and assumed that the skimmer would also be pleased by a successful challenge. The evidence suggested strongly, then, that cartoons were generally quite consistent with the 'bad news' characterization of journalism. The cartoonist might of course represent the threat favourably and the status quo with evident distaste.

"IF YOU DON'T WANT TO PLAY HOUSE, WE SHOULD AT LEAST LIVE TOGETHER AS MOTHER AND FATHER"

Aug. 24, 1977

© Tingley, *London Free Press*. Reprinted with permission

The source of these threats to social order was usually the minority group.[11] Francophones posed 76 per cent of the threats arising in their relations with anglophones. Canada provoked 55 per cent of those in its affairs with the parent countries. The provinces threatened federalism in 83 per cent of the cases, while 95 per cent of the challenges in relations between federalists and independentists came from the latter. Overall, the percentage originating with the less powerful group was 77. The less powerful group was consistently represented in cartoons as the agitator and source of social change, while the status quo was generally equated with the interests of the dominant group, even where these were the principal object of satire. Bad news consisted, then, of a series of threats to the interests of the dominant group by a subordinate who was pursuing sectional interests.

Once the analysis focused on threats to social order instead of culture and nature, the apparent anomaly of the anglophones as a dominant group identified with nature disappeared. This finding had resulted from the particular context of President de Gaulle's visit, when the leader of a parent country was shown supporting the minority group against the dominant group within Canada. The artists corroborated Ottawa's interpretation: de Gaulle's speech in favour of freedom for Quebec was an attempt by an unauthorized 'outside' dominant group to 'interfere' in Canada's 'internal affairs,' namely Canada's treatment of its minority, in a way which might alter the balance of power between them. The existence of this three-party interaction explains the anomaly that anglophones were more associated than francophones with nature, because they were the losers. It also explains the relatively equal balance between parent and child countries as sources of threats to the status quo.

The second part of the data analysis relating to hypothesis 1 studies anglophone cartoonists' responses to the threat of Quebec independence. It was expected that this would lead cartoonists to portray the Parti Québécois leaders as more villainous than previous Quebec governments. René Lévesque and his main lieutenants were therefore compared with francophone MPs and with the Quebec Liberal premiers since 1960, who espoused nationalism but not independence. In this case French- and English-language cartoons were tabulated separately.

The percentage figures for the English-language cartoonists show fairly clearly that, with the exception of keying, the major difference among the francophone personae was between the provincial and the federal politicians, the Quebec nationalists and the Canadian nationalists. The francophone MPs in Ottawa were seen almost universally as foolish and ineffective: the corresponding figures for Canadian politicians as a whole were 49 and 48 per cent. The provincial leaders, in contrast, whatever their political affiliation, were seen primarily as Quebec nationalists. They were portrayed as significantly less inclined to foolery and ineffectiveness, and slightly less effeminate, than their opposite numbers in (English) Canada.[12] This difference, which was strong in the representations by English-language cartoonists, was not observable in the works by their French-language counterparts.

Depictions of keying followed an altogether different pattern. For anglophone cartoonists, keying was slightly more characteristic of francophone politicians on the average (76 per cent) than it was of Canadian politicians in general (64 per cent). Francophone cartoonists agreed with this assessment of Quebec politicians but gave a more favourable depiction of their federal MPs, whom they showed as the most hard-working members of their profes-

TABLE 3

Portrayals of Quebec politicians by English- and French-language cartoonists

		% shown as foolish or bad among:		
Measure of	Language of cartoonist	Franco-phone MPs	Quebec premiers	PQ leaders
Foolishness				
Foolery	English	93	43	37
	French	63	57	58
Ineffectiveness	English	100	35	45
	French	46	39	48
Femininity	English	22	8	3
	French	7	9	9
Keying	English	72	78	77
	French	38	68	74
Badness				
Selfishness	English	43	65	71
	French	15	35	39
Fabrication	English	14	29	26
	French	15	19	9
Punitive representation	English	0	37	47
	French	23	4	12
Number of cartoons	English	14	49	121
	French	13	46	31

sion.[13] Artists in both languages, then, represented the gap between federal and provincial francophone politicians as substantially greater than that between the independentists and the Quebec Liberals.

Turning to the measures of badness, the federal politicians from Quebec who had been depicted as such thoroughgoing fools were shown as generally good, though inclined to be selfish. The provincial decision makers were noticeably less good on every index,[14] and were again virtually indistinguishable along party lines. Cartoonists of both languages regarded the federal-provincial or Canada-Quebec nationalist distinction as the crucial one, but the verdict of the francophones was much less decisive. They attributed less selfishness to their federal representatives but depicted them slightly more punitively.

The general picture which emerged from the English-language drawings, then, was that federalists from Quebec were inept but on the right side, whereas nationalists from the province were more effective but on the wrong side. It was also noteworthy that the Quebec nationalists were portrayed as very high on keying, suggesting that their enterprise and effort led mainly to symbolic victories. Their successes were in catching Canadian leaders off guard and embarrassing them, rather than in achieving tangible gains. The francophone artists showed their federal MPs as less selfish and much less addicted to keying. At the same time they represented them slightly more punitively, suggesting perhaps that they did not have such acceptable policies as the more selfish and ostentatious nationalists.

Thirdly, the hypothesis can be applied to regional interests situated within (English) Canada. The nineteen English-language cartoons featuring Alberta's challenges to federal policy-making corroborated this conclusion on two of the four foolishness and two of the three badness measures.[15]

The portrayals of Premier Lougheed as effective, masculine, and selfish, and the punitiveness of these drawings, were very similar to those of the Quebec premiers. The strategies of the francophone and western premiers were perceived as quite divergent, although both groups were seen as playing selfish masculine roles, sometimes effectively. Alberta had material resources to exchange with Ottawa. Peter Lougheed's approach was accordingly seen as straightforward and business-like, though he was usually shown as the fool or the victim of Ottawa's greater bargaining power. Since Quebec's resources, in contrast, were mainly symbolic, its premiers were seen to have based their strategy much more on keying, fabrication, and unbusiness-like conduct. They were represented as more skilful in these activities than Ottawa, and often as the winners, though their victories lacked the material results which accompanied Lougheed's.

This hypothesis also called for a comparison of provincial and federal leaders, where they appeared in the same cartoon. It was not possible, given the limited numbers, to make separate analyses according to topic, and the results are therefore less conclusive than one might wish. They were nevertheless quite revealing.

Although in most cartoons there was no difference in the depictions of the two, the differences which could be found were generally consistent. The prime minister was twice as likely as the Alberta or Quebec premier to be shown as foolish, but only half as likely to be depicted as bad. The sole exception related to keying, where there were no observable differences. Comparisons of the prime minister with the Parti Québécois leaders followed the same pattern but were much more extreme. While again the two were often portrayed as indistinguishable, the prime minister was four to eight times as likely as the PQ chief to appear foolish, but only one-fourth to one-eighth as likely to be shown as bad. Again, keying deviated from this pattern; where there was a difference, it was more characteristic of the Quebec premier.

Three messages were thus characteristic of the cartoons in relation to this hypothesis. First, regional and federal politicians were coloured principally by their occupation, and were generally foolish but not bad. Much more often than one would expect from chance alone,[16] they were shown as indistinguishable in these regards.

Secondly, in so far as there were differences, federal politicians were more likely to be shown as foolish and ineffective than their regional counterparts. They were, however, less likely to be depicted as selfish and bad.[17]

Thirdly, the two were connected. The more the regional politicians exhibited selfishness because their claims disregarded the national interest, the more the federal politicians were shown as incapable. Regional interests were presented as standing to some extent in opposition to national interests, and as associated with selfishness. Quebec independence was the most extreme manifestation of this. The Quebec nationalism of the province's Liberals was milder and Albertan oil policy was the mildest form. There was thus statistically significant evidence that the cartoons, whatever their region of origin, depicted national interests as good and regional interests as selfish. The foolishness of federal leaders was clearly linked to their inability to control regional interests for the sake of national ones which, as has been shown, were identified in the cartoons with those of the bourgeoisie.

In the final section dealing with the social order hypothesis, attention is turned to its fourth part, concerning the heroic representation of politicians from the cartoonist's own area.

The cartoons in this sample hardly ever included municipal figures, since French-English relations are not socially defined as a local issue except in a few trouble-spots such as Moncton, Penetanguishene, or St Boniface. The most local politicians were those operating at the provincial level, principally but not invariably the premier. It was possible to isolate and examine those drawings where a leader of the cartoonist's home province was portrayed in interaction with the federal government. The numbers of English-language cartoons were too small for elaborate analysis. There were seventeen portrayals of a leader from the cartoonist's own province, but only five of these showed him in a relationship of rivalry or conflict with federal figures. In these five, there were no noticeable differences between the representations of the cartoonist's own provincial politicians and those of the federal leaders with whom they were interacting.

There were forty-four French-language cartoons of Quebec federalist leaders and seventeen of the Parti Québécois leaders in interaction with members of the federal government. They were all drawn by cartoonists from Quebec papers. Nineteen of them showed a rivalry or conflict, though the effects of locality were at times confounded with those of language, since the local leaders were invariably francophone whereas the federal ones were sometimes anglophone. Some support for the hypothesis was found in the French-language cartoons: provincial heroes outnumbered federal heroes 7:2 on one measure and 9:0 on the other. Correspondingly, federal fools and villains outnumbered their provincial homologues by 17:12 and 19:10.[18] Provincial leaders were twice as likely as their federal counterparts to be portrayed as masculine, and only half as likely to be depicted as non-masculine. Finally, four of the nineteen cartoons (21 per cent) were heroic, compared with 10 per cent for the collection of drawings as a whole. The second half of the hypothesis thus received slight support, but only in the case where language differences corresponded fairly closely to the local-central government difference.

In summary, the social order hypothesis was strongly supported by the data, though its corollary about local politicians was confirmed only where language differences were also involved.

2: THE MINORITY GROUP HYPOTHESIS. *The richness of the politician's environment will be thinned by the exclusion of minority groups such as women, ethnic and racial minorities, representatives of local and regional interests, members of opposition parties, and Quebec independentists, except when they are shown posing threats to the social order.*

The inclusion of political and social minorities in the cartoons was unusual. The leader of the opposition attracted cartoonists' attention only when John Diefenbaker was protesting the activities of President de Gaulle, or when this office holder was unable to exercise effective control of his own party. Diefenbaker's assaults on Robert Stanfield's support for federal bilingualism policy comprised the only occasion in French-English relations when cartoonists focused on a member of the opposition other than its leader. Minority party leaders appeared in less than 1 per cent of the cartoons, and the most prominent members of the cabinet fared little better. The prime minister and the Quebec premier dominated the Canadian cartoon scene on these topics to an impressive degree (see Table 4).

Canadians from visible minorities, immigrants, and allophones were rare, appearing in about 3 per cent of the drawings. Women were rarely depicted, because editorial cartoons analyse a male-dominated field. Since Mrs Thatcher

TABLE 4
Percentage of cartoons in which political figures appear, by topic

	De Gaulle	Queen	Ottawa-Quebec	Constitution	Separation	Federal biling.	Quebec lang.
Prime minister	24	17	48	55	22	18	6
Premier of Quebec	26	9	61	21	81	5	35
Cabinet member	7	0	12	3	6	5	0
Member of other party	8	6	2	3	0	5	1
Other Canadian politician	29	5	7	39	10	5	21
N	151	63	156	67	55	83	84

NOTE: Percentages do not add to 100. Some cartoons contain none of these characters, while others contain several.

was new in office when the present sampling of cartoons stopped, the queen was the only woman who was portrayed regularly on any French-English topic. She appeared in 76 per cent of the cartoons concerning relations with Britain. Otherwise, women were seen in about 14 per cent of the drawings, the range being from 9 per cent on the effects of separation to 24 per cent on federal bilingualism policy. They occupied two principal roles; as members of the public, and as allegorical figures for a nation. In their role as citizens they did not differ from men; this facet of feminine participation will be discussed as part of hypothesis 6.

Allegorical figures were generally statuesque and suffering, though a few exhibited other stereotyped female qualities such as shrewishness. About half these figures were portrayed as foolish and ineffective, but relatively few were strongly feminine in their postures, engaged in keying, or depicted as bad. In general, cartoonists avoided both the depiction of women as significant political figures and the use of feminine poses to satirize men.

The portrayals of the royal family were in some ways similar to those of allegorical figures. About half the pictures showed them as fools and a few as feminine. They were depicted as more effective than the allegorical figures[19] but as more likely to be engaged in keying.[20] Overall, they were more likely to be shown as foolish.[21] Their form of foolishness was more likely to consist of 'going through the motions' than of passively suffering others' foolish activity. They were even less likely than the allegories of nations to be shown as bad.[22]

In general, then, women as symbolic figures were more the recipients than the initiators of political action. They were made foolish through victimage and not as a result of their own activity. They were largely innocent

TABLE 5
Depictions of allegorical figures as fools, bad people

Portrayal as	Non-fools outnumber fools by					Fools outnumber non-fools by			
	4	3	2	1	0	1	2	3	4
Foolish	–	1	8	39	13	41	2	1	–
Ineffective	–	1	9	38	9	42	5	1	–
Feminine	–	4	20	68	2	10	1	–	–
Keying	–	3	16	59	4	20	3	–	–

	Neutral people outnumber bad by					Bad people outnumber neutral by			
	4	3	2	1	0	1	2	3	4
Selfish	–	2	11	65	9	15	3	–	–
Fabricating	–	4	21	69	2	9	–	–	–
Punitive representation	–	1	14	66	7	14	2	1	–

TABLE 6
Depictions of royalty as fools, bad people

Portrayal as	Non-fools outnumber fools by					Fools outnumber non-fools by			
	4	3	2	1	0	1	2	3	4
Foolish	–	–	4	15	6	15	7	–	–
Ineffective	–	–	9	21	6	9	2	–	–
Feminine	–	1	11	23	4	6	2	–	–
Keying	–	1	3	9	6	20	8	–	–

	Neutral people outnumber bad by					Bad people outnumber neutral by			
	4	3	2	1	0	1	2	3	4
Selfish	–	1	12	26	5	3	–	–	–
Fabricating	–	1	15	27	2	2	–	–	–
Punitive representation	–	1	16	27	–	2	–	–	–

of badness. They were thus shown as relatively passive upholders of social order. The frequent association of gender roles with the culture-nature opposition was not strongly evident, but the forces of wildness and disorder were invariably represented as male. On the occasions when the culture-nature division was present, it was linked more to ethnicity than to gender in the cartoons.

3: THE CAST OF REGULARS HYPOTHESIS. *The symbolic world in the cartoons on a given topic will be limited to about ten unlabelled 'regulars' and some labelled 'visitors'. In principle, these characters could be caricatures of well-known individuals, symbols of nations or human qualities, or representations of social forces. In practice, individuals will be much more numerous than symbols or representations, because capitalist ideology attributes success, failure, and foolishness disproportionately to individuals.*

The second part of this hypothesis was readily observable in the drawings. While individuals taking action were shown in almost all cartoons, the proportion which depicted a social force or an allegorical figure was generally very small, and never exceeded one in six of the pictures on any topic.

The first part was strongly supported, with one important qualification: membership of the regular cast varies widely according to the topic. The centrality of the two leading personae in French-English relations, the prime minister and the premier of Quebec, was not at all constant from one topic to another. Table 4 showed that the prime minister was featured in 55 per cent of the constitutional but in only 6 per cent of the Quebec language cartoons. The premier of Quebec, meanwhile, was seen in 5 per cent of the federal bilingualism drawings, as compared with 81 per cent of those which focused on separation.

The constitution was perceived as a tripartite struggle between Mr Trudeau, a Quebec leader, and the premiers of the other provinces. While Trudeau and Lévesque were almost always recognizable without a label or similar clue, the federalist Quebec leaders were generally labelled when they appeared, and the other provincial premiers were labelled in about half the drawings where they were shown. The opposition, the federal cabinet, and leaders from other countries were usually excluded, and when other Canadian politicians were featured they were generally given name-tags. Members of the public and civil servants were always left anonymous.

Relations between Ottawa and Quebec were depicted as interactions of the prime minister and the federal cabinet with the premier of Quebec. Members of the cabinet, including the prime minister, were given labels in about half their appearances. This proportion was about average for the cabinet but was abnormally high for the prime minister, who was rarely identified in any other context. Quebec's premier was labelled about once in every four appearances.

The effects of separation were treated as largely internal to Quebec. René Lévesque was dominant, with Pierre Trudeau and the Quebec cabinet in the background. Lévesque was given identifying tags in about one-third of the cartoons, and his cabinet in about half. The visit of President de Gaulle evoked the widest range of political figures. The president, Prime Minister Pearson, and Premier Johnson were the three main ones, but the artists also gave some prominence to the federal cabinet, the opposition, René Lévesque, and a number of other politicians. The three main personae, the cabinet, and Mr Diefenbaker were taken to be easily identifiable. Lévesque and the other politicians, however, were labelled in about half their appearances.

Royal visit representation, in contrast, was restricted to the regal pair and the prime minister; they were taken to be immediately recognizable. Language policy was restricted to the leaders of the party currently in power; again they were so closely identified with their policies that very few name-tags were judged to be necessary.

Overall, recognizability was highest for the prime minister and the leader of the opposition, who were given labels in only about 15 per cent of the cartoons where they appeared. The queen, the Duke of Edinburgh, and President de Gaulle came next, receiving identification labels in 20 to 25 per cent of drawings. The provincial premiers averaged 30 per cent, with René Lévesque treated as slightly better known than the others. Quebec and federal cabinet ministers were judged to need name-tags in 40 per cent of their appearances. Other politicians were given labels more often than not: Mayor Drapeau, the federal NDP leader, the heads of the Royal Commission on Bilingualism and Biculturalism and the Task Force on Canadian Unity, and several opposition leaders from the Quebec National Assembly.

The hypothesis could also be tested by tabulating individuals rather than cartoons. The numbers here were larger, but the lack of statistical independence precluded detailed analysis. Roles which were never shown more than four times on any topic were relegated to the 'Miscellaneous' category.

Table 7 shows the percentage of characters who occupied one of the eleven categories which were found at least five times on one of the seven topics. Several of them were broad enough that a cartoon could have contained more than one role from this category. A drawing of 'Other MPs' could have included the leader of the opposition, a third party spokesperson, and a cabinet member. In practice, this happened so rarely that the distortion could safely be ignored.

'Other Quebec politicians' could have been subdivided into Péquistes and Liberals, but only on the topic of Quebec language policy. A division of the allegorical figures would have yielded additional roles only in relation to President de Gaulle's visit. These findings lend additional support to

TABLE 7

Percentage distribution of role categories by topic: all cartoon characters

	De Gaulle	Queen	Consti-tution	Ottawa-Quebec	Sepa-ration	Federal biling.	Quebec lang.
Prime Minister	14	7	20	21	10	7	3
Other MPs	3	6	4	6	–	5	–
Civil servants	4	5	8	2	–	26	10
RCMP, police	2	7	–	–	–	4	3
Quebec premier	15	4	6	24	31	–	14
Other Quebec politician	5	–	–	4	14	–	14
Other premier	–	–	9	–	–	–	–
Allegorical figure	11	–	8	7	4	–	6
Citizen	8	23	17	23	17	38	28
Foreign head of state	28	37	–	–	–	–	–
Business	–	–	–	–	–	–	7
Miscellaneous	10	12	27	13	24	21	15
Number (all characters)	368	164	181	364	115	221	189

hypothesis 3, that cartoons on French-English relations deal with a limited cast of about ten roles, although their importance varied widely from one topic to another.

Attempts to study patterns of interaction were not very fruitful. Cartoonists often include the minimum number of persons required to make their point. Only one or two principal characters were usually depicted. Minor ones were frequently omitted, and interaction would have had to be inferred in most cases.

4: THE IMAGINARY CANADA HYPOTHESIS. *The participants in partisan or national conflict will be depicted as formally equal rivals, similar in size and power, and not as adversaries with quite unequal resources. Cartoons will thus perpetuate the myth of the Imaginary Canada. If third parties are present, they will be depicted as bystanders or as moderating influences who take a position between the two sides. They will be shown to be hurt by the dispute.*

Hypothesis 4 concerned depictions which corresponded to Wilden's Imaginary Canada. The results show that, for francophone cartoonists, all topics except federal bilingualism generally centred around a dispute. For anglophone cartoonists, this was not the case on those topics where their own symbols were dominant: the queen's visit, the constitution, and federal bilingualism. However, their drawings were structured around a dispute when their own symbols were not dominant.

Only a minority of disputes were depicted as involving equally matched pairs. These results suggest that representations of the Imaginary Canada are widespread but not predominant in cartoons. Overall, they occurred in 22 per cent of the drawings. They were most frequently found where direct interaction between Ottawa and Quebec was illustrated. This was to be expected, since Wilden saw equality between Ottawa and Quebec as a central pillar in the structure of the Imaginary Canada.

It was also found that, where the parties were presented as unequal, the dominant country was not consistently drawn larger or placed more centrally in the cartoon, as artistic conventions would lead one to expect. There was a slight tendency for de Gaulle to be portrayed as more prominent than the Canadian leaders. There were no significant differences, however, between Canadian politicians and those of the parent countries. The same was true in the few comparisons between federal and anglophone provincial leaders.

Third parties were rarely shown acting as moderators or mediators, openly or in the subtler ways in which journalists do. Since cartoonists see themselves as more akin to columnists than to reporters, one would not expect them to pose regularly as moderating influences. They usually present themselves as satirists who propose a pox on both parties, or as moralists who take a political position favouring one side.

Portrayals of suffering third parties were not very common. They occurred in only 18 per cent of drawings which featured a dispute, with a range from 4 per cent in the case of the constitution to 27 per cent on the topic of federal

TABLE 8
Cartoons structured around dispute between equals

	De Gaulle	Queen	Consti- tution	Ottawa- Quebec	Sepa- ration	Federal biling.	Quebec lang.
Language of cartoon	E F	E F	E F	E F	E F	E F	E F
No. of cartoons showing two sides and:							
No dispute	10 28	21 9	34 4	40 8	19 4	39 10	16 3
Dispute	33 80	21 12	24 5	80 28	25 7	31 3	40 25
No. of cartoons showing dispute between:							
Unequals	23 54	20 11	13 4	42 11	14 4	17 3	30 20
Equals	10 26	1 1	11 1	38 17	11 3	14 –	10 5

bilingualism. Suffering was fairly often depicted in the other 82 per cent of cartoons which showed a dispute. It was usually attributed to the losing party in the dispute, however, and not to innocent bystanders.

5: THE DOUBLE STANDARD HYPOTHESIS. *Business leaders will be portrayed much less regularly in cartoons than political leaders. The percentage of foolish and disorderly people will be much higher in portrayals of politicians than in depictions of business executives; the former will engage much more in keying, fabrication, and disputes.*

Hypothesis 5 concerns the portrayals of the public and private sectors. The private sector of the economy is an important news focus, and it contributes most of the advertising material on which newspapers depend. Nevertheless, according to Gans (p. 12), the economically powerful are rarely in the news. Furthermore, most of the topics which constitute French-English relations are not socially defined as closely related to the economy. The exception is Quebec language policy, which was expected to influence (English) Canadian and American investment in the province. It was therefore scarcely surprising that only 3 per cent of the 659 cartoons showed either actual or allegorical business figures, and that only 21 or 1.3 per cent of the 1,602 characters on these seven topics were business people. By contrast, well over 70 per cent of the characters were political leaders or government employees, most of the rest being citizens. A fuller study of the extent of business portraiture can be made in chapter 7 from the cartoons on Canadian-American relations, for these are socially defined as primarily economic.

The type of portrayals which business and politics received was measured on the two broad dimensions of foolishness and badness (described in detail in Appendix B). The analysis of foolishness had four aspects: foolery, ineffectiveness, femininity, and keying. Eight cartoons showed a single person from business, while five showed two each, and one portrayed three.

In 43 per cent of these cartoons business leaders were shown more often than not as engaging in foolery; in 36 per cent they were generally shown as ineffective. In 7 per cent they were drawn mainly as feminine, and in 14 per cent as mostly engaged in keying. While these numbers were too small to be reliable, in the overall pattern the minority were shown as foolish and the majority as serious.

Politicians had similar profiles in certain respects, but appeared quite different in others. In 49 per cent of the cartoons they were generally depicted as engaging in foolery. A similar result, 48 per cent, obtained for representations of ineffectiveness. Femininity was attributed in 6 per cent of cases.

The proportion pictured as mostly engaged in keying was 64 per cent. Four independent comparisons of the representations of political and business figures could be made, using the U-test. This more thorough examination showed the differences to be highly significant.[23]

There were thus some marked differences in the degree of foolishness attributed to business and politics, which support the concept of a double standard. They can be summarized in another pair of statistics: depending on the measure, 45 to 65 per cent of cartoons in which a politician was the central character portrayed that person as foolish. Only in 15 to 35 per cent of the cartoons focusing on a business leader was that person portrayed as foolish.

The three measures of badness were applied to the cartoons: selfishness, fabrication, and punitive representations. Thirty-six per cent of cartoons showed most business people as selfish rather than normally pursuing their own interests; 14 per cent represented business punitively on the whole, while 79 per cent showed it laughingly or descriptively. None presented business as engaged in fabrication.

On the same measures, 36 per cent showed Canadian political figures as mainly selfish and 18 per cent depicted them punitively. Fabrication was seen as the practice of 12 per cent in politics. In general, then, politicians were judged slightly but not significantly more harshly than business executives in terms of goodness.

The figures for these cartoons, showing business people in the context of French-English relations, could be compared with their depictions on business topics. In view of the variability from one topic to another, it was conceivable that those who were represented favourably when they were a minor element in ethnic relations would be depicted quite differently when they were the central focus. The larger number of cartoons would also offset the problems of reliability which arise in such a small sample. The results for foolishness were, however, very similar: business chiefs were slightly more prone to foolery and ineffectiveness when they were the centre-piece of the cartoons, but were slightly less apt to be shown as feminine or as active in keying. The differences never reached statistical significance, and tended to cancel out. But executives were more likely to be seen as bad when they were the central focus.[24]

In summary, business leaders were rarely seen in cartoons. When they did appear, they were only infrequently shown as evil and in most cases they were not seen as foolish. In general, they were seen as serious, good people who contributed positively to society. Two qualities could be said to distinguish between these two groups and the social institutions in which they were dominant: competence and orderliness. There were insufficient cartoons of particular business figures to examine whether special attention was being given to individuals who were guilty of unusual financial foolishness.

Other data supported this argument. Overall, 68 per cent of the drawings portrayed someone as foolish; of these, 83 per cent portrayed only politicians in that manner, while 17 per cent showed others in this light, perhaps in addition to politicians. Among fool-making cartoons on the spousal theme, politicians were depicted as the only fools in 98 per cent of cases; on the in-law theme the figure was 88 per cent. Only on the children theme was there an important representation of other fools, nearly always citizens or civil servants. Almost 50 per cent of fool-making cartoons on this theme included non-political figures.

It is clear from these results that the display of foolishness among political leaders was disproportionate to its display among those in other occupations.[25] Consequently the overall message is that politics and elected representatives are the primary sources of threats to social order, whereas business and its leaders are one of its main supports. The public is represented as the principal victim.

One of the most frequent messages in cartoons is that politicians' main activity is keying: posing, pretending, and going through the motions. One might conclude from this that in the capitalist state, public dramas govern political action, just as market mechanisms govern economic action. Politics is the marketplace for resolving conflicts about values through debate and bargaining. It is taken as self-evident that economic action is serious and therefore cannot threaten social order. It is taken as questionable whether political action is serious; consequently it is presented as a threat to social order. The viewer is implicitly offered two alternative resolutions for the puzzle of politics. If politics as an institution is inherently comic, it should be treated as light entertainment. If it is serious, then stern measures should be taken to restore order in a domain where the forces of disorder and foolishness are so regularly portrayed as rampant.

Business leaders thus fit Klapp's deft description of practical leaders who do things through 'active command, management, contributions, works and the like' (1964: 42). Political leaders are better described in Klapp's account of the mock symbolic hero (1962: 159–69). Real symbolic heroes make vicarious winners of their audience, reinforcing their sense of security that social change is understandable and still within human control. They personalize change in a dramatic and simplified form, combining integrity with showmanship as they conquer evil and restore social solidarity (1964: 25, 44). The mock hero fails to emulate this, but relieves the audience's alienation and sense of insecurity by offering a chance to laugh at the institutions and those who seek success within them.

The present analysis is taken further. While Klapp sensitively relates satire and mock heroism to popular alienation, oligarchy, and impersonality (1962: 119–23, 162–6), he does not ground these in the nature of capitalism and its view of politics. He observes that 'politicians have suffered badly in cartooning' (1962: 165) and that celebrities have difficulty in maintaining a private life because they feel treated as public property (1964: 15, 17). He is careful not to identify the practical leader with the business executive or the symbolic leader with the politician. He recognizes the possibility that some political leaders will acquire an image as practical persons, while some business persons will be portrayed as clowns. Perhaps as a result, he does not probe the significance of the double standard by which public figures are fair game and have virtually no recourse when pilloried, while private figures in business have ample legal and social protection. Analysis of cartoons, however, suggests that most politicians are pressured by the demands of their symbolic role into foolishness because the public figure 'will find that a dramatic sense of symbolic requirements is a very different thing from practical requirements' (Klapp, 1964: 64).

6: THE PASSIVE CITIZENS HYPOTHESIS. *Ordinary citizens and politicians will be depicted as foolish in about the same proportion of cases. However, the depiction of politicians as active will contrast with the portrayal of ordinary citizens as their passive audience. In general, politicians will be shown as having little contact with those who have elected them.*

Politicians were shown as less inclined to foolery and more effective than citizens; in short, they were more adept at the necessitous aspects of political work. The stronger depiction of foolery among the citizenry was quite pronounced on two topics and fairly clear on three others; across the set of seven topics it was highly significant.[26] Their greater ineffectiveness was pronounced on three topics but not observable on the other four; overall it was again highly significant.[27] However, politicians were more effeminate than citizens[28] and much more likely to be engaged in keying.[29] Their frivolity as symbolic actors exceeded that of the electorate.

This pattern was more complex than had been anticipated. The strongest difference related to keying, and was in the expected direction: this behaviour was portrayed as the speciality of politicians and as the clearest defining trait of the political system. These leaders have the opportunity to exercise power but instead, the public is informed, they play at politics by competing for popularity and symbolic advantages. They mistake appearance for substance and make phoney alliances which reveal their true characters. Conjoined to this is the greater effeminacy of politicians, because these pursuits which they substitute for action are stereotypically viewed as characteristic of women.

The cartoonists repeatedly stressed that the persistent foolishness of politicians implied a similar if not greater foolishness in those responsible for letting them continue in office. In these cartoons the electorate ranks as the most ineffective and the most prone to foolery. This is rarely a partisan statement, in which the cartoonist contrasts the foolish and ineffective voters for one party with the good if not heroic supporters of another. Their depictions did not often change when the party in power did, and the rare portrayals of the opposition leaders were no more flattering. The artist asserts that politicians do not attain their positions in a social vacuum, but as a result of decisions by their constituents. If the leaders are foolish, this necessarily reflects adversely on their supporters.

This 'self-evident truth' of capitalist democracy masks the many elements which influence a candidate's chances of winning nomination by a major party (Forcese and deVries). It also masks the differential ability of the parties to replenish their resources and to sway the electorate. Politics is thus divorced from its material base and re-presented as 'part of entertainment and leisure' rather than as work. It becomes private, voluntary, and for most people passive, rationalized on the grounds that the public is incompetent and should leave decisions to the experts (Wilson: 228, 249). Cartoonists reject the part of this ideology which urges citizens to defer to politicians and civil servants; but their selective attack on politicians and the public promotes, perhaps unintentionally, government by business leaders as the modern ideal.

One might summarize by saying that politicians are shown as active fools, committed to symbolic action and keying, who sometimes succeed in extricating themselves from victimage through their high level of activity. Perhaps the classic Canadian example was McNally's cartoon of Diefenbaker sprouting wings and flying out of the corner into which he had painted himself. The public, meanwhile, are more victims than fools, straightforward people who expect but never get practical action, as exemplified by Macpherson's little man. They are generally victimized by the politicians because they are relatively passive and resourceless.

In respect to keying, hypothesis 6 was strongly confirmed. While citizens were generally shown as greater fools than their elected leaders, the citizens had one redeeming trait in these depictions: they tried to do their job. Politicians, in contrast, substituted all kinds of play for their work: they were

the crickets of Aesop's fable, who were not even going through the motions of doing work. Instead, they were devoting their considerable energies to posturing, quarrelling, and seeking self-aggrandizement. Only the business leaders combined honest work habits with effectiveness. The ordinary citizens were a blend of these two opposites, honest but ineffective workers. The moral for democracy and social structure was clear: if one desired honest effective government, ordinary citizens could not be counted upon. They persistently chose leaders whose energies were misdirected. They should, instead, entrust government to those whose business experience was the best assurance that they could handle public property and whose business success served as the guarantee of their goodness and seriousness. This portrayal of business and its executives glosses over the essentially self-seeking nature of their enterprise and its perennially undemocratic structures.

The cartoonist, then, invites the public to see themselves in his or her special provocative mirror. While it has sometimes been proposed that the passive spectator is the desired goal of capitalist ideology, Barthes (p. 92) and Williamson (pp. 19, 41–2) among others have shown that this view is much too simple. The ideal, rather, is active consumership, participation directed toward capitalist goals. It can be argued, similarly, that this is one of the goals of cartooning. By portraying citizens as sheep, it is suggested, these artists try to provoke them into activity designed to curb the foolishness of their politicians and to render them more business-like.

Table 9 examines the various roles which cartoonists assign to the public in their analyses of contemporary politics. The first and largest category consists of cases where the public is absent from the scene. These account

TABLE 9
Role of the public in editorial cartoons, percentage by topic

	Constitution	Ottawa-Quebec	Separation	De Gaulle	Queen	Federal biling.	Quebec lang.	Total
Absent	60	75	68	83	82	51	48	68
Invisible audience	11	3	13	1	–	1	4	4
Visible audience	9	3	4	4	6	2	10	5
Participating	7	4	2	4	1	2	6	4
Interacting with self	13	15	13	8	11	44	32	19
Number	67	156	55	151	63	83	84	659

on the average for two-thirds of the drawings, the range being one-sixth in each direction. The second category consists of a small number of cartoons which show no members of the public, but where the main character is looking straight at the skimmer, as if addressing an invisible audience. This type included 4 per cent of cartoons on the average, but as many as one in eight on two topics – the constitution and the effects of separation. The third category contained those drawings where the viewer could see members of the public acting as an audience, before whom political leaders were expounding their foolishness. The cartoonists treated them as a rule with the same satirical touch that was applied to the politicians. This, too, was a small category, and called for a low level of activity by citizens. The fourth category showed the public as participants interacting with political leaders. Some of them were responding actively to the deeds of public figures and taking an active part in shaping events. Lastly, the fifth category showed members of the public interacting with one another, in response to the initiatives of absent political chiefs.

Table 9 reveals that passivity and activity were about equally common in the relatively small number of cartoons which showed direct interaction between political leaders and the public. There were thirty-four examples of a passive and twenty-eight of an active response by citizens. When the 'invisible audience' cartoons were included, the ratio of passive to active representations of citizens reached two to one. When all the drawings were categorized it increased to more than three to one. Skimmers were most likely to see themselves omitted; when portrayed, they were more often passive or absent watchers than active participants in politics. In these hyper-ritualized performances, skimmers are fairly consistently informed that politics is foolish, that they are foolish when they enter it, and that they normally remain detached from its fool-making potential. This may not of course be the message which most glancers receive, but it certainly predominates among those being sent.

An even more consistent message in the drawings is that politics and the public operate in separate spheres. Even if the invisible audience cartoons are counted as examples of interaction between citizens and leaders, only one cartoon in eight showed any such interaction directly or implicitly. The other seven-eighths portrayed only one or the other. Political leaders occupy a social space from which the public is nearly always excluded, according to these artists. The citizenry reacts to political decisions – very extensively in the case of language legislation – but generally does so in private spaces where politicians do not venture. Citizens and their representatives discuss matters of public interest largely within their own social circles. Political matters are mostly privatized, and the genuinely public sphere is narrowly circumscribed.

This chapter has reviewed the evidence relating to six hypotheses about the ideological content of editorial cartoons on French-English relations. Using the cartoon as the unit of analysis, strong support was found for the social order hypothesis. Among the cartoons which presented characters from a dominant and a minority group in interaction, almost 80 per cent featured a threat to social order, usually emanating from the minority group. As a rule, order was not re-established within the limited narrative of the cartoon, and in this respect it echoed the bad news orientation of the news pages. Some drawings featured a local hero standing up to a larger and more distant power, but these comprised a tiny fraction of all cartoons.

The minority group hypothesis was also confirmed strongly. Gender, ethnic and racial, political, and regional minorities were rarely featured, except when they were disturbing the social order. The cast of regulars hypothesis was also confirmed for each topic, but not necessarily across topics. Particular topics such as the constitution were treated as the pre-rogative of a small number of role players, but these were not the same ones who were portrayed in relation, say, to Quebec's language legislation.

The Imaginary Canada hypothesis received considerable support in one respect: Ottawa and Quebec were often treated as formally equal in their relations. This was not the case for Canada's relations with Britain, France, or its own provinces, however. The double standard hypothesis received strong support in certain respects and substantial support overall. Business figures were rarely caricatured, but were portrayed as less foolish than politicians when they were shown. This was especially striking in relation to keying and ineffectiveness. Finally, the passive citizens hypothesis was confirmed: most drawings showed the electors as passive and rarely in touch with those who governed them.

The general message which emanates from these cartoons, then, is that the dominant group, and especially business, is shown as defending the status quo, while minority groups, and sometimes politicians in general, are shown as disruptive. Although cartoonists may be strongly satirical in their portraits of the present social order, the general thrust of their work gives it ideological support. They laugh at its foibles and the excesses in its politics, but rarely challenge its basic capitalist foundations.

In conclusion, two observations will be offered which arose as this analysis proceeded. The first concerns the role of the skimmer as constructed by the conventions of cartoonists, the second the changing significance of cartooning itself.

Editorial cartooning as an art-form is affected both by the medium within which it appears and by the artists' responses to the conventions of their profession. The medium restricts cartoonists to black, white, and shading. As a result, the conventions and psychological messages of colour cannot be part of the artist's repertoire. The assumption that most readers skim the cartoon defines it as a drawing whose message should be grasped very quickly by most viewers. While a delay of two or three seconds in getting the point, seeing the incongruity, or reading the accompanying text is acceptable, cartoons are expected to reveal their overt message almost immediately; they are akin to headlines and at the opposite extreme from crossword puzzles.

In order to work successfully within these restrictions, several forms of simplification are widely used. Most cartoonists, especially francophones, drastically curtail their cast of characters, their wealth of background detail, their use of words. Most of the personae are drawn in two and not three dimensions: the researcher can tell only in very broad terms which part of the character's anatomy is level with the eye of the artist.[30] There are, of course, striking exceptions: Macpherson sometimes delights in elaborate scenarios, while Barron and Norris include little gags in their backgrounds. On the whole, however, the focus on exaggerating certain traits of the main characters is highlighted by a relatively scanty treatment of the others.

The need to produce simplified and scanty drawings, it should be emphasized, makes the artist's task harder. To represent a bored audience or an arrogant ruler may be much more difficult if the conventions oblige him or her to do so in a few strokes. Simplicity implies that background details should be redundant, serving to repeat the main theme, perhaps with slight variations, but not to generate new ones. Barron's living-rooms become excessively suburban, while Norris's potted plants or signs of poverty are superabundant. The viewer has the opportunity to revel in the repetition of displays of opulence, tattiness, or idleness. Again, some of Macpherson's work constitutes an exception, for he may introduce scenes from sub-plots or themes which complement rather than reproduce the main one. The discerning viewer is then offered the complexity of comedy rather than the simplicity of farce.

These conventions have important repercussions for the social construction of the glancer role. As a glancer, one is offered the task of decoding the artist's message, seeking the butt of the humour, and enjoying the satire.

Since this activity is designed to be of very short duration for the average skimmer, the trail is well sprinkled with clues. Where the artist is referring to an 'obscure' news item or a minor personality, explanatory labels are likely to be included. Some cartoons are simply visualizations of a popular saying, such as 'The prime minister has put his foot in it.' Some show a public official with the features of an animal, a legendary figure, or an occupational group, whose main characteristic is well known through stereotypes: a donkey, a cave-dweller, or a doctor, for example. Others rely on dramatic or situational irony or on antiphrasis to show the incongruities between the characters' words, deeds, and situations.

In these respects, it is suggested, most cartoonists require their skimmers to show powers of decoding roughly equivalent to those needed for a single clue in a crossword puzzle. There is little evidence, in cartoons, of the modern tendency in literature and the theatre to expect substantial audience participation, either in performing the work, in Eagleton's sense (1976b: 66–9), or in examining the conventions on which it is based (Hutcheon, 1984: 139–52). Nor is there evidence that the cartoons provoke readers to peaceful or to violent action, as often happens among sports spectators (Smith, 1979; Critcher, Clarke).

The changing significance of cartooning itself also deserves comment. In the era of partisan newspapers with opinionated owners, the cartoonist's task was to satirize the opposing party, especially where its leaders had similar colourful qualities to those of the owner. Within their partisan framework, one party stood for social order, another for disruption and social evils. Low satire and personal attacks were the mainstay of the artist's work, and the glancer was invited to take the side of good government. The cartoonist was expected to purvey the official line wittily and incisively.

As local monopolies have become the dominant form in the newspaper industry, cartoonists have switched to a 'professional role' as non-partisan commentators. Their verbal and artistic skills are now directed against the party in power, whatever its policies and popular base may be. While low satire and personal fool-making may still, on the surface, be common, the deeper implications of monopolization and professionalization are quite different. The old-style cartoonist was an optimist, who equated foolishness with certain individuals and prophesied a golden age when they were displaced. The modern-style cartoonist proves to be a pessimist, who equates foolishness with politics itself, since any prime minister will engage in the same practices – even those who come from a strong business background.

Below the surface, then, the cartoonists' target has gradually shifted from the individual to the system, since politicians of one party are only marginally better or worse than those of another, like brands of detergent. Constant lampooning of the democratic decision-making process may, as Press argues, be a form of tinkering, if the effect is simply to correct small errors. There is, however, a much less flattering interpretation: that cartooning, like the whole newspaper enterprise in which it is embedded, constitutes a continuous attack on public and democratic decision-making, from the vantage point of private decision-making. At another level, then, cartoons undermine democracy as trivial and ineffective by comparison with more autocratic forms of governance.

The chapter thus ends with a paradox. Although, individually, editorial cartoonists are deeply democratic, their art-form itself may be becoming more undemocratic in its messages as it becomes more professional.

7

Canadian-American Cartoons as Capitalist Slogans

This chapter closely parallels the two preceding chapters, but studies cartoons about Canadian-American relations. In this context (English) Canadians, who were the dominant group in the earlier analysis, are the minority, and Québécois become invisible. We begin with a brief report on the extent of regional and topical differences in the cartoons (full details are given in Appendix C). Since Americans were featured in very few French-language drawings, no search for language differences could be made. The chapter then tests the six hypotheses about content against this fresh set of cartoons.

REGIONAL DIFFERENCES IN THE CARTOONS

Regional differences were sought in the structure of the drawings, the main characters, and the extent of pro- or anti-American sentiment. There were strong differences on only two of the twenty-six characteristics of the cartoons. Satire by Ontario cartoonists was directed more against individuals and less against political institutions than satire from the other regions. Ontario cartoonists were more likely to represent politicians as the only fools in their drawings. In this respect the central region's critique of politics remained closer to the capitalist mythology – that politics is uniquely the home of foolishness and that individuals rather than social structures bear responsibility for what takes place.

The topical differences were again much stronger, and coalesced into a pattern which displayed military interactions with the United States as graver, starker, and subject to more intense pressures than economic discussions. Canada was shown as having even less power and less room to negotiate in military than in economic affairs. Military independence was represented as involving greater costs for Canada than economic independence from the United States. Among the possibilities mentioned were a U.S. invasion, CIA infiltration of the RCMP, and the military use of Canada – as a missile testing site, a decoy for missiles aimed at the United States, or as a Soviet–United States battleground.

At the same time, the drawings made plain that there were major overlaps between economic and military policy. American military policy was seen as closely tied to trade. This happened both directly, through the pressures on Canada to buy u.s. military equipment regardless of its utility, and indirectly through the state's role in repressing any signs of Canadian independence from the promotion of American capitalist interests. The state was thus portrayed as both the salesperson for capitalism in dealings with compliant dependent nations, and also as its enforcer in relations with those who resisted.

When attention was turned to regional differences in the cartoon characters, the analysis again showed that topic was much more important than region. While region had some utility in predicting foolishness among Canadians, only topic had general value as a discriminator.

Finally, the extent of anti-Canadian and anti-American bias was examined, following the model of analysis developed in the corresponding part of chapter 5.

A clear rank-order was revealed. Western cartoons were the most pro-Canadian, while those from Ontario were the least pro-Canadian. Drawings from English Quebec and the Maritimes were intermediate. Ontario cartoons were the most likely to picture Americans. They were also the most likely to attribute foolishness to Canadian politicians and to citizens who participated in politics. Those from the West were the most likely to show only the local impact of American policy, depicting Canadians more positively as passive non-participants in politics.

There were also differences in national bias from one topic to another. Overall, Canadian governments were credited by cartoonists with the ability to perceive their economic interests, though they were often portrayed as unable to assert and defend them effectively. However, they were often shown as unable to conceptualize their military interests except by imitating those of the United States. In particular they were often accused of uncritically buying u.s. equipment, which rarely if ever worked as it was intended to.

The remaining sections of this chapter closely parallel those of chapter 6. They test the six hypotheses against the sample of 197 drawings on Canadian-American relations. Once again the cartoon and not the single character was the unit of analysis. Thus a work which showed several politicians as foolish was regarded as a stronger statement than one which showed only one in this light; but each drawing was counted once in any table.

1. The Social Order Hypothesis

The nature-culture distinction was quite important in the military cartoons, since 44 per cent introduced this metaphor. The economic drawings, however, relied on it in only 24 per cent of cases. There was a significant tendency, when this metaphor was utilized, to associate the Americans more with culture and the Canadians more with nature.[1] Canada was generally shown as the country with natural resources, and innocent and technologically backward people. The United States was portrayed as the user of natural resources, a sophisticated and technologically advanced nation which maintained its position with a blend of persuasion and force.

The culture associated with the United States was, however, very different from that which the artists had attributed to the parent countries. Britain and France represented 'pure culture,' expressed through state visits in formal attire. These renewed the symbolic ties between relatives who saw each other only occasionally and who engaged mainly in ritual exchanges. The participants acted as symbolic leaders, though infrequently the prime minister or the French president might 'stoop' to seek partisan or economic gain from the occasion. The United States, in contrast, represented 'everyday culture,' expressed in working talks conducted in shirt sleeves. Practical matters were negotiated between close neighbours who saw each other regularly and who engaged principally in material exchanges. The participants acted as bargainers, though occasionally one of them might 'rise' to a public relations gesture promoting goodwill. Economic ties, which dominated relations with the United States, were treated as virtually absent from relations with parent countries. The tools used in building and maintaining family solidarity were altogether different from those needed for success in economic or military negotiations. This polarization of the pure and the material nations in Canada's political environment is, of course, an additional element in cartoon mythology.

Canada's previous dependency on Britain and France was portrayed as quite unlike its present dependence on the United States, just as relations with distant and aging parents differ from those with close neighbours of one's own age. The two types of government were shown in a manner which reinforced this opposition. Britain was always represented by the queen and never by its prime minister. It was therefore shown as symbolically important, economically unsullied, and powerless. British self-interest was never portrayed, either in allegorical form or through the behaviour of its leaders. Its values were shown to centre around pageantry, aristocratic leisure, and symbolic work. Conversely, the United States was almost always represented by an energetic working president who was vigorously pursuing the

© Aislin, Montreal *Gazette*. Reprinted with permission

commercial interests of his country. American culture existed only in the form of trade and technology, both of which were used mainly for purposes of social control. Consequently, American patriotism and culture could never exist for their own sake but only as conduits and thin covers for hard-working self-interest. American values, correspondingly, are depicted as based upon industry, the bourgeoisie, and necessitous work.

France was portrayed in an intermediate role, a sometimes uncomfortable amalgam of these two extremes. President de Gaulle was American in his enterprise and hard work, but European in directing it mainly to symbolic accomplishments more suited to a pre-industrial era. He was self-interested and sophisticated, but frequently ineffective, and his particular blend of European and American qualities was shown, in these exclusively English-language cartoons, as mainly destructive.

Since the nature-culture metaphor was found only in a minority of the drawings, a search was again made for a more dynamic structure focusing on social order. This once more proved fruitful: among the cartoons in which both Canadians and Americans were shown as participating, 94 per cent of those on military relations and 74 per cent on economic relations featured a threat to social order from one nation's representatives. A few depicted threats by a third nation, or a joint threat; some were ironic, in depicting a threat which would be clear to the skimmer but which both parties conspicuously failed to see.[2] Almost four out of five of the cartoons featured bad news, in the sense of a threat to social order from one of the two principals.

Where the threat came from the minority group, Canada, there was almost a 50 per cent chance that the dominant group would be able to restore the status quo.[3] Where the threat came from the dominant group, the probability fell to one in eight.[4] The difference was highly significant statistically.[5] In this context, unlike that of French-English relations, significantly more threats came from the dominant group than from the minority.[6] The Americans were seen as the main source of disruption, pursuing their own interests with little regard for social order in Canada.

In this context, the second part of hypothesis 1 implied that nationalistic Canadians might be portrayed as local heroes in relation to u.s. dominance. In the North American setting, it was unlikely that the Canadian bourgeoisie would define its own interests as regional and therefore selfish, in relation to those of the United States. The view of continental interests as good but national interests as selfish would probably not be upheld by these data. In the French-English context, where most cartoonists were drawing for skim-mers from the dominant group, capitalist ideology about minorities was

TABLE 10

Canadian and American politicians practising foolery

	Non-fools outnumber fools by					Fools outnumber non-fools by			
	4	3	2	1	0	1	2	3	4
Canadian	–	–	3	21	3	52	6	2	–
American	–	–	–	35	1	12	1	1	–

$z = 3.90, p = 0.00005$

frequently part of their armoury. In the Canadian-American setting, where their art was consumed by the minority group, this world-view did not correspond with the skimmers' perception of social reality. Cartoons which incorporated it would be unlikely to seem funny and likely to offend. For these reasons, the presence of heroic representations might be much more extensive when the audience was the minority group.

In practice, the results were more complicated than had been predicted. Considering first the data on business, 55 per cent of the nine cartoons showing Canadian business leaders in their relations with Americans represented most of them as ineffective and as practitioners of foolery. This was true in only 20 per cent of the twenty-five which featured American tycoons. In three of the nine, Canadians were drawn mainly in feminine poses, while no Americans were shown in this way. The proportion shown as engaged in keying was identical at 11 per cent for both nationalities. The differences pointed consistently to a portrayal of the Canadian economic elite as more foolish than the American, and the Americans as bad to a greater degree than the Canadians. Although the numbers were small, the greater foolishness of the Canadians was highly significant,[7] while the greater badness of the Americans was significant.[8] Overall, the pattern was highly significant.[9]

The introduction of nationality and national interests broke up the relatively simple picture presented in chapter 6, of business leaders as generally serious and good people. Goodness, along with foolishness, was ascribed mainly to those who stood for Canada's economic interests. Seriousness, alongside badness, was attributed principally to their commercial rivals, who were generally pictured as stronger and more ruthless. The foolishness of Canadian business consisted more of ineffectiveness than of stupidity or childishness. They were victims of the toughness of their adversaries and not of their own mistakes. North American culture, however, places such

"As long as I hold the mortgage on the rink I'll write the rules!"

February 15, 1966

© Chambers, Halifax *Chronicle-Herald*. Reprinted with permission

a stress on winning that the distinction between the bumbling loser who should have succeeded and the gallant but outclassed loser was severely blurred in the drawings. Efforts to categorize them separately proved to be quite unreliable and they were eventually treated together as fools. There was little to suggest heroism here.

It is appropriate now to study whether the impact of nationality on the portrayals in politics is similar to that which has been found in commerce and manufacturing. Table 10 shows how far the political chiefs of the two nations were shown to differ in their practice of foolery. The differences on the foolishness measures as a set were highly significant[10] and in the expected direction. Canadians were again seen as more foolish than Americans when occupation was held constant. In terms of badness, the now familiar pattern recurred: Americans were represented as more bad than Canadians.[11] Once more, the overall pattern was highly significant.[12] In the comparisons of Canadians and Americans, then, the former were consistently and significantly depicted as more foolish, while the latter were shown as more bad.

These results will now be compared with those which were described in chapter 6. In each case, the anglophone Canadian cartoonists perceived their own group as foolish and the out-group as bad, even though in the one case 'they' were a minority which sought independence and in the other 'they' were a dominant neighbour. The distinction between 'we' and 'they' proved to be more useful for prediction than the differences in power. The drawings presented threats to the interests and social order of (English) Canada from neighbouring nations which were also pursuing their own interests, and pointed up alleged weaknesses in the policies of their own group's leadership.

It was found in the last chapter that the hypotheses about capitalist ideological content were illustrated fairly openly when (English) Canadians were the dominant group. Where they were the minority, this content was more often masked, and at times became a source of laughter. In this more complex situation, the same ideology was serving simultaneously to curb Canada's internal minorities and to generate discontent with (English) Canadians' own situation as a minority in North America.

In chapter 6, the threat of regionalism to national interests was examined in the setting of the federal government's relations with the provinces. In the setting of Canada-u.s. relations, the threat took the form of Canadian resistance to American goals. This portrait of Canadian foolishness and American badness can be reviewed in the context of threats to social order. The regional minority (in this case the Canadians) is portrayed once more as foolish losers, and the integrity of the power hierarchy is preserved.

However, the minority group with regional interests is now associated with goodness and not badness. The moral positions of the dominant and the subordinate group have been inverted as the cartoonist looks up rather than down the power hierarchy from the vantage point of an (English) Canadian. In this regard the artists identify in their work more with national than with international or American capitalism. Their nationalism does not deter them, however, from regularly ridiculing Canadian politicians who are reluctant to recognize that the prevailing social order is American.

While the cartoons promulgated a certain version of Canadian nationalism, their evaluation of it was by no means uniformly favourable. Canadian nationalism might be laudable, but its fool-making power was considerable. Canadian economic and political leaders alike were foolish and impotent before the greater power and seriousness of the Americans. Indeed, they were unable even to seem heroic in their inevitable defeat. By painting an association between goodness and failure, badness and success, cartoonists offered the skimmer a version of politics which was a potion of satire and tragedy. The heroes were parodied as inept while the villains were presented as potent. This scenario is deeply unsatisfactory for the skimmer. It is so structured that, if one accepts the version of reality beneath its comic surface, its tensions can be resolved only in two ways. First, the skimmer may identify with the 'bad' Americans and convert them into heroes because they are successful. Secondly, one may introduce a new hero, a Canadian Economic Superperson, whose business genius can overcome the villains in the name of Canada. The few cartoon representations of the current Canadian economic elite do not suggest that cartoonists see them as able to satisfy this need.

2. The Minority Group Hypothesis

The exclusion of political minorities was very apparent. The prime minister appeared in 39 per cent of the cartoons, and members of the governing party, generally cabinet ministers, in 21 per cent. Cabinet ministers occupied noticeably more of the spotlight in this setting than in French-English relations, where they were observable in less than 10 per cent of the cartoons. Representatives of the opposition parties, however, were shown in only 5 per cent. In relations with the United States, the prime minister and the cabinet were portrayed as more dominant among the political figures than they had been on any topic concerned with French-English relations. Together they comprised 85 per cent of the Canadian politicians featured in the economic cartoons and 96 per cent of those in the military drawings.[13] The cartoonists allocated very little space in international relations to either the provinces or the opposition parties.

Members of minority groups were rare, appearing in 5 per cent of the drawings. Women could be seen in four of the military cartoons: a prostitute, a naked lady accosted in her bath-tub by an insurance salesman, an unidentified member of the Kennedy clan who got a black eye playing touch football, and a reluctant plump warrior/grandmother. They could be seen in twenty-two of the economic cartoons: a waitress, a customs officer, three allegories of Canada, one enterprising tourist, and sixteen wives and girl-friends. Where they were active, it was nearly always within the family setting. Women were thus treated as largely irrelevant outside the family context, having little significance either as political actors or as metaphors for male ineffectiveness.

In both Canadian-American and French-English cartoons there was a relatively sustained focus on the disruption of (English) Canadian goals by the other group portrayed. This distinction between the in-group and the out-group tended to outweigh the distinction between the dominant and the minority groups.

3. The Cast of Regulars Hypothesis

This hypothesis was again supported strongly. The cast of characters was consistently limited, and once more varied from one topic to the other. Individuals again far outnumbered symbols and representations.

When all the role categories were included, several differences according to topic became apparent. Most obviously, security personnel were the largest single category in the military cartoons, but were virtually absent from those on the economy. In return, the economic sphere was populated more by citizens, business leaders, civil servants, and a range of miscellaneous characters. The major political leaders and the allegorical figures were equally prominent in both contexts, though the u.s. cabinet was shown taking a more major part in military than in economic decision-making.

Recognizability depended on nationality and political position. The president and the prime minister were the most readily identifiable without a written clue. Members of their cabinets and of the opposition in Parliament were less recognizable. They were felt to require labels in about one-third to one-quarter of their appearances. Provincial premiers were verbally identified in 50 per cent of their depictions. Business leaders were unique in being labelled nine times out of ten, but this figure cannot fairly be compared with the others. The purpose of most tickets attached to business executives was to identify their industry and not their occupation. Cartoonists had no difficulty in drawing immediately recognizable business chiefs. They lacked the conventions, however, to distinguish visually between an oil executive and one from the auto industry unless the background was unmistakeably a refinery or a production line.

The variations in labelling by nationality were not strongly significant. It was nevertheless interesting to note that, when parallel positions were compared, the Americans were less often identified than the Canadians. The prime minister was slightly more likely than the president to be labelled, and the Canadian cabinet members were slightly more likely than the vice-president or members of the u.s. cabinet. The differential was not statistically significant on either topic.

4. The Imaginary Canada Hypothesis
This hypothesis was not confirmed: only about one drawing in five showed the two countries as formally equal, the proportion being fairly constant from one topic and region to another. This myth was not an important structural feature of these works.

Suffering third parties were even rarer in the Canadian-American than in the French-English setting: they were observable in only 6 per cent of the cartoons on each topic. There was, however, a clear tendency for Americans to be displayed as more masculine and more prominent than Canadians in the cartoons.[14] Depictions of their unequal power were visually reinforced by their portrayal as more central and more formidable figures.

5. The Double Standard Hypothesis

Since Canadian-American relations are defined primarily in economic and secondarily in military terms, it is likely that economic policy and business interests will be featured much more prominently in drawings on this topic than they were in the context of French-English relations. It will be recalled that only 3 per cent of French-English cartoons included a business figure and only 1.3 per cent of the characters were representatives of commerce and manufacturing. In cartoons on Canadian-American relations, by contrast, 13 per cent featured at least one character from the American business world, while 5 per cent depicted a Canadian business person.[15]

The increase in representation was highly significant.[16] By comparison with the attention given to business news, however, the caricaturing of business leaders was unusual. It was narrowly restricted to instances where a single industry was viewed as trying to gouge the government or the public. Cartoonists' ridicule was reserved for cases of clear corporate malfeasance, but such deviance was represented as far less common in the business than in the political world.

The cartoonists' national perspective, as was seen earlier, had a considerable impact on their portrayal of Canadians and Americans. It was therefore imperative that this hypothesis be tested only by comparing business and political leaders from the same country. When this was done, the data generally confirmed the positive image of business.

When American business and political leaders were compared, there were indeed significant discrepancies in the depictions of the two. The differences according to the four measures of foolishness were highly significant,[17] especially in terms of keying, which is shown in Table 11. They were in the predicted direction.

The differences in keying between the Canadian economic and political elites were also in the predicted direction. They were statistically significant, but only at the 0.05 level, owing to the very small number (nine) of Canadian business figures. When the differences in keying for the two nationalities were combined, the differences between business and politics in this regard were highly significant.[18] Those for the other three measures of foolishness were supportive, but were themselves significant only for the American characters.

For the three categories which were portrayed in substantial numbers,

TABLE 11

Differences between U.S. business and political leaders in keying

	Non-keyers outnumber keyers by					Keyers outnumber non-keyers by			
	4	3	2	1	0	1	2	3	4
U.S. Business	–	3	3	14	–	1	–	–	–
U.S. Politics	–	1	2	11	–	36	–	–	–

$z = 4.76, p < 0.00001$

the order of foolishness was clear. United States' business was significantly less foolish than U.S. politics, which in turn was significantly less foolish than Canadian politics. At the same time, Canadian business was slightly less foolish than Canadian politics. For each nationality, therefore, the hypothesis was confirmed whenever the numbers permitted an analysis.

The differences in terms of badness were in the expected direction but were not significant overall. Although there were strong hints that Canada was being tricked into buying expensive and worthless American military equipment, the main thrust of both economic and military cartoons was a recognition of the power differential and the use of straightforward strong-arm tactics to ensure Canadian compliance with U.S. policies. The general pattern for foolishness and badness, taken together, was highly significant.[19]

It had originally been thought that capitalist cartoons on foolishness might concentrate on the waste of public money which was alleged to characterize government. Wastage could be direct, as public funds were spent on projects which were deemed unproductive in terms of either material products or broader social benefits. This was sometimes the case in the drawings on Canadian-American military relations. Wastage could also be indirect, as decisionmakers themselves were seen spending their time in fruitless debates on petty details, giving the public little tangible return for paying the salaries and expenses of the politicians and those who administered their policies. Waste was an important but not the dominant theme in the cartoons on Canadian-American relations. Nor was the economic cost of maintaining Canada's nationhood and limited independence. Together they occurred in less than 10 per cent of the drawings.

Similar conclusions emerge when the distribution of fools is studied. Overall, 21 per cent of the drawings showed no fool; of the remainder, 70 per cent displayed political leaders as the sole source of foolishness. The predominant message was once more that politics was the principal nest of foolishness. Similar figures were noted in chapter 6. They further substantiate the view that politics is seen as the main threat to the social order, whose mainstay is business. Although foolishness was shown as especially chronic among politicians, its victims in public life were not portrayed as more acute sufferers than those found in private life. Sixty-four per cent of the Canadian-American cartoons were structured around a conflict between two sides; in 45 per cent of these the artist was judged to be illustrating its unproductive nature, and in the others it was treated as neutral.

6. The Passive Citizens Hypothesis

In testing hypothesis 6, nationality was again held constant, since it had an important and consistent influence on the drawings. Portrayals of u.s. citizens were too infrequent[20] to justify comparing them with u.s. politicians. Reliable results were therefore obtained only for the comparison between Canadian political leaders and Canadian citizens on the topic of relations with the United States.

The results matched those found in chapter 6. Citizens were significantly more foolish and ineffective than their leaders,[21] but less effeminate and much less apt to engage in keying.[22] The analysis which was made earlier has been confirmed. Once again, the politicians were represented as blameworthy: they were depicted as significantly more bad on all three measures.[23]

Table 12, like Table 9, examines the passivity of the public in editorial cartoons on Canadian-American relations. Activity and passivity were about equally common in the portrayals of direct interaction between citizens and politicians on military topics, a finding which supported those observed in the last chapter. For economic relations, however, this was less true; although the numbers were smaller, passive audiences were rare in this context. When both topics were combined, the three middle categories showed a ratio of nearly two active portrayals to one passive representation. The

TABLE 12
Role of the public in editorial cartoons, percentage by topic

	Absent	Invisible audience	Visible audience	Participating	Interacting with self	N
Economic	76	1	2	7	14	160
Military	81	–	11	8	–	37
Total	78	–	4	7	11	197

"I suppose one simply must have faith in a country that produces the whitest wash, the softest hands, the coolest smoke, the fastest relief from acid upset . . ."

"The president's on TV . . . or don't you care how he runs the countries?"

© Norris, *Vancouver Sun*. Reprinted with permission

inclusion of all five categories, however, made the balance four to one in favour of passivity. Skimmers were again likely, then, to see themselves depicted as relatively passive spectators or absentees in economic policy.

SUMMARY AND CONCLUSIONS

The change of setting, from French-English to Canadian-American relations, produced some differences in the results obtained, along with some important continuities. When (English) Canadian cartoonists portrayed the relations between (English) Canada and Quebec, their position as members of the dominant group was paralleled by their consistent portrayal of capitalist ideology toward minorities. The first four hypotheses presented minorities, in this perspective, as frequently disruptive, with considerable potential as fool-makers; at other times they could be ignored. When they depicted relations between Canada and the United States, their own position as members of the minority group was paralleled by fairly consistent modification of capitalist ideology toward minorities. They perceived most of the disruption to their social order as originating with the dominant group, which was viewed in negative moral terms. They did not represent Canadians and Americans as formally equal; the latter were both more powerful and more successful. The pursuit of national interests was not glorified, but treated with great ambivalence as a potent formula: for making fools if one were from the minority group, and for making enemies if one were from the dominant group. The nationalist, then, was more a fool than a hero or villain.

In the setting of Canadian-American relations, then, four major capitalist myths were markedly less central than they had been in the context of French-English relations. The conspicuous exceptions were the two which are crucial to editorial cartooning: the foolishness of politicians, politics, and electors by comparison with business, its executives and (implicitly) consumers, who are courted throughout the newspaper. These represented the bottom line for the editorial cartoon. They were the dogmas which were not to be challenged by the jester, when all others were treated as legitimate targets for laughter and criticism. They firmly withstood the threats to their dominance posed by Quebec independentism from within, by American imperialism from without, and by the presumed Canadian nationalism of most of the viewers. National and ethnic groups might vary widely in their susceptibility to representation as good or bad. When nationality was held constant, however, the gap between a nation's politicians and its business chiefs remained significant in every context where it could be examined.

This generally favourable representation of business distracts the glancer from wondering whether the answer to political foolishness might lie in a radical alteration of the capitalist economic system. The skimmer is offered little reason to hope that the current tragi-satiric situation will change, and little encouragement to think that it would be worth taking action to induce social change. In these respects the ideology of the cartoons is quite consistent with that of the media in general. They depict an alienated capitalist world where political action is foolish, and where nationalism is noble but ineffective. Individual consumerism is represented as the only rational form of action. Politics is bad news, not in the apocalyptic sense which the headlines often convey, but as the abode of foolishness on the home front and badness abroad.

The findings of this chapter are at first glance open to two interpretations. First, one could note that American business figures were prominent in cartoons on these topics, and that u.s. culture was closely identified with the most advanced form of capitalism. One might then conclude that the United States served in the drawings as a very thinly disguised metaphor for capitalism itself, in its most exploitive and rapacious form. The cartoonists, in this perspective, were offering a penetrating critique of capitalism and in particular of its invocation of the state apparatus of persuasion and coercion. This would explain why there were very few Canadian business figures, and why the few who were shown tended to be portrayed as small persons committed to old-fashioned technologies and business methods. It does not offer a satisfactory explanation, however, of the double standard: business leaders in both countries were portrayed more positively than political figures.

The second interpretation seeks to respond to this weakness. The cartoonists' critique is not aimed at capitalism per se, but at certain features of monopoly capitalism which are not consistent with a free market of relatively small independent producers and traders. It appears that the traditional ideology of the Chamber of Commerce lives on in this corner of the local monopoly press. The objectionable features of American monopoly capitalism include the appropriation of the state, the rapacious search for raw materials, the trampling of the small entrepreneur, and the use of market strength as a monopoly weapon. Economic nationalism is perhaps courageous and certainly foolish when power is unevenly divided. Canada's raw materials are the only weapon which could be used to augment the country's independence. There is profound ambivalence over taking such a stand, given the aggressiveness of u.s. enterprise and Canada's constant vulnerability.

The hostile physical environment which has been such a dominant theme in Canadian literature (Atwood; Frye, 1971; McGregor) has here been transformed into a hostile economic environment, where little Canada is pushed around by big United States and is often deeply divided in its assessment of the best response.

Summary and Conclusions

The preceding chapters have generated and tested a set of hypotheses about the ideological content of Canadian editorial cartoons on intergroup relations from the 1960s and 1970s. Symbolic action was valuable in providing ideas about the structure of cartoons. Marxism was the most useful framework for relating these insights to their setting in newspapers, and understanding the place of papers in the social structure.

The first chapter elaborated the main analogy underlying this book, that cartoonists are the jesters of the bourgeoisie. Medieval jesters carefully respected the power of their protectors, who were the source of their livelihood. Their task was to mock the status and pretensions of the clergy and the courtiers, who were their protectors' major rivals for individual and institutional power. As power gradually passed from the monarchs to the merchants, the position of the court jesters wilted. Later, as elected representatives became the chief holders of political power, caricaturists and then cartoonists began to appear. The early ones were engravers and entrepreneurs who sold humorous political prints. Subsequent ones were employees of party newspapers and periodicals, ridiculing the leaders and policies of the opposing parties. Today cartoonists work for oligopolistic newspapers and laugh at politics on behalf of business, which by buying advertising space has become the major patron of the newspaper. In this setting the cartoonists' task is to illustrate the foolishness of public life and politicians and, by implication, the wisdom of business leaders and private enterprise. Most artists do this by concentrating their fire on the current political power-holders, regardless of party.

The second chapter discussed the principal themes of symbolic action. The symbolic work of acting out public dramas is, in Burke's view, just as important for society as the necessitous work of producing material goods and services. Politics is largely symbolic work. Abstract principles and concrete interests alike become embodied in particular leaders who champion them. The leader's success then becomes the success of free trade, or communism, or clean government, over an opponent who represents government restriction, capitalism, or corruption. Successful public dramas thus make the social order concrete and meaningful to ordinary people. They also maintain confidence that the social order will give fair recognition to competing interest groups and to opposing principles, such as helping the unsuccessful and rewarding the enterprise of the successful.

Parliamentary debates are public dramas which make heroes, villains, and fools of these champions and their causes. Sometimes the drama of public debate and persuasion is enough to maintain such a balance between opposites. When this drama fails to provide an acceptable result, the public drama of sacrifice is likely to be invoked. Sacrifice implies conflict, suffering, atonement, and reconciliation. Through these four processes it is publicly confirmed that one principle or interest has priority over its opposite, and the champion of the losers is publicly sacrificed to commemorate the victory. An election campaign is a sacrificial drama. The winning party is elected and elated. The losers are humiliated and relegated to the ranks of the opposition. At the same time they are not annihilated, and they promise to play their role loyally and without rancour against the public or the victors. They and the interests and principles they represent begin to regroup in preparation for the next ritual combat. In the long run, defeat may indeed have the effect of strengthening them, though their current champion will not survive a series of defeats.

The cartoonist creates an imaginary world and uses it to offer a commentary on politics: Ben Wicks's *Outcasts* and Pogo's swamp are well-known examples. Distant events, personalities, and relationships are domesticated: a clever analogy transposes them into something familiar and everyday. Quebec's desire for independence is abstract and remote from the daily experience of many (English) Canadians; consequently it is difficult for them to understand. The cartoonist suggests that it is like a wife's desire for liberation from her husband's rule. American policy toward Nicaragua is also hard to grasp; but one can think of it as a heroic resistance to communism or as a form of mean bullying.

In bringing distant events within the skimmer's grasp, cartoons demonstrate the tremendous potential of politics for making fools of people. They show today's leaders stumbling to balance symbolic with necessitous work, or opposing ideals and interests with each other. They explore the powerful irony that those in western society who attempt to bring social order through democratic debate appear to succeed only in increasing the disorder.

Symbolic worlds are not morally neutral; they are used by their creators and owners to convey certain messages. Newspapers are symbolic worlds which reflect certain ideologies, notably that of the bourgeoisie. In so far as cartoons promote this world-view, their underlying message includes at least six core features: it equates the dominant political organization with social order, and treats sectional and more local interests as narrowly selfish; it ignores minorities except when they are seen to be disturbing the social order; it portrays power and decision-making as confined to a narrow circle of regulars, and depicts social change as the result of outstanding individual effort; it re-presents unequal relations of conflict as rivalries between equally strong opposites; it equates business with social order and goodness, politics with social disorder and badness; and lastly, it represents voters as passive and relatively isolated from political decisions. In short, economic leaders are portrayed as struggling for the national good in the private domain, using their expertise in managing the economy. Politicians, meanwhile, are shown struggling for individual glory in the public sphere, using their lack of expertise to mismanage the economy. Cartooning is therefore a public service, which alerts the citizens to the misrepresentation which politicians practise through official documents and party publications.

The third chapter sought further clues to the nature of cartoons by examining the structure of newspapers themselves. Papers make money by attracting readers whose attention they can sell to advertisers. Most are now local monopolies, dependent on mass circulation and the ability to appeal to all kinds of consumer. They seek maximum readership by presenting news in the form of interesting stories, and by offering provocative opinion columns. Most cartoonists, like columnists, are now contributors who have the freedom and responsibility for expressing their own viewpoints. At the same time, like reporters, they seek to be non-partisan – exposing foolishness wherever it is found in politics, but looking principally among the leaders of the party in power.

In their irreverence for politics they portray the capitalist state and its chief executives as a threat to the capitalist enterprise, and to the present social order. By presenting business and politics as opposites, cartoons and other newspaper features distract public attention from the massive overlap and collaboration between government and business. According to one pithy attempt to summarize newspapers' relations with business and the state, newspapers 'cleanse by publicity.' They cleanse the state by publicizing examples of government waste, incompetence, and intrusions into privacy. They cleanse business by printing only favourable news and publicity material about it, as long as it lives up to its own values.

The conventions of newsgathering include story-telling and rhetorical oppositions. In the individual news story, strongly conflicting positions are presented. They may then be reconciled by the reporter, though sometimes the reader is left in suspense until the next issue. In the paper as a whole, political news is enlivened by focusing on its more exciting and threatening aspects, setting up a stark contrast between the bad news which reporters detail and the good news offered by the advertisers. Stories are frequently taken out of their broader context and presented as unconnected elements from largely separate social worlds, generally far from the reader's own experience and thus immune to the critical scrutiny which familiarity might offer.

Chapter 4 set out the principal hypotheses about cartoon content which had been derived from this conceptual framework. It then discussed possible assumptions about the role of the skimmer, and the methods used to collect and analyse the cartoons. Chapter 5 examined the cartoons on French-English relations. It found few differences according to the region of Canada from which the drawing originated, or the language of the cartoonist. However, there were widespread differences according to the topic of the cartoon. Consequently, it was generally possible to combine English- and French-language drawings from all parts of the country on the same topic when the hypotheses were tested. Cartoons on different topics were analysed separately wherever the numbers permitted.

Chapters 6 and 7 tested the hypotheses which were identified in the previous chapters. Compared to the importance of business news in the dailies, cartoons about business were rare on all the topics stemming from French-English and Canadian-American relations. First, the social order hypothesis was examined. A dynamic study of threats to social order proved extremely fruitful. Culture served in most cartoons as a metaphor for social order, while nature represented social disorder. In French-English cartoons, the challenges of francophones to the status quo were widely portrayed as catching anglophones off guard, shaking their social control, and reducing them temporarily to a state of disorder. In most French-English drawings, the minority was depicted as the agitator and source of social change. In this regard it made little difference whether the francophones were federalists or independentists. Francophones played this role in relation to anglophone Canadians, the provinces played it in dealings with the federal government, independentist Quebec in opposition to federalist Canada, and Canada in interaction with Britain though not with France.

The status quo was associated with the interests of the dominant group. Most threats to social order were not successfully countered; the impression of disorderliness persisted and very little reconciliation took place. The cartoonists often made it clear that they did not favour the particular status quo which they were portraying. Nevertheless, their work nearly always represented bad news, in the particular sense that stability was being threatened and not restored. In relations between Canada and the United States, the latter was generally shown in the (English) Canadian cartoons as the main source of disruptions. In this instance, 'they' were depicted as the originators of the disorder, even though they were the dominant group.

In a small minority of drawings, a local politician would be shown as a hero in relation to representatives from a larger political unit; though such persons were more likely to be shown as victims or fools. The first hypothesis, then, found strong support in the French-English cartoons, but disturbances in Canadian-American relations were shown as coming mostly from the dominant group.

The minority groups hypothesis was strongly supported in the French-English cartoons. Members of gender, regional, linguistic, and political minorities were all shown disproportionately rarely. Allegorical and real women were rarely depicted, and both tended to be confined to stereotypical roles. Members of dominant groups were shown in disproportionately large numbers. The same conclusion held in the case of the Canadian-American cartoons, but there was one exception: Canadians were much less conspicuously underrepresented than any other minority in portrayals by their own artists.

The cast of regulars hypothesis was supported in both sets of cartoons. Major policy issues were thus portrayed as the preserve of a small number of central figures. They were predominantly individuals; allegorical symbols of nations and qualities were not often found, and representations of social forces were uncommon. While the cast was always small, its composition varied widely from one topic to another. The prime minister, for example, might be shown as central to certain topics but peripheral to others.

The Imaginary Canada hypothesis proposed that conflicting social groups or political units would be shown as formally equal rivals, when even a superficial study of their relative resources showed that one regularly exploited the other. Relations between (English) Canada and Quebec were quite likely to be portrayed in this manner, as the hypothesis predicted. Canada's relations with its provinces, or with other countries, however, rarely conformed with this hypothesis.

The double standard hypothesis proposed that political leaders would be portrayed as much more foolish and disorderly than business leaders. This hypothesis was consistently supported in both sets of cartoons, especially in relation to keying and effectiveness. Business was generally shown as serious rather than foolish, and good rather than bad. Exceptions occurred only when a particular company or industry was reported as greedy (the oil companies), overbearing (the auto makers), huckstering (the sellers of nuclear weapons), or unpatriotic (Sun Life).

Since business was portrayed as orderly and positive, only its deviants deserved to be even occasionally caricatured. Political leaders, by contrast, were presented as much more foolish and slightly less good than those in business. Laughing and not punitive satire was the usual underlying mood. The cartoons were dominated by a few principal office-holders: the prime minister, the American president, and the Quebec premier. Although cabinet ministers were quite often prominent in the Canadian-American cartoons and in those dealing with relations between Ottawa and Quebec, other political figures were rarely in evidence except on the constitutional issue and President de Gaulle's visit. France, the United States, and Great Britain were represented by their president or queen; the French and British prime ministers were hardly ever shown. The cast of characters was generally limited to about ten well-known roles, mostly politicians, along with their entourages, or allegorical figures.

It had been expected that independentists would occupy a unique position as the villains of Canadian politics and the scapegoats for anti-French sentiments. In practice they were scarcely distinguishable from Quebec nationalists such as Robert Bourassa and Daniel Johnson. All these figures were perceived as provincialists who put Quebec first. They were strongly contrasted with the federalist MPs from Quebec who were presented as putting Canada first. The latter were portrayed as inept but on the right side, whereas the nationalists were more effective but on the wrong side. The nationalist victories were represented as largely symbolic, however, and therefore as trivial. Cartoonists showed some sympathy for their own local politicians – those from Quebec when opposed to the federal government, and those from Canada when opposed to the United States. These nationalists were depicted as good but quite foolish.

Canadian and United States' politicians were found to be much more prone to foolishness than business leaders from the same country. Politics was depicted as the headquarters of foolishness: in 70 to 80 per cent of the drawings which showed a fool, politicians alone fitted this description. Keying was the clearest single indicator: whereas others worked, politicians only pretended to work. Squabbling was another trait which was particularly associated in the drawings with politics. Many issues were presented in the form of a political dispute, though only in dealings between Ottawa and Quebec were the two disputants misleadingly treated as formally equal rivals. Where a dispute set regional against national interests, the regional politicians and their interests were shown as less foolish and less good. The inability of federal politicians to restrain the regional interests of Quebec and Alberta was seen as one important aspect of their ineptitude. When Canadian politicians were unsuccessful in promoting the nation's interests against those of the Americans, they were similarly shown as inept.

The passive citizens hypothesis predicted that electors would be both foolish and passive. Members of the public were indeed shown, in both sets of cartoons, to be quite as foolish as politicians. Whereas the latter were seen as active fools, however, citizens were generally shown as their passive victims. The differences were again most pronounced in respect to keying, which was the best distinguishing mark of the politician. According to this critique, they have the opportunity to exercise power but instead they play at politics for the sake of popularity and symbolic advantages, mistaking appearance for substance. The public is victimized but keeps re-electing similar people to office. Citizens who were shown as active were generally interacting only with other citizens. They were rarely seen with members of the political or economic elites.

The keying which is shown as characteristic of politicians contrasts with the honest and effective work habits attributed to business people. The moral for democracy is clear: ordinary citizens cannot be relied on to elect good governments. Decision-making should be left to those who can handle property, for business success is the best assurance of seriousness and capability if not of goodness.

Very few cartoons showed third parties who were suffering as a result of the politicians' activities, however. The skimmer was left free to judge whether politics as an institution was inherently comic and ought to be treated as entertainment, or whether it should be taken seriously and purged of its disorderly and foolish elements.

The results of testing the first four hypotheses enable one to elaborate on the cartoonists' treatment of patriotism in a capitalist society. Patriotism was observable whenever anglophone cartoonists represented (English) Canadians more favourably than either francophones or Americans. While this could have taken the form of a contrast between good members of 'our' group and bad members of 'theirs,' such overt chauvinism was infrequent. It was most widely found in connection with disturbances of the status quo: (English) Canadians were generally shown as the victims of the other group's disruptive initiatives, which they were rarely able to counter effectively. While francophone cartoonists were more likely than anglophones to view the status quo unfavourably, there was general agreement that francophone leaders were usually the source of the disruption. As a result, anglophone Canadians were more likely than either Americans or francophones to be depicted as the fools and losers, whether the setbacks were symbolic or material.

Patriotism was also evident behind the portrayal of provincial interests as narrowly selfish compared with the common good of all Canadians. This is perhaps the central myth of the capitalist state. It corresponds to the conviction of management that its priorities reflect the good of the company as a whole, whereas those of the workers are sectional and selfish. Québécois and Albertans were shown, especially by Ontario cartoonists, as persons whose self-seeking initiatives made the federal government look flat-footed and foolish. The same message was thus found in both contexts. 'Their' disruptive behaviour has once more made 'our' politicians look foolish, and 'our' material or symbolic interests have again been mildly harmed. The method was generally one of laughing satire: where the threat was perceived as more serious, the artist switched to a punitive representation of 'them.'

Capitalism was the central element in the cluster of findings relating to hypotheses 5 and 6. The principal conclusion, as has been emphasized, was the double standard: politics and politicians were systematically represented as foolish, whereas business and its executives were generally depicted as sensible. Keying was the clearest example: business leaders were portrayed as people who work, while politicians were shown spending a great deal of energy in simply playing at decision-making. Cartoonists have established their legal right to almost unlimited criticism of public figures, while those in the private sphere are protected by legislation in which the burden of truth is firmly on the critic. While individual business leaders or industries might sometimes do something foolish, politicians as a group were never displayed doing anything constructive. If individual politicians were being constructive, others were shown undermining them; and frequently the only persons depicted were foolish politicians.

Politics was also firmly associated in the cartoons with symbolic work, to the exclusion of necessitous labour. Business, meanwhile, meant necessitous work to the exclusion of what was symbolic. Symbolic work was systematically disvalued in comparison to necessitous work. The contrast between the utility of business and the futility of politics was thus markedly exaggerated.

The second important finding about capitalism was the emphasis on individual responsibility and achievement. There was little recognition that social forces or social contradictions played a part in social change. In the present context, this implied that business figures should take credit for constructive achievements, politicians should take the blame for destruction and for failures. Individual responsibility was over-emphasized, and the importance of social forces was masked. These rhetorical devices further strengthened the message that business and politics were inherently opposed rather than profoundly intertwined.

The third key finding was the depiction of the public as passive victims of political but not of business decisions. Indeed, the power wielded by business was rarely illustrated on any of these topics. When, for example, unemployment was portrayed, it was shown as the burden of politicians and not of business executives. Similarly, the responsibility for political squabbling and ineptness was laid on the politicians, and occasionally on those who elected them. None was placed on the capitalist system which obstructs political reform. The implication that business leaders could choose much better cabinet members and run the country more successfully was thinly veiled. There was no hint at the possibility that different skills or values might be desirable in the two spheres, or that democracy would be preferable to autocratic or team leadership geared to profit-making.

Patriotism and capitalism modified each other in the cartoons, just as the capitalist state and the capitalist enterprise influence one another. More of the capitalist myths were evident when the cartoon was drawn for an audience from the dominant group than when the readership came from the minority. Evaluations of a group's economic interests as good or bad were influenced by the expected allegiances of the readers. Conversely, patriotic respect by citizens for their leaders was overwhelmed by ridicule of politics as an institution and of its leading exponents.

The lampooning of the capitalist state by the capitalist economy represents the central paradox addressed by this book. News reports and cartoons alike exaggerate the contrast between politics and business in favour of the latter. In so doing they mask the very extensive overlap between them in a capitalist society. The major political parties are largely financed by business, and in turn government offers massive grants to enterprising companies. In a mixed economy of large and often monopolistic organizations, the lines between public and private enterprise are blurred, with a continual and major interchange of personnel between the two sectors. Business leaders run for political office or are seconded into the public service, retiring politicians and former public servants take positions with large private corporations. In a detailed case study, Fournier (chaps. 5, 8–10) showed how the Quebec Liberal government of the early 1970s engaged in extensive consultation with business for a long period before informing the public of any major changes in policy.

In business ideology, however, these striking similarities are masked. Newspapers elaborate the differences between government and business, and disputes between them over property rights are often carried on the news pages. The two are re-presented as implacable enemies, locked in struggle on such issues as the amount and pattern of taxation, the extent of government regulation and subsidization, access to private and public information. Bourgeois ideology grounds these arguments about boundaries and power in fundamental oppositions – between the public and private spheres, between unproductive and productive enterprise, between vague and precise criteria of success, between inefficiency and efficiency, between talking and doing. Cartoons are conduits for this ideology, which associates the first, uncomplimentary member of each pair of opposites with the government, and the second, complimentary member with business.

It was noted earlier that the Imaginary Canada hypothesis found relatively little open support in these data. Cartoonists do not usually disguise major political inequalities behind an appearance of formal equality, though sometimes this was done in the case of relations between Ottawa and Quebec. They recognize and depict differences in power quite clearly in most instances. One might suggest, however, that the major finding of this book about the double standard simply illustrates that the Imaginary Canada is very much alive in representations of the relations between business and politics. Cartoon messages both downplay the worth of politics and exaggerate its distinctiveness from business. It could be argued that these ideological processes are the same ones which can be found behind the verbal illustrations of the Imaginary Canada which Wilden found. The power of the minority group is exaggerated through its depiction as equal to the dominant group; and its members' actions and motives are downgraded in the process of comparison. Editorial cartoons, on this view, are not often structured around the Imaginary Canada in their portrayal of Canada's relations with parent and neighbour countries toward which Canada is the minority group. They are more often structured in this manner when the dominant group views its own relations with those of its constituent units which are engaged in mild rebellion. They are nearly always structured in this way when politics is compared to business, whatever the cartoonist's perspective and group membership might be. In this respect cartoons, like the newspapers in which they appear, play a somewhat specialized and very important role in the social construction of the Imaginary Canada. They develop the Imaginary version of the relations between politics and business.

The cartoon, it has been argued, domesticates distant and complex events and personalities for the skimmer. It presents vivid allusions and metaphors which locate these puzzling news items immediately within commonsense categories of thinking. Cartoons can achieve this in a more holistic and light-hearted way than editorials or columns. Instead of serious, step-by-step reasoning, drawings rely on the glancer's instantaneous grasp of images. They enlist humour to slip across a serious message, appealing to the skimmer's desire to laugh at authority figures and to express ambivalence about those whose decisions affect our lives. By allying a picture with a text they involve more of the skimmer's senses. They offer a suggestive pattern to be seized as a whole, rather than a discourse which must be read and perhaps criticized one line at a time. Their latent message may slip more successfully than an editorial through the filters with which skimmers protect themselves from ideas which run contrary to their interests.

Newspapers have become more monopolistic, and cartoonists more professional and non-partisan. In so doing they have gradually shifted their sights from individual politicians of a certain party to politics as an institution. The low satire of earlier generations highlighted individual weaknesses, and held out the hope of better things with the next change of regime. The medium satire of the current professionals satirizes whoever is in office, implying that politics as an institution is inherently a humming centre of squabbling, posturing, waste, and destruction. While their drawings individually act as watchdogs, barking at particular acts which leave something to be desired, their cumulative contribution comprises a systematic ridiculing of democratic procedures because those who are supposed to practise them regularly fail to live up to their ideals. Implicitly, and regardless of the political preferences of individual cartoonists, their art praises the alternative model offered by business, drawing a veil over its autocratic and self-serving features.

The change in the cartoonist's status, from political camp-follower to relatively independent professional, has been an important one. It has, however, had significant side-effects which have rarely been recognized. Attention has been drawn to two of these, which have followed from the implicit assumption that an editorial cartoonist is nearly always a *political* commentator. By satirizing politics more than business, what began as the pursuit of individual foibles has gradually become a veiled attack on democracy, even though this is contrary to the intentions of most cartoonists. By satirizing politics more than business, cartoonists have contributed to the portrayal of a largely imaginary relationship between them, based on the traditional capitalist outlook toward each. In striving to share their insights about individuals and situations with a public which is increasingly divorced from direct contact with the sources of news, cartoonists have, ironically, contributed to the misrepresentation of relations between the economic and political systems.

Cartoons are delightful medicine for one's anxieties about political events; but they are also dangerous. They pack a punch, not only for the politician who is made to look foolish, but also for the glancer who may swallow a hidden message along with the laugh.

Coding Guide

The coding for this book was a content analysis of the cartoons and the cartoon characters by the author and one of the research assistants. A copy of the coding guide is given below. Much of it was relatively straightforward, since cartoonists strive for easy identification of the persons portrayed and the points being made. Judgment was called for in a number of places, however. The points of difficulty will now be reviewed, beginning with the variables relating to the cartoon characters. In each cartoon, up to four characters were analysed individually. A few cartoons contained more than four, but these were nearly always crowd scenes where the individuals did not play discrete roles. In general the four largest characters were selected, as measured by the distance from the highest to the lowest visible points on their bodies and clothes. An exception was made in the small number of cases where this would have excluded any person who played a distinctive role. This procedure ensured that all the significant role players were included, since most cartoons restricted themselves to less than four characters and placed the main ones centrally and in the foreground.

The first point which involved judgment was attribution among the four comic types. Frye's *Anatomy of Criticism* served as the basis for identifying them. Although Frye does not set the four types up, in the approved sociological manner, as polar opposites along two dimensions, a careful reading of his work generated a list of adjectives, and occasionally nouns, which could be used to differentiate them. It is inherent in Frye's conceptualization that the types shade into one another, so they are better represented as segments of a circle than as clearly separable points. For this reason the classification was often ambiguous between two or occasionally three of the types. The coders therefore made up to two categorizations of each character, giving primacy to the one which appeared more accurate.

Klapp's social types proved to be both a suppler and in some ways a more appropriate classification scheme. In this case the earlier scheme of heroes, villains, and fools proved more workable than the later, more refined scheme. It was generally a straightforward task to distinguish among the three basic categories, but more difficulty arose in making the subtler distinctions between heroes and pseudo-heroes, fools and victims. As a result, these overlapping categories were combined in the statistical analysis. A similar attempt was made to classify the motives of each character as selfish, ordinary, or noble. The central category was used in all cases where there was doubt or where reasonable pursuit of one's own interests was shown. The extremes were preferred only when there was a clearly negative or positive portrayal. There was thus some overlap between the assessment of motives and the classification into villainous and heroic social types.

The representations of characters in glorifying, descriptive, laughing, or punitive terms also correlated to some extent with motives and social types. The final character-based item which presented some ambiguity was Goffman's concept of keying, since it involved judgments of what constitutes 'real' politics as opposed to 'playing at politics.' This problem was resolved by drawing up a list of forms which keying might take, and counting as keys only the relatively clear cases.

The codes relating to the cartoon as a whole required a number of judgments. The presence of a nature-culture contrast was coded only when it was clearly illustrated, by subhuman or 'primitive' traits or by ultra-sophistication. Food and sex were treated semiotically rather than metaphorically or psychoanalytically. They were said to be present when a cartoon could clearly be read in terms of rules about sexual access, ingestion, or excretion. Metaphors about table manners were thus excluded, and no evaluation of sexual symbolism was made. The crossing of taboos was noted only when it was clear. The judgments on irony presented some problems, where there was ambiguity over whether the character was aware of the irony.

In many instances it was possible to conclude that the cartoon scene excluded certain persons who had an interest in what was taking place: when for instance two persons were talking about a third person who was absent. There were few examples of tragedy or comedy, the choice usually being between low satire against an individual and medium satire aimed against social conventions. In addition to the elements of capitalist ideology outlined in chapter 3, searches were made for two specific elements of bourgeois ideology in the cartoons: the presence of latent messages that conflict was unproductive, and the treatment of all issues as disputes between two sides. Latent messages were inferred from the portrayal of politicians as mutually destructive in their squabbling.

The stress measure was an operationalization of Dondis's work. It required careful assessment of the symmetry and stability of the cartoon, based on the location and shape of its major lines and its centre of gravity. Finally, Zijderveld's characterization of jesters as respecting power but not social position proved very fruitful. There were many instances where ridicule of one socially important character was combined with respect for the power of another.

This guide reproduces the coding instructions which were used. The underlying rationales for some of them will be found in Appendix B, pp. 181–99.

I. CHARACTERISTICS OF EACH CARTOON USED IN LOG-LINEAR ANALYSIS

1. *Food, sex as cartoon themes*
   o Neither is present
   1 Food only is present
   2 Sex only is present
   3 Both are present
2. *Clarity of target for satire*
   o Target is unclear in at least one instance
   1 Target is clear and only one person
   2 Target is clear and two or more persons
   3 No satirical target
3. *Crossing of taboos in cartoon: humans depicted as subhuman, sacred persons as profane, breaking of sexual or other taboos*
   o No crossing of any taboo
   1 At least one is crossed
4. *Presence of antiphrasis: words openly contradict deeds or sentiments*
   o Not present
   1 Present
5. *Presence of dramatic irony or dramatic understatement, where skimmer is aware of contradiction between words or expectations and reality, but at least one person in the cartoon isn't*
   o Not present
   1 Present
6. *Presence of situational irony: at least one actor finds self in ironic situation, which makes words or actions inappropriate*
   o Not present

    1 Present

7. *Missing persons: at least one person involved or referred to in the scene beyond those shown*
   - 0 No missing persons
   - 1 At least one

8. *Minorities: at least one person present from a racial or ethnic minority group, other than French, British, Québécois, or (English) Canadian*
   - 0 None present
   - 1 At least one present

9. *Non-Canadians: at least one non-Canadian present*
   - 0 None present
   - 1 At least one present

10. *Reconciliation: cartoon shows alliance, restoration of harmony between anglophone and francophone or Canadian and American*
    - 0 No reconciliation
    - 1 Some reconciliation

11. *Genre of cartoon*
    - 1 Tragedy (hero in tragic situation)
    - 2 Romance (hero pursuing and overcoming villain)
    - 3 Comedy (mildly good characters, happy ending)
    - 4 Medium or high satire (against conventions, values)
    - 5 Low satire (against particular individuals)

12. *Labelling: number of characters with identifying label*
    Code the number of characters

13. *Unlabelled: number of characters with no identifying label*
    Code the number of characters

14. *Alternative reading: Could comic or social types of at least one character plausibly be coded in more than one way?*
    - 0 No
    - 1 Yes

15. *Double meaning: Do words in text or caption constitute pun, other kind of double meaning?*
    - 0 No
    - 1 Yes

16. *Viewpoint: Is cartoon drawn from the viewpoint of someone other than an adult spectator – from ground level, high in air, etc.?*
    - 0 No
    - 1 Yes

17. *Cartoonist, public shown: Is either the cartoonist or a member of the public shown in the cartoon?*
    - 0 No

1 Yes

18. *Collaboration: Does the cartoonist show conflict as unproductive and suggest that people should collaborate because they have the same interests?*
   o No
   1 Yes

19. *Dispute: Does the cartoon display a dispute between two 'sides'?*
   o No
   1 Yes

20. *Equal disputants: If a dispute, is it shown as a dispute between two equal rivals, or as a reverse of the normal power hierarchy?*
   o No, neither
   1 Yes

21. *Are any persons besides politicians shown as fools?*
   o No
   1 Yes

22. *Personification of groups, social forces: Are any groups or social forces personified in the cartoon?*
   o Neither
   1 Social forces (inflation, bilingualism policy)
   2 Groups (taxpayers, political party)

23. *Stress measure: Score one point each time one of the following statements holds true:*
   − the centre of gravity of the picture falls off its central vertical axis
   − the centre of gravity of the picture falls off its central horizontal axis
   − the centre of gravity of the picture falls off the diagonal from lower left to upper right
   − the centre of gravity of the picture falls off the diagonal from upper left to lower right
   − more of the shaded part of the picture lies above than below its central horizontal axis
   − more of the shaded part of the picture lies to the left than to the right of its central vertical axis
   − the major shapes in the picture are asymmetrical

24. *Power not position: Does the cartoonist show respect for those who have power and disrespect for the social position of others?*
   o No
   1 Yes

25. *Suffering third party: If cartoon shows two parties in conflict, does it show a third who is suffering from the conflict?*
   o No

1 Yes

26. *Bad language: Are there examples of incorrect French or English (as opposed to slang, regional, or working-class speech) in the cartoon?*
   0 No
   1 Incorrect French
   2 Incorrect English
   3 Both

II. CHARACTERISTICS OF EACH CARTOON USED ONLY IN CHAPTERS 5 AND 7

27. *Presence of culture: One or more persons depicted as sophisticated, with exaggeratedly refined features, formal clothing, neat appearance, emotions under tight control. Use only if another is depicted as nature.*
   1 Canada in relation to Britain or France
   2 France or Britain in relation to Canada
   3 Province(s) in relation to Canada
   4 Canada in relation to province(s)
   5 Independentist Quebec in relation to federalist Canada
   6 Federalist Canada in relation to independentist Quebec
   7 Francophone in relation to anglophone
   8 Anglophone in relation to francophone
   9 Canada in relation to United States
   0 United States in relation to Canada

28. *Presence of nature: One or more persons depicted as natural, with long hair, untidy appearance, primitive costumes, grotesque facial features, emotions not under control. Use only if one or more others are depicted as culture.*
   Coding as for item 27

29. *Source of disruption to social order*
   Coding as for item 27; leave blank if no disruption

30. *Ability of other group to restore social order*
   0 Unable
   1 Able

III. CHARACTERISTICS OF EACH CARTOON CHARACTER USED CENTRALLY IN DATA ANALYSIS

In each cartoon, analyse up to four characters. Where more than four are shown, select the four largest, in terms of measured height, ignoring any parts of the body which are not visible. If only head and shoulders are shown, for example, measure only head and shoulders and do not try to estimate height of rest of body.

Where choice of the four largest omits an important role altogether (because a key figure is shown very small in the background) include this person instead of the smallest duplicate figure.

Foolishness Measures

1. *Social type*
   1 Villain, including fanatic, brat, revolting person, bigot
   2 Hero
   3 Fool
   4 Victim, loser
   5 Puppet, thing, no mind of own
   6 Pseudo-hero: winner in scene shown, but not particularly villainous or admirable
   7 None of the above
   Those classified as 3, 4, or 5 were considered to be engaged in foolery.
2. *Ineffectiveness, as seen in cartoon*
   0 Clearly ineffective
   1 Ineffective in some ways, effective in others
   2 Clearly effective
   Those classified as 0 were considered to be ineffective.
3. *Femininity: presence of feminine traits in portrait*
   Begin with score of 5; add 1 for presence of each masculine trait, subtract 1 for each feminine trait, to maximum of 9 or minimum of 1. Ignore features which are not shown at all, such as hidden hands.
   – Fingers, hands. Fem: touches self, caresses object or person, traces outlines. Masc: grasps, manipulates object or person
   – Leadership. Fem: passive follower, admirer, subordinate. Masc: active leader, instructor.
   – Position relative to others. Fem: within family group. Masc: slightly aloof in gaze, posture.
   – Body position. Fem: reclining, defenceless, snuggling. Masc: protecting, upright.
   – Position of head, body. Fem: tilted, bent. Masc: erect.
   – Expression on face. Fem: smiling, unserious. Masc: serious.
   – Concentration. Fem: withdrawn, off in another world. Masc: focused on matter in hand.
   Those scoring 1, 2, or 3 were considered in feminine poses.

4. *Presence of keying: Person is 'playing at' politics, only pretending to combat other party or government, treating politics as a game, contest (of appearances or popularity), or ceremony. Includes clearly phoney alliances, sequences exposing 'true character.'*
   o No keying by this person
   1 Keying by this person

Lack of Importance

5. *Position of person in cartoon: sum of scores for each dimension*
   (a) *Vertical*
   o Low (head in lower third of picture)
   1 Medium (head in middle third of picture)
   2 High (head in upper third of picture)
   (b) *Horizontal*
   o Side (head in outside fifth of picture, from right or left frame)
   1 Intermediate (head in intermediate part of picture)
   2 Central (head in middle fifth of picture)
   (c) *Foreground/Background*
   o Background (whole body visible – 'public distance')
   1 Middle ground (most of torso visible – 'social or business distance')
   2 Foreground (only head and shoulders visible – 'personal distance')
   Those scoring o, 1, or 2 were considered not to be prominent.

6. *Internal or external relations: person seen along with others from homologous or larger political units*
   o All others come from same political unit as this person: a provincial politician is seen in the company only of others from the same province.
   1 Some from same unit, others from outside it; or only one person shown.
   2 No other comes from same political unit as this person.
   Those classified as o were considered not to be prominent.

Badness

7. *Selfishness of person*
   o Person shown as selfish, narrow, as opposed to reasonable pursuit of own and sectional interests.
   1 Person shown as reasonably pursuing these interests.
   2 Person shown as concerned for wider interests, at expense of own group.
   Those classified as o were considered to be selfish.

8. *Fabrication: person engages in deception, stage whisper, hidden thoughts which aim to trick another person shown or referred to*
   o No fabrication by this person
   1 Some fabrication by this person
9. *Overall representation of this person*
   1 Glorifying – shown in clearly positive terms
   2 Laughing – as foolish person
   3 Punitive – shown in clearly negative terms
   4 Descriptive – none of the above
   Those classified as 3 were considered to have been shown as bad.

IV. BACKGROUND CHARACTERISTICS OF CARTOON CHARACTERS
WHICH WERE CENTRAL TO THE ANALYSIS

10. *Ethnic or national origin of person*
    o Canadian, ethnic origin unspecified or unclear
    1 English Canadian
    2 French Canadian, Québécois
    3 White Canadian, neither English nor French
    4 Native person
    5 Black Canadian
    6 American
    7 British
    8 French
    9 Other, nationality unknown
11. *Identity of person*
    91 categories used
12. *Comic type of person*
    1 Alazon – rigid, pretentious, bound by protocol, squabbling, old-fashioned, vain, elderly
    2. Eiron – scheming, power-hungry, cliquish, secretive, hypocritical, conspiratorial
    3 Buffoon – joker, childish, play-acting, ostentatious, scared, clown, entertainer, parasite, bully
    4 Churl – rustic, butt, prig, killjoy, innocent, blind, deaf, untidy, disorganized, helpless, has something missing
    5 None of the above
13. *Sex (actual)*
    o Not known, does not apply

    1 Male
    2 Female
14. *Canadian political party affiliation*
    0 Not Canadian; party not known
    1 Liberal
    2 Progressive Conservative
    3 New Democratic
    4 Social Credit
    5 Parti Québécois
    6 Union Nationale
15. *Presence of 'competing representatives': persons from the same ethnic group at the same level of government, who belong to a different party*
    0 None present
    1 One or more present
16. *Presence of 'supporting representatives': persons from the same ethnic group at the same level of government, who belong to the same party*
    0 None present
    1 One or more present
17. *Presence of non-human traits*
    0 Subhuman: person is shown with creature's features or portrayed as tiny, alcoholic, skeleton, ancient, Nazi
    1 Only human traits
    2 Super-human: shown as spirit, angel, giant, ghost, genie, devil
18. *Dual signification: person has clothes, part of body, whole body of someone/something else*
    1 No, person is simply presented as self
    2 Yes, person has dual signification

French-English Cartoons: Regional, Topical, and Ethnic Differences

This appendix gives more detail on the regional, ethnic, and topical analysis which lay behind the conclusions which were sketched in chapter 5. The sections are given the same titles as the corresponding parts of that chapter to facilitate cross-referencing.

REGIONAL DIFFERENCES IN THE STRUCTURE OF THE CARTOONS

It was possible to identify seven topics which were treated in at least nine French-language and nine English-language cartoons. Nine was chosen, arbitrarily, as the smallest reasonable number for this part of the analysis. Since all seven topics were featured in over forty English-language cartoons, some examination of regional differences was possible in every case.

The seven topics were grouped into three themes for purposes of reporting the results. The theme of relations with the parent countries, France and Britain, included two topics: visits by French presidents or prime ministers, and visits by Queen Elizabeth and members of her family. Since Canada is most often made meaningful through the metaphor of the family, this theme will be referred to as the 'parent' or occasionally as the 'in-law' theme.[1]

The theme of relations between francophones and anglophones included three topics: Ottawa's dealings with Quebec, discussions on a new constitution, and the possible effects of Quebec's separation. In the metaphor of Canada as a family, this is the 'husband-wife' or 'spousal' theme.

Finally, the theme of bilingualism included two topics. The first was the Royal Commission on Bilingualism and Biculturalism, and the Trudeau government's subsequent bilingualism policy. The second was the Quebec government's policy on the use of English in the province, as embodied in Bills 22 and 101. This will sometimes be referred to as the "children" theme, since it concerned the paternalistic treatment of a language minority by the dominant group.

The regional breakdown was much less elaborate than one might have

wished, owing to the uneven regional distribution of the cartoons themselves. There were seldom enough drawings from English Quebec or Maritime newspapers in the sample to treat these regions separately; their combined
total was always less than twenty. The situation was only slightly better for
the Prairies and British Columbia, where the total only once exceeded twenty-
five. The regional analysis was therefore very limited; it was practicable only
to compare cartoons from Ontario with those from western and those from
eastern Canada. This simplified regional breakdown did nevertheless permit
a useful distinction between the centre and the periphery[2] of English Canada.
No regional analysis was attempted for the French-language cartoons, since
nearly all came from the Montreal papers. Quebec City and Trois-Rivières
were only lightly represented, and no French-language drawings emanated
from the other provinces.

For the log-linear analysis reported in this section,[3] the dependent variables were the twenty-six structural features of each cartoon described in
the first part of Appendix A. On two of them there were strong regional
effects, which made the overall set of regional differences statistically significant.[4] The two variables which showed strong regional differences were
the presence or absence of non-Canadians in the cartoons[5] and the representation of politicians as the only fools.[6] In the former case, western cartoonists were much less likely to include non-Canadians in their cartoons
on either topic from the in-law theme (Table 13). Their commentary on 'in-
law relations' was mainly devoted to the repercussions on Canada's internal
affairs. English-language cartoons from eastern Canada and Ontario, in
contrast, were much more likely to portray the visitors and their interaction
with Canadian leaders directly. This was to be expected, since two of the
three tours by the 'parents' were limited to eastern and central Canada.

The other significant difference was less straightforward. On five of the
seven topics, Ontario cartoonists were more likely than those in other parts
of (English) Canada to single out politicians as the only persons who merited
depiction as fools. Artists to the east and west were more likely to direct
some of their fool-making at other sections of the public. No other regional

TABLE 13
Presence of non-Canadians by region of cartoonist

Non-Canadians shown	President de Gaulle			The Queen		
	East	Ontario	West	East	Ontario	West
No	1	2	4	2	1	7
Yes	8	24	4	5	22	5

differences were uncovered by the present research, however, and the importance of regional variations was small by comparison with the variations in content between one topic and another. As a result, it was concluded that there were no patterns in the structure of English-language cartoons according to the measures tried in this research.

Differences according to the topic of the cartoon were observable on all twenty-six measures of its content.[7] Topic was clearly a much more important influence than region on the make-up of cartoons about French-English relations. It has a consistent effect on who was portrayed, in what manner and from what standpoint they were represented, and what the cartoonist's message was.

LANGUAGE DIFFERENCES IN THE STRUCTURE OF THE CARTOONS

The topics were grouped into the same three themes, in order to examine the impact of topic and ethnicity on the twenty-six features which were used to study regional differences. Once again, variability was most marked according to topic: there were significant differences on twenty-seven of the seventy-eight comparisons, as compared with fifteen according to ethnicity[8] and thirteen where joint effects were observable.[9]

The results varied widely from one theme to another. Perception of the two parent countries was the theme on which French- and English-language cartoons differed most consistently. The in-law theme was the main focus of language differences, ten of the twenty-six reaching significance. There were also seven differences by topic and five significant joint effects on this theme.[10] This was, indeed, the one setting in which the topic was not the most important source of variation. On the spousal theme there were important variations by topic and a modest but significant number of language and joint differences; it was, so to speak, the median theme.[11] The children theme showed significant differences between the two topics on about half the items. In this case the predictive value of the topic was particularly high. The number of joint effects was significant,[12] and there was only one instance of a French-English difference. One might summarize this general pattern metaphorically by concluding that French-English disagreements focus on the in-laws rather than on the spouses or children, and on the past rather than the present or future.[13]

The greater emphasis on collaboration in the English-language cartoons[14] was apparent in relation to six of the seven topics; on the average they were twice as likely as the French-language cartoons to feature this message. These results are consistent with the dominant position of the English audience and their desire to retain the status quo in relations between the groups. The one exception was language policy in Quebec: here the francophone artists were nearly three times as likely to seek collaboration. In this situation the roles were reversed, and francophones had the vested interest in pleading for collaboration from the minority.

The differences on the stress measure[15] derive from the work of Dondis, who argued that asymmetrical and unbalanced representations evoke more stress in the viewer than those which are balanced and symmetrical.[16] Asymmetry is not, of course, the only technique by which the artist can induce stress: Macpherson sometimes draws white figures on a black background to produce a gothic effect, while some cartoonists prefer the blunter approach of representing certain characters as evil.

On the in-law theme, though not elsewhere, the French-language cartoons were significantly more likely to have a clear target[17] and were significantly less ambiguous.[18]

As one might expect, figures connected with President de Gaulle or with Quebec bilingualism were more likely to be labelled in English- than in French-language cartoons. Those connected with the queen's visit or federal bilingualism were more likely to be labelled in French-language cartoons.[19] The differences on the spousal theme also supported this argument, though they did not reach statistical significance. English-language cartoons used labelling twice as regularly as French cartoons in relation to Ottawa-Quebec collaboration and the effects of separatism, where francophones were prominently portrayed. French-language cartoons used labels three times as regularly on the constitutional issue, where most of the leading actors were (English) Canadians. As an alternative, a cartoon would sometimes make reference to a person whose features would be unfamiliar to many viewers, but without depicting this character. The distribution of 'missing persons' by topic and language was consistent with the distribution of labelling.

REGIONAL DIFFERENCES IN THE CARTOON CHARACTERS

Initially, regional portrayals by English- and French-speaking artists were compared for each political leader separately. It was apparent, however, that the results could not be satisfactorily tested statistically, since the depictions of several characters in the same cartoon were not independent of one another. A heroic portrayal of one person implied that another would be shown as villainous in order to complete the scenario; the role played by one could be predicted from knowing the role played by another. To permit statistical analysis, the cast of characters in a cartoon had to be treated as a single unit.

One could then test how far cartoonists from Ontario perceived ethnic groups in the same way as those from other English-speaking parts of the country.

While this perspective could be applied straightforwardly to characters who were present, it created difficulties in the case of those who were not shown. The absent persons might be the subject of an allusion or a whole conversation, and might be crucial to the incident. Their absence, however, obliged the researcher either to ignore them or to infer the traits which a normal reader would give them. Their absence might be important in liberating the characters in the picture to be frank about them, to damage their plans, or to repair the havoc which they had caused. In order to avoid making questionable inferences about those whom the cartoonist had deliberately omitted, it was decided to analyse only those who were actually portrayed.

In this instance the most appropriate form of tabulation was to summarize the data for each measure and to conduct a log-linear analysis.[20] The characteristics of the set of persons in the cartoon would be the dependent variables, the independent variables being region and topic. When ineffectiveness was the measure, for example, the goal was to see whether the presence of ineffective anglophones correlated with the presence of ineffective francophones and whether this relationship was stronger on some topics and in some regions than in others.

In Table 14 it will be seen that when an Ontario cartoonist shows no ineffective francophones in the drawing, the chances are eight to six that no ineffective anglophone will be shown. When at least one ineffective francophone is depicted, the chances are nine to three that no ineffective anglophone will be portrayed. The same pattern holds in other regions of (English) Canada, though the correlation there is slightly stronger: only one ethnic group is ever shown as ineffective in any one drawing. Along with this

TABLE 14
Incidence of ineffective francophones and anglophones, by region:
English-language cartoons of President de Gaulle

Number of ineffective anglophones shown in cartoon	Number of ineffective francophones shown in cartoon			
	Ontario		Rest of (English) Canada	
	None	One or more	None	One or more
None	8	9	6	4
One or more	6	3	7	0

similarity there is also a difference. Ontario cartoonists are more likely to show francophones (in nine pictures) than anglophones (in six) as the only ineffective persons. Artists in other regions, by contrast, show ineffective anglophones in seven drawings but ineffective francophones in only four.

Regrettably, the greater number of cells into which the jointly dependent variable had to be divided made it possible to distinguish only between Ontario and all other provinces in this section of the analysis. Although there could have been important differences among the other regions, the requirement of sufficient numbers for four cells on the dependent variable made such a subdivision possible only in one or two instances. Nevertheless, this simple regional breakdown permitted a useful distinction between the centre and the periphery.

Nine measures were used to judge the extent of differences in portrayal. They clustered into three dimensions whose negative poles were foolishness, lack of importance, and badness. Foolishness comprised four aspects: foolery, ineffectiveness, keying, and femininity. Lack of importance was signified when the character was relegated to the background or was pictured only with local rather than with national or international figures. Badness consisted of selfishness, fabrication, and punitive representation by the artist.

The four measures of foolishness will now be described. First, foolery referred to those characters who were portrayed as fools rather than as heroes, villains, or neutral people.[21] Secondly, ineffective persons were those who emerged as losers in the incident shown. While there is overlap between fools and losers, or between heroes and winners, the two assessments were certainly not identical. Thirdly, keying referred to characters who were 'playing at' politics – only pretending to combat the other party, treating politics as a game, a ceremonial or a contest of appearances and popularity. Drawings which revealed phoney alliances or the 'true character' of the subject were also treated as examples of keying. Finally, femininity was judged according to Goffman's criteria for masculine and feminine poses: use of the fingers and hands to grasp or to caress; taking an active lead or being a passive follower; standing aloof or within the group; posing in an upright protective or in a reclining defenceless way; having an erect or a tilted head; having a serious or a smiling expression; and concentrating on the matter in hand or appearing withdrawn into another world.[22]

The first measure of unimportance was lack of prominence in the cartoon. Prominence was defined in terms of one's location. Those pictured toward the top, in the centre, and in the foreground scored 2 in each respect. Those found near the bottom, toward the edge, and in the background scored 0 on each. The placement of the body in relation to the top and side was measured carefully, and in cases of ambiguity the face was regarded as the central feature. Foreground figures were those whose face and torso alone could be fitted within the frame, whereas middle-ground figures could be fully shown and background figures occupied less than one-third of the height of the picture. This measure reflects the conventions on prominence described in texts on artistic composition. The second measure of unimportance looked at the company the character kept. Some were shown only with others from their own or more local levels of government; they were portrayed as moving only within these restricted circles. Others were shown with persons from higher levels of government, or with those from other governments at the same level. They were depicted as moving in wider circles than their own, sometimes on the international scene.

The first measure of badness concerned the motives which the cartoonist was attributing to the character. It aimed to distinguish those who were portrayed as clearly selfish from those who were shown as reasonably pursuing their own interests. While this may sound quite arbitrary, it was soon found to be fairly simple to recognize those instances where the artist was obviously depicting a grasping or selfish person. In cases of reasonable doubt the subject was not classified as selfish. The second measure of badness, fabrication, was taken from Goffman. It referred to the activity of those engaged in stage whispers, deceptions, or hidden thoughts which aimed to trick another person. The final measure drew on Coupe's distinction between glorifying, descriptive, laughing, and punitive representations. This proved relatively straightforward, since cartoonists are generally aiming to convey an image which will be comprehended very quickly. Characters who were represented punitively, as villains, were contrasted with those represented in one of the other three ways.

Seven log-linear models were used to examine the effects of region, in comparison with those of topic. Two joint dependent variables were used in a series of tables organized like Table 14. This approach was admirably suited to revealing differential representations, since it measured variations in the ratio of cartoons falling in the principal diagonal (No, No or Yes, Yes) to those falling in the other diagonal (No, Yes or Yes, No). A perfect positive correlation would be one model for the complete absence of bias: whenever an ineffective member of one group was shown, an ineffective member of the other group would also be shown. A correlation of zero would indicate that bias against each group was strictly proportional to the frequency of its appearance in the cartoons. The ratio of negative to positive depictions of one group would be the same whether or not the other group was depicted alongside it. Perfect negative correlation would mean that both groups were sometimes shown, and that every negative portrayal of one group would be accompanied by a positive depiction of the other. The strength and sign of the correlation, however, does not tell whether the bias is disproportionately directed against one group, and if so against which. This is one limitation to the log-linear analysis of these particular tables. The value of this part of the analysis lies, rather, in revealing which variables most influence the pattern of negative and positive representations.

Regional differences in the extent of negative representations would be revealed by variations in the strength of the correlation from one section to another of tables like Table 14. The analysis would accurately compare the strength of regional differences with the clarity of differences according to topic, which was also included as a variable in this analysis.

A complication inherent in this approach is that of establishing statistical significance for the results when the dependent variable is not dichotomous. A second set of sub-tables like Table 14 could be produced to show how often anglophones or francophones were depicted as effective, and a third showing the frequency of the middle category, partial effectiveness. The sub-tables are not necessarily of equal value, since one response may be too rare to give significant results from samples of this size. Where there was a set of such tables relating to the same polytomous dependent variables, the most significant result from the set was reported, for each log-linear model.

The first log-linear model asserted that the two dependent variables were indeed uncorrelated: no combination of topics or regions would influence the probability that either ethnic group would be depicted negatively. The second model was that a correlation existed between the two dependent variables, but that it was not influenced by either the topic or the region from which the cartoonist came.

The third model postulated that the two independent variables, topic and region, would jointly affect the treatment of French- but not of English-speaking characters. The fourth proposed, conversely, that they would jointly affect only the representation of English-speaking characters. The fifth argued that the correlation between the two dependent variables would vary by topic but not by region. The sixth suggested that this correlation would vary according to region but not according to topic. This was the model of greatest interest, but its confirmation depended on the discrediting of some of the others. The other theoretically possible models were rejected in advance. Some specified only a relationship between one of the independent and one of the dependent variables, without reference to the other two. The saturated model allowed for the possibility that every conceivable log-linear relationship would occur – a model which is true by definition, but also trivial.

It had been expected that these models could be tested for all seven topics, but this proved impractical. The joint dependent variables could not be studied on certain topics because the portrayal of either francophones or anglophones was too infrequent. The distribution of the shortfall in numbers followed a complex pattern, and different aspects of badness, unimportance, and foolishness were unexaminable on different topics. As long as the log-linear analysis was subdivided into seven topics, small numbers made some of the results quite unreliable. The topics were therefore grouped into the parental, the spousal, and the children themes. Only the most statistically significant result from the two or three topics within each theme was utilized. For those themes on which a highly significant result occurred alongside one or two statistically insignificant results, this procedure exaggerated the significance of the findings. Conversely, where two or three highly significant results were found within the same theme, the procedure underestimated their joint significance. On balance, the two types of error were likely to cancel out, but it was recognized that the procedure was less than ideal.

A similar strategy was used in relation to multiple tests of the same joint dependent variable. There were, for example, three tests in the set comprising the masculinity measure. One related to the presence or absence of anglophones and francophones who were shown as strongly masculine in their poses. The second related to the presence or absence of moderately masculine members of each group, and the third to the presence or absence of weakly masculine members. There were nine such sets of measures on each of the three themes. These tests were clearly not independent of one another, and some were quite unreliable because of the very small numbers. Again, the most significant test was reported while the others were omitted, leading to the same kinds of error. In order to offset this error, rather higher levels of significance than usual were adopted, though it was recognized that this approximation was very inexact. These procedures combined to yield one independent test for each of the nine measures of foolishness, badness, or unimportance on each of the three themes, a total of twenty-seven tests for each model.

The first model – that there was no relationship between the two joint dependent variables – was decisively rejected. On thirteen of the twenty-seven tests there was at least one correlation which was significant at the 0.001 level, and on only nine was there no significant difference even at the 0.05 level.

Rejection of the second model, that the relationship between the joint dependent variables was constant, was even more decisive. There was at least one result significant at the 0.001 level on twenty-four of the twenty-seven tests, and on only one was there no significant result. There were thus clear differences in the portrayals of the two dominant groups, the strength of these differences varying according to the topic and the region.

The other models were much more precise than the first two, in that they posited a relationship of a particular form. The most successful of them was the fifth, according to which the topic alone would have a noticeable effect on the correlation between the two joint dependent variables, and would thus be the major identifiable factor influencing the extent to which anglophones and francophones were portrayed differently. This more precise model was of little predictive value when parental relations formed the theme of the depictions.[23] It was very important on the husband-wife theme: among the nine tests, five had at least one difference which was significant at the 0.001 level. The three topics which comprised this theme – relations between Quebec and Ottawa, the constitution, and the effects of separation – led to very different patterns for portraying francophones and anglophones. Finally, there were less pronounced but still quite significant differences for this model on the children theme: in three of the nine sets there was at least one significant difference.[24] The two topics related to bilingualism, then, produced somewhat different portrayals of the two dominant groups.

The next most successful of the more precise models was the third, according to which topic and region would jointly affect the presence of francophones but not of anglophones. This model had no predictive value for the parental and spousal themes, but was highly significant for the children theme. In five of the nine tests it produced a single significant difference, although only one of these reached the 0.001 level. There were thus some indications that topic and region together had a modest impact on the presence of francophones in cartoons about bilingualism. The observed differences in these cases all followed the same pattern. When the subject was federal bilingualism, the Ontario cartoons more often depicted English-speaking and omitted French-speaking Canadians than did the cartoons from other parts of Canada. When, however, Quebec language policy was the focus, the Ontario cartoons were more likely than those from other provinces to omit English-speaking and to depict French-speaking Canadians.

The same pattern of ratios held in the other cases where the third model led to a significant result. In relation to language policy, then, there was a modest effect involving region and topic together. Ontario cartoonists stressed more the role of the politically dominant group: anglophones in the case of federal bilingualism, francophones in the case of Quebec language policy. Artists from the other provinces, meanwhile, elaborated more on the role of the minority group. Ontario cartoonists did not, however, present either group in a more or a less favourable light than their colleagues elsewhere. There was no tendency for either 'region' to depict one language group as more heroic or successful, the other as more villainous or inept.

The two remaining models, four and six, had no significant predictive value, reaching significance on only two of the twenty-seven tests. The fourth model proposed that topic and region would have a joint effect on the English- but not on the French-speaking characters; the sixth posited that region would have a direct effect on the relationship between the joint dependent variables.

LANGUAGE DIFFERENCES IN THE CARTOON CHARACTERS

It was possible to study how far depictions by French- and English-language cartoonists differed from one another, and how much variation there was from one topic to another. The models used were the same as those chosen for regional differences; in the absence of widespread regional variations it was decided in nearly all cases to combine all English-language cartoons. The independent variables were thus the topic and the ethnicity of the cartoonist. The joint dependent variable was again the depiction of anglophones and francophones as foolish, unimportant, or bad.

The first model, that there would be no correlation between the two dependent variables, was again decisively rejected. Of the twenty-seven independent tests, sixteen produced at least one result which was significant at the 0.001 level. There were thus widespread differences in the representations of English- and French-speaking Canadians. This is, of course, only a first step toward demonstrating bias. It is quite possible that cartoonists from the two groups agree in ridiculing the leaders of one language group on certain issues and those of the other group on other issues; if so, model five will be strongly supported. It is also possible that in some respects each group is harder on its own leaders than on those of the other group: the chi-squared tests do not indicate the direction of the differences which have been observed.

Closer examination of the results from the first model showed two main patterns. First, there was a widely prevalent tendency for laughing satire to be directed mainly against the cartoonist's own ethnic group. Members of the artist's group were consistently and significantly more likely to be presented as ineffective, effeminate, and engaged in keying. Secondly, the examples of punitive satire were more often directed against the other language group. There was, however, no difference in the selfishness of motives ascribed to one's own and to the other group, or in the tendency to see the other group as deceptive. The data thus gave some support to the argument that light humour was more often directed against the artist's own language group, while more punishing humour was slightly more often directed against the leaders of the other group. This finding will be examined in more detail later, to see whether particular individuals or subgroups served as scapegoats for ethnic hostility.

The second model, that the portrayals of anglophones and francophones were correlated but did not differ according to the topic or the ethnicity of the cartoonist, was also rejected at least once at the 0.001 level on every one of the twenty-seven tests.

According to the third model, topic and ethnicity both influence the portrayal of anglophones, but not that of francophones. This model found significant support at least once on fifteen of the twenty-seven independent tests, four of these being significant at the 0.001 level. The model was the dominant one in relation to the in-law theme, where it produced a significant result on eight of the nine tests. The other models had no significant impact on this theme.

The pattern was relatively clear-cut and simple. Cartoons from both language groups showed a reasonably even balance of francophones and anglophones in their scenes from President de Gaulle's visit, and the same was true of French-language cartoons on the queen. English-language cartoons about the queen, however, almost completely omitted any francophone figures: only four could be found in the forty-two cartoons.[25] This major difference concerned the extent to which, not the manner in which, the two groups were displayed.

On the spousal theme this third model was less important, though still statistically significant.[26] On the children theme it was again important, reaching significance on two of the three badness measures and two of the other six.[27] In the federal bilingualism cartoons anglophones were shown as overwhelmingly innocent if no bad francophone was present; but in the company of a bad francophone they were unlikely to be innocent. The general picture, then, was that both sides were to some extent blameworthy, in the judgement of cartoonists from both language groups. When the topic changed to Quebec's language policy, however, the anglophones were shown as almost wholly innocent of villainy, especially in the English-language press.

The fourth model, conversely, looked for joint effects of ethnicity on the portrayal of francophones alone. The results were considerably less striking: significant differences occurred at least once on only eight of the twenty-seven independent tests, and only one of them was significant beyond the 0.05 level. Six of them were found on the spousal theme, and two in relation to the in-laws. The former was extremely significant; the latter was not.[28] Although there were often differences on the in-law theme, these did not form very clear patterns.

Indeed, only two patterns were observable. First, on the topic of the constitution, francophones were depicted much more negatively when in the presence of foolish or bad anglophones than otherwise. This was especially true when the artist was working for an English-language newspaper. Secondly, the results were much more stereotyped on the badness than on the foolishness or unimportance measures. On the topics of Ottawa-Quebec relations and separation, however, francophones were depicted more negatively when in the presence of anglophones than in their absence. In French-language cartoons there was some tendency to attribute bad relations between the language groups to the francophones. This was much stronger in the English-language cartoons.

For the selfishness variable, the first three rows of Table 15 reveal that when no anglophone was illustrated as selfish, the chances were over six in ten that a selfish francophone would be shown. The chances were lower for the fabrication and punitive representation variables, one in four and one in three respectively. For these two variables, however, the second and fourth rows showed that over 90 per cent of those represented as fabricators (twenty-eight of thirty) or punitively (forty-two of forty-five) were francophones, compared with 77 per cent (sixty-four of eighty-three) when selfishness was the criterion.

Once again, there was some evidence here that foolishness and unimportance were more often attributed to one's own than to the other group.

TABLE 15
Three measures of badness in Ottawa-Quebec relations:
English-language cartoons

	Selfishness	Fabrication	Punitive representation
No one shown as bad	39	90	75
Only francophone shown as bad	62	28	42
Total with no bad Anglophone	101	118	117
Only anglophone shown as bad	17	2	3
Both shown as bad	2	0	0

However, badness was more often attributed to the other group than to one's own, especially on the Ottawa-Quebec topic, which was dominated by English-language cartoons about René Lévesque.

The fifth model proposed that differential representation, and the correlation between depictions of the two groups, would vary from one topic to another. It yielded significant results at least once in thirteen of the twenty-seven cases, seven of these being at the 0.001 level. It was very influential on the spousal theme,[29] moderately influential on the children theme,[30] and altogether without importance on the in-law theme.

The sixth model, wherein ethnicity had an independent effect on the correlation between representations of the two groups, was the weakest, with a significant result on only five of the twenty-seven tests.[31] Only in relation to masculinity and badness was there any indication of a consistent effect. The scattered differences which were observable nevertheless had one dominant feature. In relation to the queen's visit, the constitution, and federal language policy, anglophones were seen as the initiators. Cartoonists from both language groups saw anglophones as the main villains in relation to the constitution, the tendency to do so being stronger among francophones. On the two other topics, each group was likely to single out its own as the principal villains, this tendency being much stronger for the English- than for the French-language cartoons. In relation to President de Gaulle, Ottawa-Quebec relations, separation and Quebec language policy, where francophones were seen as the initiators, both groups were likely to focus on francophones as the villains. It was noted earlier that French-language cartoons were more likely than those in English to have a clear satirical target, and were less likely to leave the verdict to the viewer's interpretation. Nevertheless, when blame for badness was distributed, the francophone cartoonists were more likely to spread it reasonably evenly between the groups on any given topic, while those working in English

TABLE 16
Villainy: the queen, federal bilingualism, and the constitution

Language of		Topic			
Cartoonist	Villain	Queen's visit	Federal bilingualism	Constitution	Total
English	English	17	27	11	55
English	French	5	2	10	17
French	English	2	1	6	9
French	French	9	3	–	12

TABLE 17

Villainy: President de Gaulle, Ottawa-Quebec relations, separation, Quebec language policy

Language of		Topic				
Cartoonist	Villain	De Gaulle	Ottawa-Quebec	Separation	Quebec lang.	Total
English	English	4	22	3	11	40
English	French	50	132	48	50	280
French	English	40	5	1	3	49
French	French	55	25	4	10	94

were more likely to focus their spleen on one group to the exclusion of the other, in a stereotyped manner.

REGIONAL BIASES IN THE CARTOON CHARACTERS

The analysis detailed in the two previous sections proved unsatisfactory when the focus turned to the direction of bias. In the first place, the tables failed to discriminate between cases where no francophone was portrayed and those where the francophones who were portrayed did not have the characteristic in question. One of the difficulties which pervaded this research was to decide how far it was legitimate to impute traits to characters and to an ethnic group which was not shown. In a few cases other signs in the drawing or the text conveyed the artist's intentions. In general it was hazardous to draw conclusions, from observing the portrayal of the one group which was shown, about the depiction of the other group when it was not. Decisions about these missing data would have important effects on the results, and it was by no means obvious how they should be made.

The second difficulty derived from the organization rather than the content of tables such as 14. Entries in the main diagonal denoted the absence of bias: both groups were treated in the same favourable or unfavourable manner. If the attribute was negative, cells in the upper right corner denoted bias against francophones while those in the lower left corner denoted bias against anglophones. The earlier analysis, however, did not combine the unbiased categories and compare them with the extent and direction of bias. A reordering of the table was needed before this could be done. Furthermore, it was desirable to examine the extent of bias *within* a cartoon: four negative portrayals of members of a group make a stronger statement than a single negative image.

The data were therefore rearranged and amplified. For each region and topic, tabulations were made which showed the relationship between the ethnicity of the characters and the bias in their representation. Table 18 corresponds to the first half of Table 14; it shows the presence or absence of ineffective portrayals of English and French speakers in Ontario papers on the topic of President de Gaulle's visit. The variable displayed in the columns is the extent to which French- and English-speakers predominate among the principal personae in the cartoon. The first column lists the cartoons where anglophones outnumber francophones by four;[32] in the second, the difference in favour of anglophones is three;[33] in the third the difference is two.[34] Continuing the series, the fifth signifies equal representation[35] and the last means no anglophones to four francophones.

The variable displayed in the rows of Table 18 is the extent to which designations of ineffectiveness are concentrated in one group. Here, portrayals of ineffective francophones were combined with portrayals of effective anglophones to give a score for the extent of pro-anglophone sentiments in a drawing. Depictions of effective francophones were then combined with depictions of ineffective anglophones to give a score for the extent of pro-francophone sentiments in the same drawing. The two scores were then added to indicate the extent of bias in the cartoon. The first row contains cartoons in which pro-anglophone sentiments outnumber pro-francophone sentiments by four; the second contains those where the difference is three; and so on.

The entries in Table 18 are to be read as follows. In four of the cartoons in the sixth column, where francophones outnumber anglophones by one, pro-francophone sentiments are in the majority by three: there are two

TABLE 18
Extent and direction of bias: Ontario cartoons on ineffectiveness during de Gaulle's visit

Numerical predominance		Anglophones outnumber francophones by				0	Francophones outnumber anglophones by			
		4	3	2	1	0	1	2	3	4
Pro-francophone	4									
sentiments exceed	3						4		1	
pro-anglophone	2					1		3		
sentiments by	1						4		1	
	0			1		2	3			
Pro-anglophone	1				1					
sentiments exceed	2							4		
pro-francophone	3									
sentiments by	4					1				

effective francophones and one ineffective anglophone. These drawings show bias in favour of francophones, since Frenchness is associated in them with effectiveness twice and Englishness with ineffectiveness once. In the other four cartoons which fall in that column, there is one more francophone than anglophone, while pro-francophone sentiments are in the majority by one.

In order to avoid problems of deriving overlapping tables from the same data, the analysis was restricted to the nine negative traits discussed at the beginning of the previous section, for which the answer could be treated as a dichotomy: each character either was or was not shown negatively. For each topic there were four independent tests of whether one group was more likely than the other to be shown as foolish, two of whether it was shown as more unimportant, and three of whether it was more often depicted as bad.

Entries in the diagonal from top left to bottom right refer to cartoons where there is equal and negative treatment: all characters of French or English background are shown to be ineffective. Entries in the diagonal from bottom left to top right refer to cartoons in which there is equal and positive treatment: all English and French characters are shown to be effective. There were eleven such cartoons in this set; these were the eleven which were recorded as 'No, No' or 'Yes, Yes' in Table 14. There are six entries above this diagonal which show bias in favour of francophones: in Table 14 these were the cartoons which contained ineffective anglophones but no ineffective francophones. There were nine entries below this diagonal which showed bias in favour of anglophones: in Table 14 these were the drawings which included ineffective francophones but not ineffective anglophones.

Tables such as Table 18 are difficult to read and to compare. For each one a simplified table such as Table 19 was therefore produced. Since the focus was on negative representations, the diagonal from lower left to upper right was taken as the baseline for unbiased depictions; in cartoons falling into this diagonal none of the personae were shown as fools. In Table 18 there were eleven cartoons which fell into this main diagonal. In the new

TABLE 19
Pro-French and pro-English biases in Ontario cartoons on
President de Gaulle's visit: ineffectiveness

	Predominantly pro-French representations				Predominantly pro-English representations			
Score	−4	−3	−2	−1	0	1	2	3	4
Frequency	0	0	0	6	11	4	5	0	0

Table 19 derived from it, they occupy the central position, as befits a neutral category. Cartoons in the adjacent diagonal, one cell up and one cell to the left, were one degree more favourable to francophones and one degree less favourable to anglophones. In the new table they are shown immediately to the left, or one degree more pro-French, than the neutral category; they number six. Correspondingly, those who fell one cell below and one cell to the right of this diagonal were one degree less favourable to francophones and one degree more favourable to anglophones; they appear in Table 19 immediately to the right of the neutral category. The entries in Table 18 have thus been compressed into a single row showing the degree of pro-French or pro-English representation.

The Mann-Whitney U-test was then used to test whether the distributions for Ontario and the other provinces differed significantly, when the topic and the dependent variable were the same. On the foolishness dimension, twenty-eight tests were possible, since there were four measures of foolishness and seven topics. Eight of these yielded moderately significant differences.[36] In every case the cartoons in Ontario papers showed francophones more negatively and anglophones more positively than did the cartoons from the other anglophone provinces. Similar though less pronounced results were found on the dimensions of unimportance and badness.[37] These, too, were all in the same direction, and the overall pattern of results was quite significant.[38]

On one of the seven topics, Quebec language policy, there were enough cartoons from English-language newspapers in Quebec and the Maritimes to distinguish these from the western papers. The patterns for these two peripheral regions were almost identical on foolishness, unimportance, and badness.

On two of the topics, portrayals of characters from France and Britain were sufficiently frequent to permit comparisons between French and Québécois, and between British and (English) Canadian figures. First impressions suggested that leaders from the parent country might have quite different significations from leaders of the same language within Canada. No regional differences were found in English-language depictions of French and Quebec leaders. While the French leaders were presented as slightly more foolish and bad than those from Quebec, this was equally observable among English-language cartoonists in Ontario and among those working elsewhere. When showing anglophones, however, cartoonists from Ontario were likely to present the British as more foolish than (English) Canadians, while the reverse was true for artists working in the other anglophone provinces. The difference was significant,[39] but was not duplicated on the measures of either unimportance or badness.

LANGUAGE BIASES IN THE CARTOON CHARACTERS

On the foolishness dimension the tests yielded a significant pattern. English-speaking cartoonists showed anglophone characters more negatively and francophone characters more positively than did their French-speaking counterparts. This finding was extremely significant statistically.[40] On the unimportance dimension there were significant differences in the same direction: cartoonists of each language group were more likely to concentrate on showing members of their own ethnic group and to depict them as less important than members of the other group.[41] Fool-making, then, was directed primarily and disproportionately against one's own group.

On the badness dimension the results were quite different. On the five topics from the spousal and children themes there were no significant differences: neither group was attributed a disproportionate share of selfishness, deceptiveness, or other bad qualities. On the two topics from the in-law theme, however, there were some significant results. When French visitors were shown, cartoonists from each ethnic group were very significantly more likely to make negative judgments about the other group than about their own members.[42] Conversely, when British visitors were featured, there was slight but not significant evidence that cartoonists were more likely to make negative judgments about their own ethnic group.

These results can be studied in more detail. In cartoons on the in-law theme, but not elsewhere, it was possible to distinguish British from (English) Canadian, and French from Québécois figures. On the other themes, the number of British and French characters was negligible. A slight tendency was observable among the English-language cartoonists to present the French as more foolish and more bad than the Québécois characters. The reverse was true for Québécois cartoonists, who quite consistently[43] showed their own politicians to be more foolish and sometimes[44] showed them to be less good than those from France. British leaders were generally portrayed as more foolish than (English) Canadians among artists of both language groups.

Regional and Topical Variations in the Canadian-American Cartoons

Several differences between Appendices B and C should be noted at the outset, because they affect the comparability of the results in this appendix with those reported earlier. There were fewer cartoons, and they could be divided only into two broad areas: economic and military policy. While there were certainly cartoons on a number of themes – Arctic sovereignty, cultural invasion, and tourism, for example – their numbers were small because they generally related to specific incidents which quickly lost their newsworthiness. Furthermore, they were generally represented in terms of economics and the control of resources. One hundred and sixty cartoons were available on economic relations with the United States, the most frequent single topic in the present collection. Most were from Ontario, but there were subsets of sixteen from the Maritimes and Quebec, and twenty-seven from the western provinces. The second topic, military relations, generated thirty-seven drawings: three were from the Maritimes and Quebec, twenty-eight from Ontario, and six from the West. As a result, the measurement of interaction between region and topic was not very reliable. The topical analysis consisted of a comparison between the economic and the military cartoons, while the regional comparison involved differences between three parts of the country.

REGIONAL DIFFERENCES IN THE STRUCTURE OF THE CARTOONS

The log-linear analysis examined the effects of topic and region on the same twenty-six characteristics of each cartoon as a whole. There were statistically significant variations by topic and/or region on four of them, and nearly significant variations on two others. Overall, the pattern of variations was pronounced enough to reach statistical significance.[1] The interactions between topical and regional effects were insignificant on every characteristic except one – whether politicians were the only people to be portrayed as fools – and as a pattern they were similarly insignificant.[2]

Regional differences alone were not significant overall,[3] though there were two exceptions among the twenty-six measures. The first strong regional difference concerned the genre of the cartoon. Those from Ontario engaged much more in low satire than those from the other regions, where medium satire was the usual practice. The ratio of social (medium) to personal (low) satire was at least 3.5:1 in western and eastern cartoons on economic and military relations. In Ontario, however, it fell below two to one.

Many writers have noted the tendency of the capitalist press to credit or blame individuals for social change, masking the influence of the social structures within which they operate. Phenomena such as social class are rarely mentioned, the emphasis being on the determination and enterprise of individuals. Low satire reproduces this myth, by blaming individuals and not structures for failure and foolishness. It is noteworthy that this happened most frequently in cartoons from the dominant economic region, where one would expect this myth to be propagated most consistently. Even in this case, however, social satire was more widely found than individual satire. The artist's commentary was directed more against politics as an international institution than against the foolishness of the present incumbents. When these office-holders had previously been in opposition, they had doubtless joined with the cartoonists in ridiculing their predecessors for engaging in the practices which they themselves were now perpetuating.

The second regional difference showed that Ontario cartoonists were more likely than those from other provinces to single out politicians as the only people who should be portrayed as fools. Eastern and western artists generally included other segments of the population in their satire, whereas those from Ontario concentrated their fire much more exclusively on politicians.[4] The same phenomenon was noted in chapter 5, in the context of French-English relations; thus the finding appears to have some generality.

TABLE 20
Genre of cartoon, by region

	East, Quebec		Ontario		West	
	Economic	Military	Economic	Military	Economic	Military
Non-satirical	–	–	8	5	–	–
Medium satire	14	3	59	15	21	5
Low satire	2	–	50	8	6	1

$\chi_2^2 = 17.42$, $z = 3.51$, $p = 0.00023$

The argument of the earlier chapters has underlined the particular place in capitalist thinking occupied by the lampooning of politicians; within this framework the Ontario cartoons constituted purer examples of ideological art. This may be connected with Ontario's traditional position as the centre-piece and chief beneficiary of capitalist development in Canada. Its economic success has perhaps partly blinded the province to the political factors which have contributed to that prosperity, permitting it to maintain a myopic contempt for government intervention in the economy. Artists from the other provinces showed foolishness as more widely distributed, even though, in their world, commerce still remained largely untouched by it.

Differences by topic were once more very pronounced, even though only two topics were distinguished.[5] The largest differences occurred on the ambiguity and stress measures.[6] Military cartoons from all regions were less symmetrical and potentially more anxiety-provoking than those on eco-nomic affairs. They were at the same time less open to alternative interpre-tations by the skimmer. Fools, heroes, and villains were more strongly demarcated in the military than in the economic cartoons. The military drawings were more likely to use the infringement of taboos as a means of emphasizing the message.[7] Their targets were more often drawn in duplicate or triplicate, indicating that American military pressure was more a group or gang phenomenon than American economic pressure. The president would often be depicted without advisers when the economy was the centre of discussion; in military negotiations, however, advisers were nearly always present.[8] Finally, military cartoons more frequently included persons who were labelled.[9]

REGIONAL DIFFERENCES IN THE CARTOON CHARACTERS

The log-linear analysis of cartoon characters was closely akin to that used in the corresponding sections of chapter 5. Both topics and all three regions were included in the analysis, even though a few of the numbers were very small. The first model asserted that the portrayals of Canadians and Amer-icans would be uncorrelated: no combination of topics or regions would influence the probability that either nation's citizens or leaders would be shown negatively. This model was again decisively rejected: on six of the nine measures[10] there were significant differences. The overall pattern was very strong.[11] Similarly the second model, which postulated a constant re-lationship between depictions of Canadians and Americans across all regions and both topics, was strongly refuted by the data.[12]

The other, more precise, models varied in the support which they received.

There was no evidence for the third model – that topic and region would affect the portrayal of Americans but not Canadians. There were some indications that topic and region affected the portrayal of Canadians but not Americans as foolish.[13] This result faded from significance, however, when the model was further tested on the unimportance and badness measures.[14] Model five proposed that topic would have an impact on the depiction of both Canadians and Americans. This was the best of the more precise models in predicting the patterns to be found in the data: on foolishness its utility was outstanding[15] and on badness it was the most successful of a very modest set.[16] Model six posited that region would have an independent effect. This model had some validity for the foolishness measures[17] but overall did not produce significant results.[18]

The general conclusions of chapter 5 were thus confirmed; chapter 7 therefore makes separate analyses by topic wherever this is practicable, but combines cartoons from the different regions.

REGIONAL BIASES IN THE CARTOON CHARACTERS

The method of comparison to be used in this section was discussed in chapter 5. In view of the very detailed breakdowns and the limited numbers of eastern and western military cartoons, it was necessary to undertake separate analyses for region and topic. The material relevant to the regional comparisons will be presented first. The data base for this part of the analysis was the set of 160 drawings on Canadian-American economic relations.

The statistical part of the regional comparisons proceeded in two stages. First, the smaller western and eastern sets of cartoons were compared with one another. If there were no significant differences these two were then combined and compared with the Ontario cartoons. Table 21 illustrates the organization of the data.

The same pattern of results was visible on all the nine measures. The western cartoons were more pro-Canadian or anti-American than those from the East on every measure, though only one reached statistical significance on its own. On the four foolishness measures as a set, however, and on the three badness measures as a set, the differences were significant.[19] When all nine measures were combined into a single test, the results were again highly significant.[20]

In the second set of comparisons, western and eastern artists' work was combined and then compared with that emanating from Ontario newspapers. The western and eastern cartoonists were consistently more pro-Canadian than those from Ontario, on eight of the nine measures. The three badness

TABLE 21

Anti-Canadian and anti-American biases in the cartoons on Canadian-American relations,
by region: selfishness measure

Region	Predominantly Anti-American representations					Predominantly Anti-Canadian representations			
	−4	−3	−2	−1	0	+1	+2	+3	+4
Eastern	–	2	1	5	5	2	1	–	–
Western	2	1	8	5	9	2	–	–	–
E vs. W: $z = -0.90, p > 0.10$									
East + West	2	3	9	10	14	4	1	–	–
Ontario	3	2	12	45	40	7	5	2	1
E + W vs. O: $z = 0.32, p > 0.10$									

measures as a set showed statistically significant differences,[21] and when the nine measures were merged into a single test the results were again highly significant.[22]

More detailed examination showed that the Ontario cartoons were more likely than those from the other provinces to portray Americans; those from the West were the least likely to do so. As a set, these differences too were statistically significant.[23] The observed regional differences resulted mainly from two tendencies. First, cartoonists in the East, and particularly in the West, were more likely than those in Ontario to focus on portraying Canadians. They showed relatively few Americans in their drawings on Canadian-American relations. They concentrated more on the impact in Canada of policies initiated in the United States, and less on analysis of the persons seen as originating or symbolizing those policies. In this regard their drawings were more overtly regional. Secondly, cartoonists in the West, and to a lesser extent those in the East, were more positive than their Ontario colleagues in their depictions of Canadians, and less inclined to depict them as foolish, unimportant, or bad. These differences in the representation of Canadians outweighed any variations in the tendency to portray Americans negatively.

These regional differences were more impressive in their consistency than in their individual strength; they were found, to a very moderate extent, on seventeen of the eighteen measures. Their meaning was less readily apparent, however. The eastern group was the most heterogeneous, since it combined the Maritime provinces with Quebec. For this reason, perhaps, it occupied an intermediate position, though the numbers were too small to show whether English-language Quebec cartoons differed from those which appeared in the Maritimes. According to the conventional wisdom on regional differences, Alberta and British Columbia have traditionally been the most alienated from the metropolis of central Canada, the most open to and dependent on U.S. investment, and the most inclined to perceive that their regional and economic affinities lay with the United States. Ontario, in contrast, sees itself as Canada's core, the source of national policy and the heart of resistance to American economic takeover and cultural domination. Accordingly, Ontario is more critical of Canada's weak position vis-à-vis the United States, and readier to blame 'its' national politicians for their inability to alter this.

An alternative explanation might be sought in the possibility that the differences were due to regional variations in the meaning of Canada. Two hypotheses connected with this explanation were studied. First, the Canadians who were viewed more positively in the West might be provincial politicians, whereas those depicted in the Ontario cartoons might be members of the federal government. The evidence gave little support to this, however. There were 109 portrayals of Canadian politicians in their relations with the United States; 58 of these showed the prime minister,[24] and another 34 depicted members of the federal cabinet. Eight were francophones from Quebec. There remained seven MPs from the opposition parties and two anglophone provincial politicians who might have been regional heroes of (English) Canada; but only three of these last nine appeared in cartoons drawn by western artists, and this number was too small to influence the statistics.

The second hypothesis about possible differences in meaning concerned the depiction of citizens. Western cartoons might focus more on the depiction of citizens and on the public impact of Canadian and American policies. Ontario drawings might centre more on the political figures who were credited with initiating policies. This hypothesis found highly significant support in the data: in the western cartoons 39 per cent of the characters were citizens, whereas in Ontario drawings this was true of only 9 per cent.[25] Furthermore, the portrayals of citizens in the western cartoons were significantly more favourable than their depiction in those from Ontario.[26]

In summary, then, the provinces to the west of Ontario produced the most pro-Canadian and the least pro-American cartoons on Canadian economic relations with the United States. Those to the east were intermediate, while those from Ontario produced the least pro-Canadian and the most pro-American cartoons. Several factors contributed to this. Ontario cartoons were the most likely to feature potential policy makers, including Americans. Those from the other provinces, especially in the West, were more likely to focus on the recipients of policy, private citizens who would be perceived as local people. Ontario cartoons were more likely than those from the West to depict citizens negatively, when they featured them at all. Ontario's citizens, then, were shown as foolish and selfish participants in North American affairs. Those from the West were depicted as good and sensible persons who responded to events but who took hardly any part in them. There was thus at least a weak association between goodness or common sense and alienation, between badness or foolishness and participation.

The analysis of bias by topic anticipated that there might be regional differences in this respect. In light of the small numbers already mentioned, it was judged best to restrict this part of the study to comparison of Ontario cartoonists' work on the two topics.

In general, the military cartoons were more pro-American than the economic drawings. The results for foolishness and for lack of importance were significant;[27] those for badness were very weak, but in the same direction. When all three sets of measures were combined, the differences were consistent on seven of the nine and were highly significant.[28]

The direction of the results, and their significance on the measures of foolishness and lack of importance but not badness, was fairly readily interpretable. American military policies were less likely than American economic policies to be seen as anti-Canadian; cartoonists portrayed more consensus and less anti-American sentiment in the former than in the latter area. Canadian foolishness was more likely to emerge on military than on economic issues, where excessive faith in u.s. technology was often caricatured, especially in the early 1960s.

Notes

Chapter 1. The Fool Show and the Cartoon

1 In the same manner, plays upon words appeal to the young because they demonstrate 'that language is not a monolithic, denotative rational system invented by adults to dominate the young, but rather a wild, chaotic, irrational, hopelessly funny pot of sounds that can be recombined and grouped to produce unanticipated meanings' (Charney, 1978: 22–3).

2 Zijderveld is emphatic that such words as 'normal' should not be taken to imply that fools corresponded to those who are now labelled 'mentally ill.'

3 What is important for the mirror analogy is that most dimensions remain unchanged, so that the image remains recognizable through the transformation. In the case of the Festival of Fools, the fools' mass still took place in the church, involving a set of celebrants and sequences of activity which paralleled those of the mass. The impact of sacrilege and desecration was achieved precisely because there could be no doubt that the activity being parodied was a mass.

4 Zijderveld (pp. 74–85) sees the Till Eulenspiegel legends and Brant's poem *Narrenschiff* as early examples of bourgeois ideology which ridiculed traditional values through tales about fool-makers and fools.

5 In the same manner, a demonstration for nuclear disarmament does not remove the horror of nuclear war, but it may hide the terror of feeling powerless to do anything about it.

6 Walter Allen notes that the literary work of Smollett was mainly caricatural (p. 68).

7 See, for example, the portrayals of Queen Victoria in Davis's *Punch and the Monarchy*. Recent British cartoons on the royal family in *Punch* cluster around the theme, 'Wouldn't it be funny if they behaved like private citizens?'

8 In the United States the Pulitzer Prize, in Canada the National Newspaper

Award, and internationally the Grand Prize of the Salon International de la Caricature.

9 Available in the National Archives in Ottawa, along with the cartoons which Desbarats and Mosher considered for their book.

10 In a recent Canadian case, cartoonist Bob Bierman was found guilty of libel, but the decision was overturned on appeal.

11 Over 95 per cent of North American cartoonists have been men.

12 The term 'English Canada' is not a very accurate description of the nine provinces where English is the dominant language, and is losing its appropriateness in an age which stresses multiculturalism. The designation 'Canada' which Québécois independentists use is not accepted by these provinces. The expression '(English) Canada' is awkward, but captures some of the current ambiguity.

13 Press (p. 105) stresses the critical treatment of u.s. business during the Vietnam years, but this exception seems to be unusual and of short duration. The theme was not found in Canadian cartoons of the same period; they attributed the foolishness of Vietnam entirely to the u.s. government.

14 David Rosen is attempting to remedy this, for the inter-war period in Canada.

Chapter 2. Literary Theory: Cartoons as Symbolic Action and Satire

1 It is for this reason that Lévi-Strauss's analysis of myths can be admired but not tested. One either sees the connections which he makes or one does not; their existence cannot be confirmed or refuted scientifically.

2 Three other social types were mentioned later in his work: the victim, the traitor, and the corrupted or pseudo-hero. These were included in the content analysis for the present research, but were not found to be useful in analysing cartoons. Victims and fools, heroes and pseudo-heroes, were very hard to distinguish reliably.

Chapter 3. Newspapers: The Context for Cartoons

1 McLuhan (p. 190) attributes the phrase to Douglass Cater, *The Fourth Branch of Government.* I have been unable to verify the source, however.

2 This situation would be greatly aggravated if 'ethnic' white minorities were to be seen as the main source of discrimination and prejudice against visible minorities, as has happened in the United States.

Chapter 4. The Main Hypotheses and Methods of Analysis

1 This figure excludes 141 which were portraits of cartoonists.

Chapter 5. Regional, Topical, and Ethnic Variations in the French-English Cartoons

1 The nature of labels proved to be considerably more complex than Beniger implied, since there were many other ways besides a bald name-tag by which the artist could reveal a character's name.

Chapter 6. French-English Cartoons as Capitalist Slogans

1 Statistical tests of this hypothesis were difficult. Frequently the cartoonist would represent one person as cultural or as natural, but would leave the skimmer to infer whether persons from the contrasting group should be associated with the other pole. The artist could have been implicitly contrasting the person shown with the absent person, but could equally have been implying that the absent group had the same faults. In some instances, the presence of René Lévesque or Pierre Trudeau alone did not enable one to decide unequivocally whether he was representing a political unit, a language group, or a party. Given these sources of uncertainty, only cartoons which featured distinct group representatives were included in the analysis.

2 The ambiguity between the two last was resolved by treating Ottawa-Quebec cartoons as comparisons between federalism and independentism if they appeared after the PQ victory in 1976, and otherwise as referring to Canada and Quebec.

3 $\chi_1^2 = 14.75$, $z = 3.55$, $p = 0.0004$.

4 $\chi_1^2 = 8.50$, $z = 2.68$, $p = 0.0037$.

5 $\chi_1^2 = 3.23$, $z = 1.49$, $p = 0.068$.

6 $\chi_1^2 = 19.31$, $z = 4.04$, $p = 0.00003$.

7 Some cartoons were ambiguous, letting the glancer choose the ending. The coding for this section was based strictly on what was observable; no attempt was made to infer what was not shown.

8 This may sound strange, since about two-thirds of the cartoons were included. It must be remembered, however, that the dependent variable was divided into four comparisons: French-English, parent country–Canada, Canada-province, and federalist-independentist. Within each comparison there were up to five categories, such as 'dominant group breaks up social order, minority group fails to restore it.' There were substantial frequencies in some of these twenty cells along with many empty ones.

9 The percentage was 88 among the French-English comparisons, 70 among those contrasting Canada with a parent country, 78 where Canada was compared with one or more provinces, and 72 among the federalist-independentist contrasts.

10 The difference was not statistically significant: $\chi_1^2 = 3.00$, $z = 1.41$, $p = 0.079$.

11 $\chi_4^2 = 122.06$, $z = 9.25$, $p < 0.00001$.

12 For these three measures individually, $z = 3.42$, 3.66, 1.59. For the four foolishness measures together, $\chi_8^2 = 41.12$, $z = 4.52$, $p < 0.00001$.

13 This result was not statistically significant, because of the small numbers and the particular distribution across the nine categories.

14 For the English-language cartoons, $\chi_6^2 = 23.20$, $z = 3.15$, $p = 0.00085$; for the French-language drawings, $\chi_6^2 = 13.24$, $z = 1.76$, $p = 0.039$.

15 Fourteen of the cartoons originated in Ontario and five in Alberta. On six of the seven measures they showed a very similar pattern, but with regard to effectiveness there was a striking divergence: Ontario judged Peter Lougheed as much more effective than Alberta did.

16 The tested hypothesis was that, for both foolishness and badness, one-third of the cartoons would show federal and provincial politicians in the same way, while one-third would depict federal leaders more favourably, and one-third would favour those from the provinces. The proportion of drawings which showed them as equal was consistently much higher than this, the results for the test as a whole being $\chi_{12}^2 = 109.54$ for foolishness ($z = 8.43$) and $\chi_9^2 = 129.57$ ($z = 9.27$) for badness.

17 The tested hypothesis was that the number of 'better' cartoons would equal the number of 'worse' ones in each part of the table. This was rejected. The pattern was highly significant: $\chi_{12}^2 = 64.18$ ($z = 5.64$, $p < 0.00001$) for the foolishness measures, and $\chi_9^2 = 33.58$ ($z = 3.66$, $p = 0.00013$) for the badness measures.

18 $\chi_2^2 = 15.46$, $z = 3.27$, $p = 0.0011$.

19 $z = 2.35$, $p = 0.019$.

20 $z = 4.59$, $p < 0.00003$.

21 $\chi_8^2 = 27.09$, $z = 3.18$, $p = 0.0046$.

22 $\chi_6^2 = 24.33$, $z = 3.28$, $p = 0.0005$.

23 The z-scores from these four tables were 1.58, 1.37, 0, and 4.27 respectively. They combined to yield $\chi_8^2 = 35.10$, $z = 3.99$, $p = 0.00003$.

24 $\chi_6^2 = 13.52$, $z = 1.81$, $p = 0.0351$.

25 The percentage of members of the public depicted as fools was almost as high as for politicians, but they were concentrated in a fairly small proportion (14 per cent) of the cartoons, whereas politicians were shown as fools in more than half the entire sample.

26 $\chi_{14}^2 = 46.87$, $z = 4.06$, $p = 0.00003$.

27 $\chi_{14}^2 = 44.66$, $z = 3.87$, $p = 0.00005$.

28 $\chi_{14}^2 = 36.78$, $z = 3.14$, $p = 0.0008$.

29 $\chi_{14}^2 = 112.48$, $z = 8.09$, $p < 0.000001$.

30 For this reason, the attempt to infer much about the role attributed to the viewer by the artist had to be abandoned.

Chapter 7. Canadian-American Cartoons as Capitalist Slogans

1 $\chi_2^2 = 12.33$, $z = 2.83$, $p = 0.0023$.
2 These were, however, classified under 'no threat,' alongside the few which showed harmony. The classification was therefore fairly conservative.
3 $p = 0.49$, $N = 35$.
4 $p = 0.12$, $N = 58$.
5 $\chi_1^2 = 13.34$, $z = 3.38$, $p = 0.0003$.
6 $\chi_1^2 = 5.20$, $z = 2.03$, $p = 0.0212$.
7 $\chi_8^2 = 30.15$, $z = 3.50$, $p = 0.00023$.
8 $\chi_6^2 = 13.44$, $z = 1.80$, $p = 0.036$.
9 $\chi_{14}^2 = 43.59$, $z = 3.78$, $p = 0.00008$.
10 $\chi_8^2 = 37.66$, $z = 4.22$, $p < 0.00003$.
11 $\chi_6^2 = 30.73$, $z = 3.95$, $p = 0.00004$.
12 $\chi_{14}^2 = 68.39$, $z = 5.66$, $p < 0.00003$.
13 $N = 109$, 26 respectively.
14 $\chi_4^2 = 16.60$, $z = 2.81$, $p = 0.0025$; $\chi_4^2 = 22.86$, $z = 3.58$, $p = 0.00017$ respectively. Overall, $\chi_8^2 = 39.46$, $z = 4.38$, $p = 0.00003$.
15 The numbers of depictions were 25 and 9 respectively.
16 The significance test for the two differences together yielded $\chi_4^2 = 26.59$, $z = 3.97$, $p = 0.00003$.
17 $\chi_8^2 = 41.98$, $z = 4.59$, $p < 0.00003$.
18 $\chi_4^2 = 32.77$, $z = 4.55$, $p < 0.00003$ for keying; $\chi_4^2 = 10.71$, $z = 1.88$, $p = 0.03$ for fabrication.
19 $\chi_{14}^2 = 50.60$, $z = 4.37$, $p = 0.00005$.
20 They could be seen in 6 cartoons out of 160.
21 $z = 3.26$, 2.03; $p = 0.0012$, 0.0124 respectively.
22 $z = 2.18$, 4.51; $p = 0.0292$, 0.000009 respectively.
23 $z = 2.34$, 3.62, 4.08; $p = 0.0192$, 0.00032, 0.00006.

Appendix B

1 The framework used here is more elaborate than that used in Morris (1984), which noted the implicit assumption that the family spanned three generations, but neither located the older generation nor identified it with any group.
2 This division is closer to that obtained on measures of provincialism than on measures of powerlessness in Grabb (pp. 343–8).
3 The log-linear analysis yielded a series of values of chi-square. Depending on the context, these might refer to regional effects, topical effects, language effects, joint effects, or error terms. The chi-square values were then converted into z-scores using the Wilson-Hilferty approximation (Kendall: 296).

4 These two were each significant at the 0.0005 level; as a result, the overall set of regional differences was significant at the 0.0005 level: $\chi^2_{66} = 117.03$, which has a z-score of 3.68 and a probability of 0.00024. When these two strong differences were omitted, however, the remaining series of twenty-four tests did not yield statistically significant results: $\chi^2_{62} = 75.58$, $z = 1.20$.

5 $\chi^2_2 = 19.87$, $z = 3.78$, compared with a joint effect of $\chi^2_{12} = 10.18$, $z = 0.26$.

6 $\chi^2_2 = 21.58$, $z = 3.95$, compared with a joint effect of $\chi^2_{12} = 13.95$, $z = 0.51$.

7 Eighteen were significant at the 0.01 and eight at the 0.05 level. In this case and certain others, the probability that this result could occur by chance alone was too remote to be worth calculating.

8 $\chi^2_{96} = 200.9$, $z = 5.85$, $p < 0.00001$.

9 $\chi^2_{28} = 201.5$, $z = 3.96$, $p = 0.00006$.

10 For the set of language differences, $\chi^2_{32} = 104.68$, $z = 5.90$, $p < 0.00001$; for those according to topic, $\chi^2_{16} = 109.21$, $z = 6.15$, $p < 0.00001$; for the joint effects, $\chi^2_{32} = 57.24$, $z = 2.65$, $p = 0.008$.

11 For variability by topic, $\chi^2_{64} = 132.72$, $z = 4.73$, $p < 0.00002$; by language, $\chi^2_{32} = 62.16$, $z = 3.06$, $p = 0.0022$; for the joint effects, $\chi^2_{64} = 78.22$, $z = 1.23$, which was not significant.

12 $\chi^2_{32} = 66.95$, $p = 0.00056$.

13 This is quite consistent with the finding of most research, that there have until recently been two quite separate Canadian histories (Richert). Although independentist writers in *Possibles* propose a future quite unlike that favoured by most (English) Canadians, ethnic differences in relation to the present and future are generally quite small (Ornstein, Stevenson and Williams).

14 $\chi^2_2 = 7.33$ ($z = 1.96$, $p = 0.025$) on the in-law theme; $\chi^2_2 = 10.51$, ($z = 2.55$, $p = 0.005$) on the spousal theme. In the former but not the latter case there was also a significant joint effect: $\chi^2_2 = 8.73$, $z = 2.24$, $p = 0.013$.

15 $\chi^2_2 = 12.96$ ($z = 2.93$, $p = 0.0017$) on the in-law theme; $\chi^2_2 = 9.98$ ($z = 2.46$, $p = 0.007$) on the spousal theme. There was no joint effect.

16 The seven aspects of symmetry to which Dondis refers were all included.

17 $\chi^2_2 = 17.47$, $z = 3.51$, $p = 0.00023$.

18 $\chi^2_1 = 6.24$, $z = 2.26$, $p = 0.012$. The variable here is the possibility that at least one of the characters could have been coded as more than one of the social types and/or more than one of the comic types proposed by Klapp and Frye respectively.

19 On the in-law theme, $\chi^2_2 = 7.27$, $z = 1.95$, $p = 0.0256$; on the spousal theme, $\chi^2_4 = 7.34$, $z = 1.19$, $p = 0.117$; and on the children theme, $\chi^2_2 = 10.99$, $z = 2.63$, $p = 0.0043$.

20 John Fox and Sal Minkin were very helpful advisers at this stage.

21 Klapp's (1962) elaborations proved much more difficult to use in these assessments.

22 Each character was given a base score of 5; one point was then added for each masculine trait, to a maximum score of 9; one was subtracted for each feminine trait, to a minimum of 1. Elements which were ambiguous or not shown were scored 0.

23 The reason for this was largely technical: relatively few of the cartoons featuring President de Gaulle included any anglophone Canadians, and virtually none of those focused on the queen showed any francophone Canadians. It will be recalled that Pierre Trudeau was classified as Canadian, but not as either anglophone or francophone. He was thus omitted from all analyses of language, but not from those of nationality.

24 $\chi_9^2 = 34.28$, $z = 3.73$, $p = 0.0002$.

25 It will be recalled that these statistics exclude Mr Trudeau, who was not classified in either language group.

26 Overall, $\chi_{18}^2 = 40.7$, $z = 2.92$, $p = 0.0018$.

27 Overall, $\chi_9^2 = 34.45$, $z = 3.75$, $p = 0.00009$.

28 $\chi_9^2 = 15.35$, $z = 1.40$, $p > 0.05$.

29 There was at least one significant result in eight of the nine sets, seven of them being significant at the 0.001 level.

30 There was at least one significant result in five of the nine sets; $\chi_9^2 = 35.23$, $z = 3.82$, $p = 0.00007$.

31 $\chi_{27}^2 = 58.86$, $z = 3.37$, $p = 0.0004$.

32 Given the coding rules, there must have been four anglophones and no francophones in each.

33 I.e., three anglophones and no francophones.

34 I.e., three anglophones and one francophone, or two and none.

35 I.e., two and two, one and one, or exceptionally none of either.

36 $\chi_{56}^2 = 101.28$, $z = 3.53$, $p = 0.00042$. Since exact probabilities were available for the outcome of each U-test, the formula proposed by Cox and Hinkley (pp. 80–1) was used to assess the overall value of χ^2 for these results. The Wilson-Hilferty approximation could then give an estimate of the corresponding z score.

37 $\chi_{28}^2 = 32.33$ ($z = 0.64$) and $\chi_{42}^2 = 40.95$ ($z = 0.04$) respectively.

38 $\chi_{126}^2 = 174.56$, $z = 2.78$, $p = 0.0054$.

39 $\chi_8^2 = 18.86$, $z = 2.15$, $p = 0.032$.

40 $\chi_{76}^2 = 162.28$, $z = 5.37$, $p < 0.00001$.

41 $\chi_{34}^2 = 66.97$, $z = 3.22$, $p = 0.0007$.

42 $\chi_6^2 = 34.55$, $z = 4.31$, $p = 0.00002$.

43 $\chi_8^2 = 35.88$, $z = 4.06$, $p = 0.00003$.
44 $\chi_6^2 = 15.31$, $z = 2.10$, $p = 0.018$.

Appendix C

1 $\chi_{165}^2 = 227.83$, $z = 3.13$, $p = 0.0009$.
2 $\chi_{66}^2 = 62.12$, $z = -0.28$, $p > 0.10$.
3 $\chi_{66}^2 = 85.44$, $z = 1.61$, $p = 0.0537$.
4 $\chi_2^2 = 11.56$, $z = 2.72$, $p = 0.0033$.
5 Two were significant at the 0.001, one more at the 0.01, two more at the 0.05 level, and two others at the 0.10 level. Overall, the results were highly significant: $\chi_{33}^2 = 69.77$, $z = 3.54$, $p = 0.0002$.
6 $\chi_1^2 = 11.52$, $z = 3.14$, $p = 0.0008$ for ambiguity; $\chi_2^2 = 14.25$, $z = 3.11$, $p = 0.0009$ for stress.
7 $\chi_1^2 = 6.68$, $z = 2.35$, $p = 0.0094$.
8 $\chi_2^2 = 8.89$, $z = 2.27$, $p = 0.0116$.
9 $\chi_2^2 = 8.48$, $z = 2.19$, $p = 0.0143$.
10 Three of the four relating to foolishness, one of two relating to unimportance, and two of three concerning badness.
11 $\chi_{135}^2 = 325.56$, $z = 8.45$, $p < 0.00001$.
12 $\chi_9^2 = 65.75$, $z = 6.14$, $p < 0.00001$.
13 $\chi_8^2 = 18.17$, $z = 2.05$, $p = 0.0202$.
14 $\chi_{18}^2 = 25.89$, $z = 1.27$, $p > 0.10$.
15 $\chi_4^2 = 41.34$, $z = 5.23$, $p < 0.00001$.
16 $\chi_3^2 = 8.71$, $z = 1.84$, $p = 0.0329$. For the nine measures taken together, $\chi_9^2 = 52.06$, $z = 5.22$, $p < 0.00001$.
17 $\chi_8^2 = 18.40$, $z = 2.09$, $p = 0.0183$.
18 $\chi_{18}^2 = 24.61$, $z = 1.10$, $p > 0.10$.
19 $\chi_8^2 = 21.53$, $z = 2.51$, $p = 0.012$; $\chi_6^2 = 14.39$, $z = 1.95$, $p = 0.05$, respectively.
20 $\chi_{18}^2 = 44.13$, $z = 3.25$, $p = 0.001$.
21 $\chi_6^2 = 15.88$, $z = 2.18$, $p = 0.029$.
22 $\chi_{18}^2 = 37.89$, $z = 2.65$, $p = 0.008$.
23 $\chi_4^2 = 11.74$, $z = 2.07$, $p = 0.019$.
24 The prime minister was rarely depicted on this topic except in Ontario cartoons.
25 $z = 3.00$, $p = 0.0013$.
26 $\chi_{18}^2 = 32.85$, $z = 2.11$, $p = 0.017$.
27 $\chi_8^2 = 29.88$, $z = 3.48$, $p = 0.00024$; $\chi_4^2 = 12.33$, $z = 2.17$, $p = 0.015$, respectively.
28 $\chi_8^2 = 47.24$, $z = 3.53$, $p = 0.00021$.

References

Allen, W. 1954. *The English Novel*. London: Penguin

Allport, G.W., and L.A. Postman. 1947. *The Psychology of Rumor*. New York: Henry Holt

Arden, H. 1980. *Fools' Plays*. New York: Cambridge University Press

Atwood, M. 1972. *Survival*. Toronto: Anansi

Auerbach, E. 1957. *Mimesis*. Garden City, NY: Doubleday

Aveni, A.F., T.J. Curry, K. Meyer, and J. Seidler. 1979. 'Some Problems and Solutions in Visual Analysis Research: Notes from a Study of Political Cartoons.' Unpub. ms. Jackson State University, Alabama

Bagdikian, B.H. 1964. 'Why Dailies Die.' In L.A. Dexter and D.M. White, eds. *People, Society and Mass Communications*, 205–20. New York: Free Press

– 1980. 'Conglomeration, Concentration and the Media.' *Journal of Communication* 30 (2): 59–64

Bakhtine, M. 1970. *L'oeuvre de François Rabelais et la culture populaire au Moyen Age et sous la Renaissance*. Paris: Gallimard

Barnett, S., and M.G. Silverman. 1979. *Ideology and Everyday Life*. Ann Arbor: University of Michigan Press

Barthes, R. 1972. *Mythologies*. London: Cape

Bearden, R., and C. Holty. 1969. *The Painter's Mind*. New York: Crown

Beck, B. 1982. 'Root Metaphors.' *Semiotic Inquiry* 2 (1): 86–97

Becker, H.S. 1963. *Outsiders*. New York: Free Press

Bell, D.V.J. 1976. *Power, Influence and Authority*. New York: Oxford University Press

Beniger, J.R. 1983. 'Does Television Enhance the Shared Symbolic Environment? Trends in Editorial Cartoons, 1948–1980.' *American Sociological Review* 48 (1): 103–11

Bennett, W.L. 1980. 'Myth, Ritual and Political Control.' *Journal of Communication* 30 (4): 166–79

Berelson, B. 1954. 'What "Missing the Newspaper" Means.' In D. Katz, et al., ed., *Public Opinion and Propaganda*, 263–71. New York: Dryden

Berger, A.A. 1973. *The Comic-Stripped American*. Baltimore: Penguin

Berger, J. 1980. *About Looking*. New York: Pantheon

Bissonette, L. 1979. 'Les traces d'un satellite.' *Le Devoir*, 9 janv.

Black, E. 1982. *Politics and the News*. Toronto: Butterworth

Black, M., ed. 1962. *Models and Metaphors*. Ithaca, NY: Cornell University Press

Booth, W.C. 1974. *A Rhetoric of Irony*. Chicago: University of Chicago Press

Bouissac, P. 1976. *Circus and Culture*. Bloomington: Indiana University Press

Breed, W. 1964. 'Mass Communication and Sociocultural Integration.' In L.A. Dexter and D.M. White, eds, *People, Society and Mass Communications*, 183–201. New York: Free Press

– 1975. 'Social Control in the News Room.' In W. Schramm, ed, *Mass Communications*, 2nd ed, 178–97. Urbana: University of Illinois Press

Breger, D., ed. 1955. *But That's Unprintable*. New York: Bantam

Breton, R. 1984. 'The Production and Allocation of Symbolic Resources.' *Canadian Review of Sociology and Anthropology* 21 (2): 123–44

Brown, R.H. 1977. *A Poetic for Sociology*. New York: Cambridge University Press

Bruner, J. 1979. *On Knowing: Essays for the Left Hand*. 2nd ed. Cambridge, Mass.: Belknap Press

Burke, K. 1954. *Permanence and Change*. Rev. ed. Los Altos, Cal.: Hermes

– 1962a. *A Grammar of Motives*. Cleveland: World Publishing

– 1962b. *A Rhetoric of Motives*. Cleveland: Meridian

– 1964a. *Perspectives by Incongruity*. Bloomington: Indiana University Press

– 1964b. *Terms for Order*. Bloomington: Indiana University Press

– 1966. *Language as Symbolic Action*. Berkeley: University of California Press

– 1967. *The Philosophy of Literary Form*. Berkeley: University of California Press

Carney, J.D., and R.K. Scheer. 1974. *Fundamentals of Logic*. 2nd ed. New York: Macmillan

Charney, M. 1978. *Comedy, High and Low*. New York: Oxford University Press

Clarke, J. 1973. 'Football Hooliganism and the Skinheads.' Centre for Contemporary Cultural Studies, University of Birmingham. Stencilled Occasional Paper 42

Clement, W. 1975. *The Canadian Corporate Elite*. Toronto: McClelland and Stewart

Connell, I. 1980. 'Television News and the Social Contract.' In S. Hall, et al., eds, *Culture, Media, Language*, 139–56. London: Hutchison

Copi, I.M. 1968. *Introduction to Logic*. 3rd ed. New York: Collier-Macmillan

Corcoran, P.E. 1979. *Political Language and Rhetoric*. Austin: University of Texas Press

Cossette, C., dir. 1975. *Communication de masse, consommation de masse.* Quebec: Ed. Boréal-Express

Coupe, W.A. 1969. 'Observations on a Theory of Political Caricature.' *Comparative Studies in Society and History* 11 (1): 79–95

Cox, D.R., and D.V. Hinkley. 1974. *Theoretical Statistics.* London: Chapman and Hall

Critcher, C. n.d. 'Football since the War.' Centre for Contemporary Cultural Studies, University of Birmingham. Stencilled Occasional Paper 29

Culler, J. 1981. *The Pursuit of Signs.* Ithaca, NY: Cornell University Press

Curtis, L.P. 1971. *Apes and Angels.* Washington, DC: Smithsonian Institute

Davey, K., et al. 1970. Special Senate Committee on Mass Media. *Report,* vol. 1. Ottawa: Queen's Printer

Davis, W. 1977. *Punch and the Monarchy.* London: Elm Tree Books

de Guise, J. 1975. 'L'industrie des média ou le marché des auditoires.' In C. Cossette, dir, *Communication de masse, consommation de masse,* 227–32. Quebec: Ed. Boréal-Express

de la Garde, R. 1975. 'Les mass média québécois.' In C. Cossette, dir, *Communication de masse, consommation de masse,* 191–226. Quebec: Ed. Boréal-Express

Desbarats, P., and T. Mosher. 1979. *The Hecklers.* Toronto: McClelland and Stewart

Dexter, L.A. 1964. 'Introduction.' In L.A. Dexter and D.M. White, eds, *People, Society and Mass Communications,* 339–40. New York: Free Press

Dolle, G. 1975. 'Rhétorique et supports de signification iconographiques.' *Revue des sciences humaines* 40 (159): 343–57

Dondis, D.A. 1973. *A Primer of Visual Literacy.* Cambridge: Massachusetts Institute of Technology Press

Dooley, D.J. 1971. *Contemporary Satire.* Toronto: Holt, Rinehart and Winston

Dorfman, A. 1983. *The Empire's Old Clothes.* New York: Pantheon

Dorfman, A., and A. Mattelart. 1975. *How to Read Donald Duck.* New York: International General

Duncan, H.D. 1968. *Symbols in Society.* New York: Oxford University Press

Dyson, A.E. 1965. *The Crazy Fabric.* London: Macmillan

Eagleton, T. 1976a. *Criticism and Ideology.* London: New Left Books

– 1976b. *Marxism and Literary Criticism.* London: Methuen

Edelman, M. 1962. *The Symbolic Uses of Politics.* Urbana: University of Illinois Press

– 1971. *Politics as Symbolic Action.* Chicago: University of Chicago Press

– 1977. *Political Language.* New York: Academic Press

Edinborough, A. 1962. 'The Press.' In J.A. Irving, ed, *Mass Media in Canada*, 13–28. Toronto: Ryerson

Empson, W. 1950. *Some Versions of Pastoral*. London: Chatto and Windus

Epstein, E.J. 1975. *Between Fact and Fiction. The Problem of Journalism*. New York: Vintage

Ericson, R.V., P.M. Baranek, and J.B.L. Chan. 1987. *Visualizing Deviance*. Toronto: University of Toronto Press

Fisher, J., ed, 1980. *Perceiving Artworks*. Philadelphia: Temple University Press

Fishman, M. 1980. *Manufacturing the News*. Austin: University of Texas Press

Floch, J.M. 1979. 'La spatialisation et son rôle dans la mise en discours du récit.' *Canadian Journal of Research in Semiotics* 7 (1): 123–37

Fontenrose, J. 1971. *The Ritual Theory of Myth*. Berkeley: University of California Press

Forcese, D., and J. deVries. 1977. 'Occupation and Electoral Success in Canada: The 1974 Federal Election.' *Canadian Review of Sociology and Anthropology* 14 (3): 331–40

Fournier, P. 1976. *The Quebec Establishment*. Montreal: Black Rose Books

Fox, J.D. 1984. *Linear Models and Related Methods with Applications to Social Research*. New York: John Wiley

Freund, C., P. Steiner, D. Levine, J. Feiffer, and B. Holland. 1988. 'The Problem with Editorial Cartooning Today.' *The Comics Journal*, no. 119: 55–68

Frye, N. 1957. *Anatomy of Criticism*. Princeton: Princeton University Press
– 1971. *The Bush Garden*. Toronto: Anansi

Gamson, W.A., and K.E. Lasch. 1981. 'The Political Culture of Social Welfare Policy.' Ann Arbor: Center for Research on Social Organization

Gans, H.J. 1980. *Deciding What's News*. New York: Random House

Gieber, W. 1964. 'News Is What Newspapermen Make It.' In L.A. Dexter and D.M. White, eds, *People, Society and Mass Communications*, 173–82. New York: Free Press

Ginzberg, E. 1986. *Power without Responsibility*. Toronto: Urban Alliance on Race Relations

Goffman, E. 1974. *Frame Analysis*. Baltimore: Penguin
– 1978. 'The Presentation of Self to Others.' In J.G. Manis and B.N. Meltzer, eds, *Symbolic Interaction*, 3rd ed, 171–8. Boston: Allyn and Bacon
– 1979. *Gender Advertisements*. Cambridge, Mass: Harvard University Press

Golding, P., and G. Murdoch. 1979. 'Ideology and the Mass Media.' In M. Barrett et al, eds, *Ideology and Cultural Production*, 198–224. London: Croom Helm

Goldmann, L. 1975. *Towards a Sociological Theory of the Novel*. London: Tavistock

Gombrich, E.H. 1978. *Meditations on a Hobby Horse*. 3rd ed. New York: Phaidon

Gonos, G. 1977. ' "Situation" versus "Frame": The "Interactionist" and the "Structuralist" Analyses of Everyday Life.' *American Sociological Review* 42: 854–67

Goodin, R.E. 1980. *Manipulatory Politics*. New Haven, Conn.: Yale University Press

Grabb, E.G. 1979. 'Relative Centrality and Political Isolation: Canadian Dimensions.' *Canadian Review of Sociology and Anthropology* 16 (3): 343–55

Green, A.D. 1977. 'On the Political Economy of Black Labour and the Racial Structuring of the Working Class in England.' Centre for Contemporary Cultural Studies, University of Birmingham. Stencilled Occasional Paper 62

Groupe Mu. 1978. 'Ironique et iconique.' *Poétique* 36: 427–42

Gusfield, J.A. 1963. *Symbolic Crusade*. Urbana: University of Illinois Press

Haberman, S.J. 1978. *Analysis of Qualitative Data*, vol. 1. New York: Academic Press

Hall, P.M. 1972. 'A Symbolic Interactionist Analysis of Politics.' *Sociological Inquiry* 42 (3–4): 35–75

Hall, S. 1974. 'Media Power: The Double Bind.' *Journal of Communication* 24 (4): 19–26

– 1975. 'The Structured Communication of Events.' In *Getting the Message Across*. Paris: Unesco

Hamelin, L-E. 1982. 'Mythes d'Anticosti.' *Recherches sociographiques* 23 (1, 2): 139–62

Hannigan, J. 1983. 'Ideology, Elites and the Canadian Mass Media.' In B.D. Singer, ed, *Communications in Canadian Society*, 3rd ed, 55–61. Don Mills: Addison-Wesley

Harrison, R.P. 1981. *The Cartoon*. Beverly Hills: Sage Publications

Hartley, J. 1982. *Understanding News*. London: Methuen

Hewison, W. 1977. *The Cartoon Connection*. London: Elm Tree Books

Hewitt, J.P., and P.M. Hall. 1973. 'Social Problems, Problematic Solutions and Quasi-Theories.' *American Sociological Review* 38 (3): 367–74

Hewitt, J.P., and R. Stokes. 1978. 'Disclaimers.' In J.G. Manis and B.N. Meltzer, eds, *Symbolic Interaction*, 3rd ed, 308–19. Boston: Allyn and Bacon

Hill, D. 1965. *Mr. Gillray, the Caricaturist*. London: Phaidon

Hill, J. 1979. 'Ideology, Economy and the British Cinema.' In M. Barrett, et al, eds, *Ideology and Cultural Production*, 112–34. London: Croom Helm

Houle, G. 1988. 'Le point de vue de la sociologie.' Communication présentée à l'Association pour la recherche qualitative, Moncton, NB

Hutcheon, L.A. 1981a. 'Ironie, satire, parodie.' *Poétique* 46: 140–55
– 1981b. 'Review of Le Groupe Mu, *Rhétorique de la Poésie.' Semiotic Inquiry* 1 (3): 283–95
– 1984. *Narcissistic Narrative.* Toronto: Methuen
Jones, E. 1948. *Papers on Psychoanalysis.* 5th ed. London: Bailliere, Tindall and Cox
Jowett, G.S. 1983. 'The Growth of the Mass Media in Canada.' In B.D. Singer, ed, *Communications in Canadian Society*, 3rd ed, 158–75. Don Mills: Addison-Wesley
Kelner, M.J. 1970. 'Ethnic Penetration into Toronto's Elite Structure.' *Canadian Review of Sociology and Anthropology* 7 (2): 128–37
Kendall, M.G. 1958. *The Advanced Theory of Statistics*, vol. 1. London: Griffin
Kent, T., B. Spears, and L. Picard. 1981. Royal Commission on Newspapers, *Report.* Ottawa: Supply and Services Canada
Kesterton, W.H. 1972. 'The Growth of the Newspaper in Canada.' In B.D. Singer, ed, *Communications in Canadian Society*, 1st ed, 3–17. Toronto: Copp Clark
Kevelson, R. 1977. *The Inverted Pyramid. An Introduction to the Semiotics of Media Language.* Bloomington: Indiana University Press
Klapp, O.E. 1962. *Heroes, Villains and Fools.* Englewood Cliffs, NJ: Prentice Hall
– 1964. *Symbolic Leaders.* Chicago: Aldine
Kunzle, D. 1973. *The Early Comic Strip.* Berkeley: University of California Press
Lakoff, G., and M. Johnson. 1980. *Metaphors We Live By.* Chicago: University of Chicago Press
Lawrence, E. 1981. 'Common Sense, Racism and the Sociology of Race Relations.' Centre for Contemporary Cultural Studies, University of Birmingham. Stencilled Occasional Paper 66
Lévi-Strauss, C. 1972. 'The Structural Analysis of Myth.' In T. Sebeok, ed, *Myth: A Symposium*, 81–106. Bloomington: Indiana University Press
Levin, S.R. 1977. *The Semantics of Metaphor.* Baltimore: Johns Hopkins University Press
MacRae, D.G. 1975. 'The Body and Social Metaphor.' In J. Benthall and T. Polhemus, eds, *The Body as a Medium of Expression*, 59–73. New York: Dutton
Maranda, E.K., and P. Maranda. 1971. *Structural Models in Folklore and Transformational Essays.* The Hague: Mouton
Maranda, P., ed. 1972. *Mythology.* Baltimore: Penguin
Marchand, P. 1981. 'Admission Restricted.' *Saturday Night*, January: 32–41
McGregor, G.F. 1986. *The Wacousta Syndrome.* Toronto: University of Toronto Press

McLuhan, M. 1964. *Understanding Media*. 2nd ed. New York: Signet
Meyer, K., J. Seidler, T. Curry, and A.F. Aveni. 1980. 'Women in July Fourth Cartoons.' *Journal of Communication* 30 (1): 21–30
Miliband, R. 1973. *The State in Capitalist Society*. London: Quarter Books
Miller, E.F. 1979. 'Metaphor and Political Knowledge.' *American Political Science Review* 73: 155–70
Millum, T. 1975. *Images of Women*. London: Chatto and Windus
Molino, J. 1973. 'Critique sémiologique de l'idéologie.' *Sociologie et sociétés* 5 (2): 17–44
Moreux, C. 1978. *La conviction idéologique*. Montreal: Presses Universitaires du Québec
Morris, R.N. 1984. 'Canada as a Family: Ontarian Responses to the Quebec Independence Movement.' *Canadian Review of Sociology and Anthropology* 21 (2): 181–201
– 1985. 'Gender Advertisements and Political Cartoons: An Examination of Stereotypes and Bad Drama.' *Maieutics* 2 (1): 149–71
Mott, F.L. 1975. 'Trends in Newspaper Content.' In W. Schramm, ed, *Mass Communications*, 2nd ed, 371–9. Urbana: University of Illinois Press
Mouammar, M. 1986. 'When Cartoons Are Not Funny.' *Currents* 3 (3)
Nattiez, J.J. 1973. 'Problèmes sémiologiques de l'analyse des idéologies.' *Sociologie et sociétés* 5 (2): 71–90
Needham, R, ed. 1973. *Right and Left*. Chicago: University of Chicago Press
Nielsen, R. 1972. 'The Media: Must We Serve as Tools for Terrorists?' In B.D. Singer, ed, *Communications in Canadian Society*, 1st ed, 308–11. Toronto: Copp Clark
Nimmo, D.D. 1974. *Popular Images of Politics*. Englewood Cliffs, NJ: Prentice-Hall
Nir, Y. 1976. *The Israeli-Arab Conflict in Soviet Caricatures, 1967–1973*. Tel Aviv: Tcherikover
Nock, A.J. 1928. 'The King's Jester: Modern Style.' *Harper's Monthly Magazine*, March: 481–8
O'Connor, J. 1973. *The Fiscal Crisis of the State*. New York: St Martin's Press
Ornstein, M.D., H.M. Stevenson, and A.P.M. Williams. 1979. 'The State of Mind: Public Perceptions of the Future of Canada.' In R.B. Byers and R.W. Reford, eds, *Canada Challenged*, 57–107. Toronto: Canadian Institute for International Affairs
Panitch, L., ed. 1977. *The Canadian State*. Toronto: University of Toronto Press
Park, R.E. 1975. 'The Natural History of the Newspaper.' In W. Schramm, ed, *Mass Communications*, 2nd ed, 8–23. Urbana: University of Illinois Press
Perkins, D.N., and M.A. Hagen. 1980. 'Convention, Context and Caricature.'

In M.A. Hagen, ed, *The Perception of Pictures*, 257–85. New York: Academic Press

Posner, J.S. 1975. 'Dirty Old Women.' *Canadian Review of Sociology and Anthropology* 12 (4): 471–3

Press, C. 1981. *The Political Cartoon*. New Brunswick, NJ: Fairleigh Dickinson University Press

Price, K.A. 1980. 'The Social Construction of Ethnicity.' PhD dissertation, York University

Reynolds, H.T. 1977. *The Analysis of Cross Classifications*. New York: Free Press

Richert, J-P. 1974. 'The Impact of Ethnicity on the Perception of Heroes and Historical Symbols.' *Canadian Review of Sociology and Anthropology* 12: 156–63

Richmond, A.H. 1967. *Postwar Immigrants in Canada*. Toronto: University of Toronto Press

Ricoeur, P. 1975. *The Rule of Metaphor*. Toronto: University of Toronto Press

Rodway, A. 1975. *English Comedy*. London: Chatto and Windus

Roper, E. 1957. *You and Your Leaders*. New York: Morrow

Rosse, J.N. 1980. 'The Decline of Direct Newspaper Competition.' *Journal of Communication* 30 (1): 65–71

Rutherford, P.F.W. 1978. *The Making of the Canadian Media*. Toronto: McGraw-Hill Ryerson

Shaffer, L.F. 1972. *Children's Interpretations of Cartoons*. New York: A.M.S. Press

Shell, M. 1977. 'La publicité bilingue au Québec.' *Canadian Journal of Research in Semiotics* 5 (2): 55–76

Siegel, A. 1976. 'The Norms and Values of the French and English Press in Canada.' In W.E. Mann and L. Wheatcroft, eds, *Canada: A Sociological Profile*, 3rd ed, 144–56. Toronto: Copp Clark

Singer, B.D. 1983. 'Minorities and the Media.' In B.D. Singer, ed, *Communications in Canadian Society*, 3rd ed, 226–36. Don Mills: Addison-Wesley

Smith, M.D. 1979. 'Toward an Explanation of Hockey Violence.' *Canadian Journal of Sociology* 4 (2): 105–24

Smythe, D.W. 1972. 'On the Political Economy of Communications.' In B.D. Singer, ed, *Communications in Canadian Society*, 1st ed, 101–18. Toronto: Copp Clark

– 1981. *Dependency Road*. Norwood, NJ: Ablex

Sorell, W. 1972. *Facets of Comedy*. New York: Grosset and Dunlap

Streicher, L.H. 1965. 'David Low and the Sociology of Caricature.' *Comparative Studies in Society and History* 8 (1): 1–23

– 1967. 'On a Theory of Political Caricature.' *Comparative Studies in Society and History* 9 (4): 427–45

Sutherland, R.A. 1977. *The New Hero*. Toronto: Macmillan

Tardy, M. 1979. 'Sémiogenèses d'encodage, sémiogenèses de décodage.' *Canadian Journal of Research in Semiotics* 7 (1): 111–22

Thompson, G. 1979. 'Television as Text.' In M. Barrett, et al, eds, *Ideology and Cultural Production*, 160–97. London: Croom Helm

Tiefenbrun, S.W. 1980. *Signs of the Hidden*. Amsterdam: Rodopi

Tremblay-Querido, C. 1973. 'Introduction.' *Sociologie et sociétés* 5 (2): 3–16

Trudel, M., and G. Jain. 1969. *L'histoire du Canada. Enquête sur les manuels*. Ottawa: Imprimeur de la Reine

Tuchman, G. 1978. *Making News: A Study in the Construction of Reality*. New York: Free Press

Turner, V. 1974. *Dramas, Fields and Metaphors*. Ithaca, NY: Cornell University Press

Twer, S. 1972. 'Tactics for Determining Persons' Resources for Depicting, Contriving and Describing Behavioral Episodes.' In D. Sudnow, ed, *Studies in Social Interaction*, 339–66. New York: Free Press

Ungar, S. 1985. 'The Social Drama of Moral Categories.' Paper presented to the Canadian Sociology and Anthropology Association meetings, Montreal

Vatter, H. 1978. *The Devil in English Literature*. Berne: Francke

Veron, E. 1973. 'Remarques sur l'idéologique comme production de sens.' *Sociologie et sociétés* 5 (2): 45–70

Vincent, H.P. 1968. *Daumier and His World*. Evanston, Ill.: Northwestern University Press

Warner, W.L. 1964. 'The World of Biggy Muldoon.' In L.A. Dexter and D.M. White, eds, *People, Society and Mass Communications*, 341–57. New York: Free Press

Welsford, E. 1966. *The Fool: His Social and Literary History*. Gloucester, Mass.: P. Smith

Wilden, A. 1979. *The Imaginary Canadian*. Vancouver: Pulp Press

Willeford, W. 1969. *The Fool and His Scepter*. Evanston, Ill.: Northwestern University Press

Williamson, J. 1978. *Decoding Advertisements*. London: M. Boyars

Wilson, H.T. 1985. *Political Management*. New York: de Gruyter

Worth, S., and L. Gross. 1974. 'Symbolic Strategies.' *Journal of Communication* 24 (4): 27–39

Zijderveld, A.C. 1982. *Reality in a Looking Glass*. London: Routledge and Kegan Paul

Index